CANNIBALS
AND
EVIL CULT
KILLERS

CANNIBALS
AND
EVIL CULT
KILLERS

A Time Warner Book

This first edition published in 2006

ISBN 0-316-73253-2

Produced by Omnipress, Eastbourne

Printed in Spain
Time Warner Books
Brettenham House
Lancaster Place
London WC2E 7EN

Photo credits: Corbis
Front cover images: Jeffrey Dahmer, Ku Klux Klan,
and Charles Manson

CONTENTS

PART ONE: CANNIBALS
Introduction 9

SECTION ONE
CANNIBALISM AROUND THE WORLD

SECTION TWO
CANNIBALISM MOST MACABRE

PART TWO: EVIL CULT KILLERS
Introduction 296

SECTION ONE
CULT SUICIDES

SECTION TWO
CULT KILLINGS

SECTION THREE
CAUSE FOR CONCERN?

CANNIBALS

Cannibalism

Cannibalism, or anthropophagy, is the eating of human flesh by another human, in other words the eating of its own kind. The word actually comes from the Arawakan language name for the Carib Indians of the West Indies because they were well known for their practice of cannibalism. The same word is used in the animal kingdom and means the eating of a species by a member of the same species. For example, wolves will often eat each other when they are desperate for food.

Cannibalism among humans, as repulsive as the idea may seem, has been widespread in prehistoric and primitive peoples on all continents, and the practice is still believed to exist in remote areas of New Guinea.

Androphagi – the Greek word for 'man-eaters' – were an ancient tribe of cannibals who lived north of Scythia, possibly in the forests between the upper waters of the Dnieper and the Don. Scythia was a region which stretched from from the Altai region where Mongolia, China, Russia and Kazakhstan come together to the lower Danube river area and Bulgaria. The Androphagi were most likely Finns, and their manners were more savage than those of any other race. They did not observe any form of justice, or indeed governed by any laws. They were nomads, and the language which they spoke was peculiar to their tribe, but most of all they were true cannibals.

Archaeologists from Bristol University uncovered evidence of prehistoric cannibalism in the year 2001, when they were investigating a cave at Alveston, South Gloucestershire. The archaeologists had been working with a local caving group when they discovered numerous bones about ten metres below ground level. Carbon dating suggests that they were buried around 2,000 years ago at the very end of the Iron Age, or possibly the beginning of the Roman occupation. The remains of at least seven individuals were uncovered, and at least one had been murdered as the back of the skull showed that it had been smashed with a heavy instrument. The most interesting find was an adult human femur which had been split lengthwise and the bone marrow had been scraped out. This was considered to be very good evidence that there had been some form of cannibal activity. Archaeologists had suspected some form of Iron Age cannibalism for some time, but this was the first piece of strong evidence they had found.

Of course there may be many reasons why people practice cannibalism. It could be because there simply wasn't enough food for survival, or perhaps certain groups of people developed the taste for human flesh. However, it was normally to do with revenge or punishment for crimes, ritualistic ceremonies or sometimes magic. Particular tribes used to eat the bodies of their enemies as a form of triumphant victory. Other groups would eat the bodies of their dead relatives as a form of respect, believing that their spirits would continue to live inside their own bodies; this is known as endocannibalism. Human bodies used as sacrifices to the gods would have parts of their torso removed and eaten to identify their divine status.

The Wari tribe in the Amazon rain forest practised cannibalism until the late 1950s. The Wari were known to eat both their enemies and their own dead relatives. The eating of enemies was probablly just an act of contempt, very similar to a murderer eating his own victim. However, the eating of their dead relatives was done for a very different reason – respect. Burial was abhorrent to the Wari, so in an effort to destroy the memory of the once-living, all the belongings of the dead person were destroyed, including their own flesh. The Wari believed that by eating their dead and destroying their property that their 'spirit' would no longer haunt them or familiar places. The spirit of the dead was then free to be reborn and roam the forest as a *peccary* (type of pig). If times became really tough for the Wari, the peccary would return to the village and allow itself to be killed for food, subsequently ensuring Wari survival. It was the research carried out on the Wari tribe that gave anthropologists a further insight into cannibalism.

Of course, even civilized people have had to resort to cannibalism under desperate circumstances, just as a means of staying alive. The case that is probably the most well known is the Donner party that took place in America in the 19th century. A group of 90 immigrants being led by George Donner were caught in a blizzard high up in the Sierra Nevada mountains of California in October 1846. The survivors, who eventually made their way out in early 1847, had resorted to eating the flesh of their dead friends in order to remain alive. A more recent case happened when an airline crashed in a remote area of the Andes in the 1970s, once again the surviving passengers had to resort to cannibalism.

CRIMINAL CANNIBALISM

In modern times, the murder of a person for the purpose of eating their flesh is of course considered to be criminal cannibalism. However, in many parts of the world, indeed in Britain and the United States, cannibalism is not considered to be a felony and the perpetrator would have to be charged with a crime related to this act, for example murder, grave robbery or necrophilia.

Other cultures often consider the act of criminal cannibalism as an acceptable element of their customs. For example, tribes in Papua New Guinea allegedly consumed their Japanese enemies during World War II, which was an admissible part of their culture.

Of course we don't like to believe that cannibalism still takes place today, but there is much evidence to show that it does still happen and with more regularity than we dare believe. There have been many reported instances of cannibalism within the last hundred years and this book will outline some of the more well-known cases.

There are four primary areas of criminal cannibalism: sexual, aggressive, nutritional and spiritual/ritual. In sexual cannibalism the person may indulge in the eating of human flesh in order to reach a more intense and satisfying sexual climax. With aggressive cannibalism they may consume the flesh to achieve a sense of power and control, whereas in nutritional cannibalism the person eats it purely because they have come to love the taste. Finally in the spiritual or ritual form, the person will eat the flesh of another so that they can be as one with their deity. The technical term for the consumption of a god's body and blood is 'theophagy' and it has been considered a religious experience worldwide for thousands of years.

PSYCHOLOGY BEHIND CANNIBALISM

There are many theories about what would lead a person to commit criminal cannibalism, but perhaps the basic framework suggested by psychologists will help to understand this strange phenomenon.

One belief is that it could be the result of a trauma, especially one that is experienced in early childhood. In rare cases where a child has problems with weaning from its mother's breast, they may experience anxiety and fantasize about devouring the mother, or, in other words, oral aggression. It is possible that a child who has become excessively dependent upon its mother, due to maternal over-nurturing, is more likely to express its frustration in cannibalism.

Psychological interviews carried out with offenders have supported the theory that aggression towards the mother is one of the factors that induces cannibalism, as in the case of Ed Kemper.

Another case, that of Jeffrey Dahmer, indicates that he resorted to cannibalism as a result of stress. He murdered his first victim directly after the break-up of his family. However, this theory does not explain why Dahmer showed signs of cannibalistic fantasies in his early youth.

Most cannibals that have been studied by a psychiatrist appear to have some form of personality disorder or even schizophrenia, as in the cases of Andrei Chikatilo, Albert Fish, Edward Gein and Issei Sagawa. There were many similarities in their personalities, for example, they suffered from hallucinations, black-outs and some form of disorganized behaviour.

We can always surmise as to the reasons a certain person commits a certain type of crime, but can we ever really be sure, especially in the case of such a disgusting crime as cannibalism.

SECTION ONE

CANNIBALISM
AROUND
THE WORLD

Easter Island

Why were the mysterious people of
Easter Island maneaters and where
did they all go?

EASTER ISLAND WAS one of the world's most isolated inhabited islands and it is also one of the most mysterious. Easter Island is approximately midway between Chile and Tahiti and sits in the South Pacific Ocean 2,300 miles west of South America. The inhabitants of this charming island called their land: 'Te Pito o TeHenua' or 'The Navel of the World'.

The mystery of Easter Island and its indigenous inhabitants, the Rapanui, has intrigued both archae-ologists and travellers for many years. No-one is really sure where these ancient people originally came from. It is believed that Easter Island was colonized around ad 300 by Polynesians from the Marquesas Islands or Mangareva. It appears that this was part of an eastward migratory trend that originated in Southeast Asia around 2000 bc. From this migration perhaps one of the most remarkable cultures in all of Polynesia developed.

These people built long platforms or 'ahu' on which they placed slender statues known as 'moai'. The platforms were built near the coasts, with long retaining walls which faced the sea. Each ahu usually carried around four to six enormous moai which towered four to eight metres high. These statues, or 'aringa ora' (living faces), faced inland towards the villages as a form of protection. Some 887 moai have been discovered on Easter Island, of which 288 were actually erected on the ahu.

Most of the moai were cut from the same quarry at Rano Raraku, which contained the yellowish volcanic tuff which the inhabitants shaped with stone tools. Quite how these enormous statues were moved from the quarry to their place on their platforms still remains a mystery today. Some of the statues had a large cylindrical topknot ('pukao') carved from the reddish stone of Puna Pau. Eyes were cut out of coral and were fitted into the faces of the standing moai. By 1840 all of the moai had been thrown off their ahu, possibly by earthquakes or rival tribes.

Before the introduction of Christianity, the natives of Easter Island are said to have eaten a number of men, including two Peruvian traders. Every descendant of Easter Island is well aware that his ancestors were man-eaters, or as they knew it, 'kai-tangata'.

The cannibal feasts were generally held in remote parts of the island and women and children were generally excluded from this ritual. The fingers and toes of their victims were considered to be the tastiest morsels. The captives were held in wooden huts until it was time for them to be sacrificed to their gods.

The Easter Islanders' cannibalism was not, however,

purely a religious rite or indeed the expression of revenge, it was also induced by the fact that they simply liked the taste of human flesh. We have to remember that by 1600 there were more than 15,000 people living on the island, and the pressure over resources would have been tremendous. Unlike other cannibalistic societies, here, cannibalism wasn't so much for ritual, as for food, and the only large mammal whose flesh was available, was Man.

It was usually women and children who were the principal victims of these deep-rooted cannibals. However an act of cannibalism against a member of a family was deemed to be a terrible insult to the entire family, and the reprisals that followed this deed were acts of extreme violence. Similar to the traditions of the ancient Maoris, those men who had taken part in the 'meal' were entitled to show their teeth to the relatives of the victim and say, 'Your flesh has stuck between my teeth'. Such remarks invoked uncontrollable rage which often resulted in the murder of the perpetrator.

Over the years all the pure Rapa Nui blood died out. Connections with Chile brought new influences, and today there are only a few individuals left with any ties to the original population of Easter Island.

The Crew of the *Essex*

The crew survived for as long as possible without resorting to the inevitable, but malnutrition started to take control of their minds and they began consuming one another

PERHAPS ONE OF the most compelling shipwreck stories is that of the whaleship *Essex*, of Nantucket. This tragedy happened in the year 1820. The first of four previous voyages took place in 1802, and they were heading for whaling areas just off southern Africa. The reason for their journey was to collect whale oil, and also to head for the Pacific to obtain sperm oil.

On August 12, 1819, the *Essex* left Nantucket in southwest Florida, once again bound for the Pacific. On board that day were a crew of 20 and the Captain, George Pollard. Fifteen months later, on November 20, 1920, the *Essex* was approximately 2,700 miles west of Ecuador. Two of the ship's small boats were already out, and the Captain had managed to harpoon a whale. One of the small ships was just returning to the *Essex*, when the first mate, Owen Chase, noticed that a large sperm whale was charging at the ship.

The crew stood and watched helplessly while the

whale's massive head struck the bow of the ship. The whale then turned around and rammed the ship for a second time, this time staving in the bows and forcing the crew to abandon their ship.

Before leaving in three clinker-built whaleboats, the crew managed to salvage some food and water, two quadrants and two sextants to help with their survival, as they did not know how long they would be at sea before being rescued. They pulled away from their ship just in time to see the *Essex* sink and began their search for land. They knew the closest land lay to the west and, in fact Tahiti was only about a two-week sail away. However, very few ships had ever ventured as far west, and so the crew had no idea what to expect on the islands around Tahiti. The only knowledge they had of the islands was that there was the possibility of cannibals living there. Due to this fear they decided to attempt a far longer journey to the remote Easter Island, around 20,000 miles away.

The first mate, Chase, mentioned in his account of the forthcoming disaster that their captain, Pollard, would have preferred to take the risk of landing in Tahiti, but did not have the confidence to force his wishes upon his fearful crew. And so it was for this reason that the hapless crew set sail south and east, in the hope of reaching the latitude of the trade winds.

There was a total of three boats that left the wreck of the *Essex*, commanded by Captain Pollard, first-mate Chase, and second mate Joy. On the sixth day at sea the first mate reported that his boat had been attacked by a killer whale, although in all probability it was a shark. However, it was large enough to bite a large portion out of the stern of Chase's boat, splintering and splitting it in the process. For 22 days the crew suffered, managing to survive on the few meagre supplies they had managed to salvage from the *Essex.*

Exhausted and thoroughly despondent they managed to reach Dulcie's Island.

When they arrived at Dulcie's Island, the crew started a frantic search for essential food and water. They were successful in the search for water, but the only food they could find were sea-birds and their eggs; hardly enough to feed 21 starving men. Not knowing the area at all, they were unaware they they were only one day away from Pitcairn Island. Realising that Dulcie's Island could not support them, the men once again took to sea in search of Easter Island, leaving three of the crew behind at their own request.

It appears, however, that luck was not on the side of the crew of the Essex because, before they could reach their destination, their small craft was hit by a series of powerful storms which blew their small vessels off course, several hundreds of miles south of Easter Island. Unsure of what to do, the Captain suggested that they continue another 2,500 miles and try to make the coast of South America. Once again they were hit by a storm, and this time the three boats became separated. Chase's boat was the first one to get blown away from the others, and after a week of Chase's disappearance, Pollard's boat and the third boat also became separated.

Due to the lack of water and food, and to their constant exposure to inclement weather, the men were soon in a very weakened state. In the Pollard boat, and on the brink of starvation, Charles Rhamseldel was the first of the men to suggest that they resorted to cannibalism in an effort to survive. Pollard was nauseated by the suggestion, but as the days went by and the crew became weaker and weaker, it was obvious that they would either all die from starvation, or alternatively allow themselves to sustain one another!

In the end, Owen Coffin, finally convinced Pollard that one of the men would have to be sacrificed. Ironically enough it was Coffin himself who drew the short straw. Coffin was Pollard's cousin, and had been entrusted into his care at the age of 14 by his mother. Pollard demanded that he took his place, but Coffin denied him this and said it was his right to save the remaining crew of the Essex.

To settle the matter the crew decided to draw straws again, and this time it was the fate of Charles Rhamseldel who drew the short end of the stick. However, being the childhood playmate of Coffin, Rhamseldel pleaded with Coffin to exchange places. The matter was settled when Rhamseldel eventually executed Coffin himself, by shooting him in the head with a musket. The crew quickly devoured their companion, with the exception of Pollard who said that there was no way he could eat one of his own relatives.

It appears that the other two boats resorted to similar measures. In Chase's boat it was a black crew member who died first, only this time from natural causes, and he was simply thrown overboard. However, on realizing that this man could in fact have saved their lives, when a second black crew member died, a short time later, he was consumed by the remainder of the crew.

The third man to die in Chase's boat was yet another black sailor, only this time he was the victim of drawing straws for a cannibalistic sacrifice.

The men survived in this hellish way for several months, slowly eating one another to stave off malnutrition, all the time suffering from exposure to the salt and sun of the ocean. It would be many more days before some of the men found salvation.

The Aztecs

Cannibalism has been around for a long time and in a lot of places – the Aztecs used cannibalism in human-sacrifice rituals

THE EARLIEST RECORDS show that the Aztecs migrated from the north into the Valley of Mexico as early as the 12th century ad. They were a rather abject civilization who were forced to live on the worst lands in the valley.

They were a poor, ragged race who ate rats, snakes, and stole food, but above all sacrificed human flesh to their gods. They were considered just too wild and nasty by neighbouring tribes, and consequently they were driven from one place to another.

In 1300, the Tenochcas, as they were then known, escaped to settle on an island in the middle of Lake Texcoco. It was here that they were to build their city and started to thank their god, Huitzilopochtli, for his assistance with human sacrifices. The city they built was called Tenochtitlan or 'place of the Tenochcas'.

It was very hard to build Tenochtitlan because the Aztecs only had a very small piece of land in the surrounding marshes. The Aztecs made the swampy, shallow lake into a habitable place by piling up mud from the lake bottom. These mud islands were used as their city foundations. To start with they built a few thatched mud huts, and some small temples.

Next they built causeways and bridges to connect the city to the mainland. They dug canals and lined them with stone so that people could move easily around.

By 1376, the city was growing quickly and people came from miles around to live in the city of Tenochtitlan. The Aztecs slowly became more powerful and more skilled at defending themselves, although they had no real form of military strategy.

At least half of the Aztec population were farmers, and they worked on the reclaimed areas of the lake, which they covered with soil and then cultivated. The city itself consisted of a large number of priests and crafts people, and soon Tenochtitlan was becoming a true urban centre.

The Aztecs had two clearly differing social classes. At the bottom were the macehualles or 'commoners', and at the top the pilli or 'nobility'. All male children went to school to learn history, the religion of the Aztecs, and the art of war and fighting. Women were regarded as the subordinate of men in Aztec society, and were required to behave with chastity and high moral standards.

Aztec laws were simple and yet harsh. Almost every crime was punishable by death, while minor offences involved corporal punishment or mutilation. As an example, if they were found guilty of slander they would lose their lips.

Their religion consisted of a very complicated structure, due to the fact that most of it was inherited from people they conquered. They were dominated by three gods – Huitzilopochtli 'hummingbird wizard', Tezcatlipoca 'Smoking Mirror', and Quetzalcoatl 'Sovereign Plumed Serpent'. Under these three dominant gods were an infinity of other gods.

HUMAN SACRIFICE

The overwhelming aspect of Aztec religious life, however, was their predominance of human sacrifice. Although it is known that this was practiced throughout the Mesoamerican world, the Techochca performed it at a scale never seen before, or indeed since. The Aztecs believed that their gods would only give things to human beings if they were constantly nourished by human beings. To satisfy their gods, the Aztecs would draw their own blood by piercing their tongues, ears, extremities or even genitals. However, Aztec theologians also developed the idea that the gods would be best nourished if they were given the living hearts of sacrificed captives. This theology led to widespread fighting in search of sacrificial victims, both captured in war and paid as a tribute by the conquered people.

Some of these sacrifices were small, involving the giving up of a slave to a minor god. Others were spectacular, involving hundreds or even thousands of captives, but no matter what the size, the actual sacrifice was always carried out in the same manner. The victim would be restrained by four priests on an altar which would be placed at the top of a pyramid structure or a raised temple. The officiant then made an incision just below the rib cage and pulled out the victim's living heart. Next the heart was burned and the corpse was pushed down the steep steps. If the captive was very noble, or had been extremely brave, then his body would be carried down the steps.

Even more disturbing than these human sacrifices, was the practice of ritual cannibalism that was carried out at these ceremonies. After the hearts were removed and the bodies tossed down the temple steps, the limbs were removed and later cooked. As repugnant as cannibalism is to us today, back then to the Aztecs, cooked human bodies were looked upon as great delicacies. The favoured parts of the body were the hands and thighs, and it has been said that the Aztec emperor, Moctezuma, was reported to have been partial to cooked thighs served with tomatoes and chili pepper sauce. Although this thought might turn our stomachs, it must also be remembered that the Aztecs had no domestic livestock from which to obtain their protein, and so the ritual sacrifice was a way for the Aztec royalty to obtain vital nutrients. Thus in the Aztecs we can see a mixture of religion and nourishment which resulted in human sacrifice.

Sorcery in Guyana

*The Kanaimàs enjoy the savage delight of killing
and devouring human beings as part of a
gruesome ritual*

ALONG THE NORTHEAST coast of South America in
Guyana, there is a form of cannibalism that is known as
'kanaimà'. This is a form of 'assault sorcery' where the
dark sorcerers (or Kanaimàs) of the Guyana highlands
mutilate and poison their victims as part of a gruesome
and highly ritualized murder. This horrifying ritual can
take many years to complete, and the victims all end up
suffering a horrible death.

An anthropologist who visited Guyana in the 1990s,
had heard of the horrifying stories of the kanaimà but
believed them all to be grossly exaggerated. His original
plan was to survey the area making notes about the
villages, burial sites and caves so that he could write
about them in detail when he returned home. However,
shortly after arriving in one of the villages he was
approached by a local nurse who earnestly requested
that he turned his attention to the Kanaimàs instead.
She told him that the practice still took place and that
the natives were stalking, bludgeoning, poisoning and

mutilating their victims along the forested mountain paths.

She told him that the Kanaimàs did not kill their victims immediately, they preferred to maim and intimidate them by perhaps breaking their fingers or dislocating their necks. The intention of the first attack is purely to weaken the victim. Months or even years later, the Kanaimàs will return to their victim and carry out a ferocious attack. After suffering many months, or even years, of pain, the hapless victim has his tongue pierced with snake fangs, his mouth and anus are pierced with sharp objects, and also toxic plants are inserted into the anus.

Three days after death, the sorcerer inserts a stick into the already decomposing body and then sucks the end of the stick. If the sorcerer does not carry out this ritual, he is vulnerable to revenge by the family of his victim. The victim is chosen simply because they are vulnerable and the Kanaimàs announce their intention to attack with bird-like warning calls.

These attacks against innocent, defenceless people can be considered as cannibalism because the ultimate aim is to partake a portion of the dead body as a form of protection against evil, and is thought to appease the gods of the Kanaimàs.

The anthropologist himself, Neil Whitehead, was subjected to poisoning by the Kanaimàs, which made the horrendous stories related to him even more horrifying.

Cannibalism in the Congo

It has been reported that nearly all the tribes in the Congo Basin either are, or have been, cannibals

CANNIBALISM IS FAR from being dead in Africa, for it is almost impossible to control the natives who inhabit the bush. It is possible that thousands of natives are being eaten in the Congo every year, purely because it is difficult to break old habits. It is probably hard to believe but at one time or another nearly all the tribes in the Congo Basin either have been or are still cannibals. Races who, until recently, had no cannibalistic tendencies even though they were situated in a country surrounded by cannibal races, have now learned to eat human flesh.

The reason for this cannibalism is probably because they simply prefer human flesh to any other. Reports from men who have lived among cannibal races, said that they never came across a single case of them eating any kind of flesh raw; they invariably either boil, roast or smoke it. The custom of smoking flesh was to make it last longer, as sometimes the natives could go without meat for quite long periods. Smoked meat for sale in the African markets, could possibly be human flesh.

Studies of the different tribes has shown that they have a preference for various parts of the human body. Some cut long steaks from the flesh of the thighs, legs or arms; others prefer the hands and feet. Although not generally consumed, there are certain tribes who consider the head to be a real delicacy. Almost all the tribes use some part of the intestines due to the amount of fat they contain.

THE KUKUKUKUS

A missionary who spent some time with a tribe of people called the Kukukukus in the 1950s, reported a time when a party of warriors took an enemy tribesman prisoner. They tied the poor captive to a thin tree trunk and then carried him horizontally back to their village. To make sure that the prisoner did not escape, they broke both his legs by hitting them with clubs, bound him to a tree, and then adorned him with feathers and shells in preparation for their forthcoming feast. The women bought in fresh vegetables from the sur-rounding fields, and then the menfolk proceeded to dig a big hole in the ground to act as an oven. While all this was going on, the children were allowed to 'play' with the prisoner, using him as a target and eventually stoning him to death. This exercise is supposed to harden their children towards the act of killing. When the captive is no longer alive, the natives cut off his arms and legs with a bamboo knife. Next the meat is cut up into small pieces, wrapped in pieces of bark, and then cooked together with the vegetables. Such a banquet is attended by men, women and children, and is usually accompanied by dancing and jubilant songs. Apparently it is only the tribes' enemies that are eaten, and if the captive is a a brave, young, strong warrior, the muscly parts of the body are given to the young boys of the tribe so that they can absorb the dead man's power and courage. Cannibalism among the Kukukukus derives mainly from a shortage of meat and a deficiency of protein. Meat is indeed a rare luxury for them, and they have often been seen devouring the charred remains of rats, mice, lizards and other vermin after burning grass on the fields that surround their village.

FOR ALL TO SEE

Reports from people who have travelled through the Congo in the early 1900s, say it was difficult to pass down certain roads without seeing the horrible remains left to the jackals which the human 'wolves' had not found to their liking. Spotted by smouldering camp fires were the whitening bones, cracked and broken, which form the relics of 'human' banquets. Some of the bodies that were found along the roadside were minus their hands and feet, others had steaks cut from the thighs or elsewhere, while others had the entrails or head removed. It appeared that neither old nor young, women or children, were exempt from being served as food.

RECENT CANNIBALISM

Many acts of cannibalism have been reported from time to time in the African Congo, but one that has recently been brought to light by the press is the massacring and eating of pygmies by rebels in the dense forests of the northeast. It appears that the Ituri province was completely out of control and that cannibalism was just the latest of the atrocities taking place there. Ituri's forest-dwelling pygmy tribes were caught between fighting groups in the battles of Congo's four-year civil war. Two of the Ugandan-backed movements captured pygmies on a regular basis and sent them into the forest in search of food and minerals. If they returned empty-handed, they were killed and eaten. Reports came back of enemy commanders feeding on the sexual organs of pygmies, believing that this would give them improved strength. Also pygmies were being forced to feed on the cooked remains of their relatives and colleagues.

It seems that cannibalism has definitely re-emerged in certain parts of the Congo. Much of the enormous area of forest is now being controlled by the Mayi-Mayi, a group of tribal militia who have been united by their beliefs and also their taste for human flesh.

Just outside the Congolese town of Bunia, a horrified mother watched as militiamen roasted and then ate the severed arms of her dying daughters. She told of how the militiamen calmly cooked the human flesh over an open fire before throwing their victims, many of them still alive, into the flames.

It is stories like this that have galvanized the world to take action and do something about the horrific cannibalism that is taking place in the Congo.

The Last Known Tribe

They found natives who were completely
naked and living in the trees

THE MEDIA WERE absolutely buzzing all around the world in November 1995. The reason being that an expedition led by Doctor Cesar Pérez de Tudela (a famous Spanish climber and explorer), and professor Vicente Martínez (a journalist) had discovered what was possibly the last indigenous tribe of cannibals known all over the world.

This project was the result of ten years of intense work, and six different expeditions had been carried out in the past by different explorers.

The final expedition took the Doctor and the Professor a month and it involved climbing mountains, crossing jungles, rivers and lakes. The explorers found a few villages located near the rivers of Irian Jaya (Indonesia), where they discovered the natives were totally naked and lived in the trees. The majority of the natives were totally unaware of any civilization outside of their tribe.

They live in close proximity to the ethnic groups of Korowais and Kombais, and the local authorities and people of the surrounding villages were not aware that their neighbours had been practising cannibalism for many years and indeed still are.

The expedition saw first-hand the chopped heads of the tribe's enemies, the bodies of which had already been eaten by them. They even discovered the head of a missionary who had recently gone missing. These tribes are extremely hostile and live in very remote areas which made them very difficult to find. Although they proved that the natives ate human bodies, it is still not clear whether it is as a ritual or just their normal way of living.

Cannibalism in Russia

*An alarming thought is that cannibalism
seems to be a fairly common occurrence
in the former Soviet Union*

IN 1996 TEN people were charged with the killing and eating of other people. A rough estimate by Russian police is that around 30 people were eaten in just that one year. Reports leaked out through the press that human flesh was being sold in street markets, vagrants were being eaten or their bodies being cut up and sold. Every month the Russian police were finding the corpse of a homeless person with missing body parts.

UKRAINE

Police arrested three men and a woman on July 15, 2002, in the central Ukranian town of Zhytomyr. They were suspected of killing and cannibalizing at least six people, including an 18-year-old, in what is believed to have been a Satanic ritual. The young woman was killed in a forest and then fleshy parts of her body were removed and eaten by her murderers.

She was stabbed in the heart, scalped and also decapitated. The suspects then boiled her head in water and proceeded to eat pieces from it. The suspects were apprehended when they went to meet the young girl's parents to collect a $3,000 ransom.

CRIMEA

Police were called out to a home of a former convict in the city of Sebastopol in March 1996. Although they were used to dealing with some quite horrific murder cases, nothing could have prepared them for the carnage they were about to discover.

When the police entered the house they found the mutilated remains of human bodies that had been prepared for consumption. The owner of the flat, her mother and her boyfriend, had all been stabbed to death by the 33-year-old suspect. Not only had their bodies been neatly butchered, but the investigators also found the internal organs from two of the victims in a saucepan on the stove in the kitchen. On the table was a plate which had on it a freshly roasted piece of human flesh.

SIBERIA

'Pelmeni' is the Russian equivalent of ravioli. In the year 1996 a man was arrested in the coal mining town of Kemerovo after he openly admitted to killing and cutting up a friend, and using his flesh to fill his pelmeni. This crime was discovered when some vagrants were scavenging through a rubbish dump and they uncovered a severed human head. Investigators were soon to learn that the rest of the body had been minced up, put into pelmeni, and subsequently sold at cut-price rates on the local market.

KYARGYZSTAN

Nikolai Dzhurmongaliev, known as 'Metal Fang' because of his white metal false teeth, is possibly the king of the Soviet cannibals, slaughtering and serving up around 100 women to his dinner guests in the Russian republic of Kyargyzstan. Nikolai is known to have used at least 47 of his victims to make ethnic recipes for many of his neighbours.

Nikolai's belief was that women and prostitution were the root of all evil. His evil doings were not discovered until two of his friends found a head and some intestines in his kitchen. He was immediately incarcerated in a lunatic asylum in Tashkent, but amazingly enough he managed to bribe his way out of the institution. His case went to trial and he was found guilty of only seven murders. Once again he was put into an asylum but managed to escape in 1989.

Embarrassed by their failure to keep him locked up, the Russian authorities never admitted to the public that Nikolai had escaped, and spent two years trying to recapture him. They eventually managed to track him down in Uzbekistan. The Interior Minister, Colonel Yuri Dubyagin described him as, 'absolutely normal, but at one point he got a taste for female flesh'. Nikolai himself admitted that two women could provide him with enough delicate meat to keep him going for a whole week.

The attitude of this minister may possibly explain why there are so many high-scoring serial killers in Russia. Nikolai Dzhurmongaliev was considered not to be responsible for his actions, and he is once again under lock and key in a mental institution.

EATING A CELL-MATE

Two cases of cannibalism were reported in 2003 that involved prison inmates. Convicts that were kept in overcrowded prisons killed and ate their cellmates, claiming that they were being underfed and that they wanted to relieve the cramped conditions.

In 1996, a twice-convicted murderer, Andrei Maslich, along with another inmate, killed and ate a fellow prisoner. Offering no other explanation than the fact that he did not want to share his cell with anyone, Andrei, who was only 24 at the time, strangled his cellmate and then cut out his liver with a shard of broken glass. He placed the liver in his drinking mug along with some water, and then made a makeshift fire out of his bedding on which to cook his 'supper'. Both men told authorities that they were bored and wanted to visit Moscow, where they expected they would be sent for psychiatric examinations. Instead, the two men were sentenced to death.

Another case of cannibalism was reported in the Semipalatinsk prison in Kazakstan. Four convicts blamed their actions on the fact that the prison diet was inadequate and on newspaper articles they had read regarding instances of cannibalism in prison. The four inmates made a pact that they would kill and eat the first 'new guy' to be placed in their cell, and this just happened to be a convict named Volchenkov. They kept to their word and killed him, cutting the meat from his arms and back, cooking it and eating it. Some of the flesh was fried on a hot plate while other parts were boiled in an electric kettle which was kept in their cell.

BERGEN-BELSEN

Bergen-Belsen was a concentration camp established in 1943 originally to hold prisoners to be used in political exchanges. Administered by the SS, it included five sub-camps where some 50,000 Jews, political hostages, and other prisoners died of starvation, disease, brutality and sadistic medical practices.

Bergen-Belsen was liberated by the British in 1945. Inside the camp the horrified soldiers found piles of dead and rotting corpses and thousands of sick and starving prisoners kept in severely overcrowded and dirty compounds. The stench was intolerable even though the air was quite cold. The ground was muddy and a pile of corpses balanced carefully on one another, rose geometrically like a haystack. This was due to the fact that there was no more room in the crematoria.

The Russian prisoners who had been incarcerated in this open-air camp were given no food or water. Driven by starvation, people went mad, and eventually many turned to cannibalism.

BEREZNIKI

The grim discovery of a terrible murder involving cannibalism in the small town of Berezniki, in Perm Oblast, unfolded when a man brought a package of human flesh to the police station. He told them that he had bought the meat on the street, but his wife, on discovering skin on it, told her husband to take it to the police.

The police managed to establish the identities of the traders, who turned out to be F. A. Boldyshev, who had previous convictions, and his friend N. V. Ostanin. These traders, however, turned out to be the murderers as well. It appeared that they had been sharing a bottle of spirits with a third man, A. P. Vavilin, when things got out of hand and they murdered him. Next they dismembered his corpse and had one of their mothers cook up the best pieces of flesh. After gorging themselves on their human feast, the two men packaged up the remainder and sold it on the streets. They claimed they had committed the act in order to obtain some money for their next bottle of spirits and to save money on the cost of normal meat. Police discovered the remains of Vavilin's head, hands and feet discarded in the attic of one of their houses.

SASHA SPESIVTSEV

Twenty-seven-year-old Sasha Spesivtsev decided to take it into his own hands to cleanse the Russian streets of permissiveness. He killed at least 19 street children whom he saw as the dregs of society. The unemployed former mental patient, lured his homeless victims from the streets and local train stations in his home town of Novokuznetsk, back to his house. It was here, with the help of his mother, that Spesivtsev murdered his victims and then ate them.

Suspicions that there might be a serial killer active in the area surfaced in the summer of 1996 when body parts appeared in the river Aba near the school where Sasha's mother, Lyudmila, worked. However, the investigation moved rather slowly due to the nature of the victims – the poor children of the forgotten underclass – and the inept Russian judicial beaurocracy. During the early stages of the investigation, one of Sasha's neighbours repeatedly complained to the police of the nauseating stench and deafening music coming from Sasha's apartment. However, no investigation ensued, even though in 1991 a teenage girl was found dead in Sasha's house. A year later, when police finally entered his home they found 15-year-old Olga Galtseva dying on the couch with multiple stab wounds to her stomach. In the bathroom they found a headless corpse and in the living room there was a rib cage.

Before she died, Olga managed to tell the police that she, together with two 13-year-old friends, helped

Sasha's mother carry some bags into her apartment. Once inside they were trapped by Sasha and a fierce dog. No trace of Olga's two little friends was ever found, and the police can only assume that they also died. A search of Spesivtsev's apartment revealed 80 blood-stained pieces of clothing, and DNA tests established that none of them contained blood from anyone in Spesivtsev's family.

Sasha was eventually committed after being convicted of murdering his girlfriend. In prison he spends all his time undergoing psychiatric testing and writing poems about the evils of democracy. His mother, on the other hand, has withdrawn into herself and has not uttered a word since her arrest.

VLADIMIR NIKOLAYEV

On July 3, 1997, 38-year-old Vladimir Nikolayev was sentenced to death for the murdering and cannibalising two people in the town of Novocheboksary. Already on police records as a paricularly dangerous criminal, investigators found a pan of roasted human meat on the stove and another in the oven, when they went to arrest Nikolayev at his apartment. More bodies had been stored in the snow on the apartment's balcony, bodies which Nikolayev claimed he was storing to eat later on. When questioned later by an investigator, Nikolayev jokingly asked the officer if he would be prepared to make him a dinner using his own stores of human meat.

MANTUROVO

Manturovo is a quiet little town of around 22,000 inhabitants, situated on the tributary of the Volga river, but it was soon to be shaken by a case of cannibalism. Valentina Dolbilina, a 36-year-old mother of a four-year-old boy, and 28-year-old Vitaly Bezrodnov, a factory worker, were both accused of killing their drinking partner and then cooking and eating his flesh.

Dolbilina and Bezrodnov had been out for a night of heavy drinking. Bezrodnov said that he was feeling hungry and would like to eat some juicy meat. They eyed up their drinking partner who was asleep in the corner in a drunken stupor. However, they said that he was too skinny to be of any use to them, and they packed him off home. Then their attention turned to the fourth member of their drinking party, who had more flesh on him. Luring him back to Dolbilina's house, they ushered him into the tiny kitchen where Bezrodnov asked Dolbilina for something heavy. She immediately went and fetched and axe, and their hapless victim was hit on the head, beheaded, undressed and then cut up into pieces. When they had finished their grisly deed, some 15 pounds of meat was cut from the thigh and rump, and put into a frying pan.

The smell of the cooking meat aroused her sleeping flatmate, Boris Komarov, who came into the room and asked if he could join in the feast. However, despite the effects of a night of drinking, Boris noticed that there was something strange about the meat he was eating, and stated that 'it was a bit tough'. To put his mind at ease, Bezrodnov claimed that they had killed a stray dog on their way home, and that it was canine flesh that he was consuming. Reassured by Bezrodnov's explanation, Boris kept on eating the joint of meat straight from the pan. Little did he realise the true ghastliness of the situation – the dead man he was eating was his own brother, Leonid.

The horror of the situation did not end there, however, even Dolbilina's own son, Roma, was served a slice of the hapless Leonid. Later, when questioned, the boy blurted out: 'Mummy killed a man and served him up to her friends.'

ILSHAT KUZIKOV

Russian police are currently investigating a possible case of cannibalism in which an elderly woman is suspected of having stored bits and pieces of her dead husband in her refrigerator. The 83-year-old victim was found lying outside the couple's Kalingrad flat with parts of his body missing. When they searched the apartment, police found tin cans with the remains of muscles and meat in the refrigerator. Conclusive tests are still to be carried out.

Whatever the results, this case pales in comparison to that of Ilshat Kuzikov, a 35-year-old schizophrenic.

Kuzikov liked to marinate choice cuts of human flesh with onions and hang them outside of his apartment window in plastic bags. When the police forced their way into his home, they also found old Pepsi bottles containing blood, and ears hanging from his walls, which he claimed were his winter supply. They also found severed arms, legs, human bones and buckets of human flesh left to marinate with onions. Kuzikov tried to bribe the officers by offering them some of his choice meat along with a glass of vodka.

Kuzikov was found guilty of murdering three of his vodka-drinking friends and eating their internal organs on March 19, 1997. He is currently being held in a maximum-security psychiatric hospital at St. Petersburg. The self-confessed cannibal said he killed his first victim in 1992 after inviting him into his flat for a nightcap. He claimed that he became a cannibal because he was unable to buy enough food on his meagre $20 pension.

The American West
in 1846

Of the 83 members of the Donner Party who were trapped in the mountains, only 45 survived to tell the tale

THERE WERE VERY few white people living in the American West in the year 1846. San Francisco, originally an Indian town, was still a very small community which eventually flourished in an international farming community. Sacramento, which was originally little more than a lush river valley, was starting to gain popularity because of its fertile soil, and it soon became a prosperous land for grazing livestock. People from far and wide soon started flocking to the American West in search of a new life.

THE DONNER PARTY

James Frazier Reed was 45 at the time of the Donner Party. He was born in Ireland, but had become a well-known businessman, who owned a furniture manufacturing company and was also a member of the masons in Springfield, Illinois. During the American Blackhawk War, Reed had served in the military alongside the future president, Abraham Lincoln. He married Margaret Keyes-Backenstoe-Reed and together they raised three children, along with his stepdaughter, Virginia. Although Reed was disliked by his party for his wealth and culture, he was known to be a kind and caring man.

In the year 1846 three families from Springfield decided to move and try to make their fortunes 'Out West'. The three families in question were those of George Donner, Jacob Donner and James F. Reed. George and Jacob were brothers and they knew Reed by reputation.

The Oregon Trail officially started at Independence, Missouri and then moved along the Platte River in the Midwest, over the Rocky Mountains, through Utah, Wyoming and Idaho, and then down the treacherous Columbia River to Oregon city. The families were looking forward to their journey when they started out from Springfield. Many wagon trains before them had made the 2000-mile trek and, although most people suffered various hardships along the way, they managed to get over the Sierras and on to California in safety.

And so it was that the two Donner families and the Reed family set out from Springfield in April 1846. To help them drive the additional wagons loaded with food and luggage, the families had hired teamsters. They also brought with them their trusted family servants who had come along of their own free will, as they wanted to stay working with their employers. Margaret's mother, Sarah Keyes, was already frail when they started the journey, and by the time they reached Independence on May 11, she had weakened considerably and become virtually blind.

The Bryant party, led by William Russell, joined up with them at Independence and George Donner, aged 60, and his friend James F. Reed, aged 46, were chosen to be the leaders for the duration of the journey. At the end of May, Sarah Keyes died at a place near Alcove Springs. Further along the trail various other groups joined the Donner party and everything went smoothly until they decided to take the Hastings's Cut-off, which was supposed to be a shortcut. This was to be the first of a series of very peculiar events along their ill-fated journey. The reason they took the supposed shortcut was because somewhere along their route they met a man named Wales B. Bonney who was carrying an open letter from a man called Lansford Hastings. This letter told travellers of a newly-discovered route to the south of the Great Salt Lake, and encouraged people to go this way to save time. It pointed out that this route was shorter and would save the travellers around 400 miles. Despite being previously warned by experienced travellers not to take the shortcut, the Donners thought it sounded promising and decided to go against their advice.

Veering off from the normal route, the Donner party travelled on towards Fort Bridger, where they expected to find Lansford Hastings waiting for them. However, by the time they reached the Fort it was already quite late in the season and Hastings had already left, taking with him a large wagon. He had left directions for any parties that would like to follow him along his new trail. Convinced that this was the right thing to do, the Donners stocked up with supplies, and four days later their party of nine families, plus sixteen single men, left the Fort on the last day of July.

A little way out of Fort Bridger the party came across a fork in the road. The fork to the right would lead them up the old road towards Fort Hall, but as the tracks of Hastings's wagon were clear on the left fork, this is the way the Donner party headed. It wasn't too long before the countryside became very mountainous and the road barely passable. In certain places along the route they had to actually lock the wheels of their wagons to stop them sliding down the narrow ravines and steep hillsides. Still convinced that this was the way to go, the party continued to follow the wheel tracks made by the Hastings's wagon. They managed to make around 10 to 12 miles in a day, but by the time they reached the Red Fork of the Weber river the trail had stopped. Attached to a bush was a note written by Hastings, warning any party that decided to follow him through the Weber canyon, that the route was very treacherous. His advice to the party was for them to make camp and send a messenger ahead to catch up with him so that he could return and give them exact directions across the mountains. Reed, along with two other men were the appointed messengers, and they left on horseback to see if they could catch up with Hastings.

They waited for several days and on the fifth day Reed returned looking very weak and dishevelled. He was riding a different horse from when he left and he explained to the anxious party about the difficulties they had experienced in trying to catch up with Hastings. The other two men who had accompanied Reed had decided to stay with Hastings, as their horses were exhausted and Hastings could only spare one fresh horse. Despite his promise on the note, Hastings was not coming back to meet up with the group. However, on his way back Reed had managed to explore a route through the canyon which had been suggested to him by Hastings himself. Although he knew it would be difficult, he felt that they could get their wagons through. Although the party was very dubious, they decided to take Reed's word for it and they voted unanimously to take this route.

The determined emigrants pushed on and on as the terrain became more and more difficult to cross. They were growing weaker and weaker by the day as they had to constantly use axes, picks and shovels to clear the way, and gradually their spirits became lower and lower. It was now August 27 and not only were they totally exhausted, the fear was starting to set in. They had been on their new route for 21 days now and so far they had only managed to travel 360 miles. Their provisions were running low and they knew that soon the weather would turn against them. On August 29 the party arrived at the spot where Reed had met up with Hastings. Apparently Hastings's own party had managed to get through, and no doubt the Donner party would have been successful as well were it not for the onset of the winter weather. It seemed their fate was sealed when an unusually fierce winter storm hit the Sierra Nevada desert.

It took the Donner party five days to cross the desert. Wagons which got stuck in the deep quagmire of wet salt and sand had to be abandoned. Their oxen went mad from the lack of water and either just ran away or died. The party decided to take inventory of the provisions and it proved that they did not have enough left to last them the 600-mile trek which was still ahead of them. They camped for the night, but when they woke in the morning they saw the mountain peaks were covered with a dusting of snow, and they realised that things were not going to improve. They managed to reach the Humbolt River by September 26, but it then hit them that the so-called diversion had cost them an extra 150 miles. As their nerves became more and more shattered, so the fights broke out. James Reed killed the Graves family's leader, John Snyder – supposedly in self-defence – and he was subsequently banished from the party. He left his family behind, took a horse and rode on to California alone.

As the family reached the base of the steep summit on October 31, the snow was starting to fall more heavily. Some of the group did manage to reach the summit, but they had to turn back because they realised that there was no way the entire party could make the ascent. Overnight the snow fell continually, and by the morning the pass had become completely blocked by extremely high snowdrifts. Frustration really set in now as they had made the 2,500 mile journey in seven months only to be beaten by the weather by one day. They were by now only 150 miles from their final destination of Sutter's Fort, now known as Sacramento.

The group, now realising that they were stranded, decided to make camps to see them through the worst of the winter. Their shelters were basic and crude. Using nothing but logs for the walls, wagon parts for the doors and leather hides for roofing, they managed to make cabins which provided them with minimal shelter. As the snow fell, the Donner party knew they were trapped, with steep slopes in front and behind them, there was absolutely nowhere they could go. The Donner brothers were old men, and there were very few left in the party who had any strength left in them. Over the following four months, the remaining men, women and children huddled together in their makeshift cabins. By now all the oxen had been killed and eaten, and by mid-December they lost their first casualty to malnutrition. They had nothing to do to occupy their time, but nevertheless they made the best out of the situation by chopping wood and attempting to fish and hunt. There was very little game in the area and the surface of the lake was frozen, so in the end they resorted to eating bark, twigs and boiled hides.

Desperation set in and several attempts were made by

small groups to cross the mountains. One group of 15 men, women and children did successfully cross the summit, but only seven of them survived to reach Sutter's fort. Their arrival at the fort raised an outcry of alarm, and rescue attempts followed shortly afterwards.

NO OPTIONS LEFT

Back at the camp, food was now depleted, the snow would not let up, and the remaining members of the party left alive were losing all their strength and hope. They had nowhere to go, and as a gruesome reminder of their plight, the bodies of the dead were always in their sights. The suggestion of cannibalism had been made, but no one was sure about this, nor indeed were they looking forward to the fact that this is what they would have to resort to. Soon they had no options left . . .

Desperation set in, and four of the dead bodies at the camp, now known as 'Camp of Death' were cut up, and the meat was dried. After all nobody had been murdered, they were only resorting to this desperate measure in order to survive. The survivors were very careful about who they ate, they made sure that none of them were actually consuming any of their own relatives. Most of the dead had died from starvation so they could offer only a small amount of meat, but the little they were able to obtain provided them with enough strength to move on.

At the end of December the storm, which had held the party in their makeshift camp, subsided and some of the party were able to leave the Camp of Death, leaving those who chose to stay behind. They took as much meat with them as they could carry in their packs, and then pushed ahead as far as they could. They knew they had a long way to go and that they were still miles away from any Indians, let alone white people. The sorry party of five men and five women trudged across the Sierra Nevada in their snowshoes in a desperate effort to reach their final destination.

By early January the party had made reasonably good progress, but they still had a long way to go and food supplies were again running low. One of the party, Joe Fosdick grew terribly sick and was unable to keep up with the others. Understandably he was left behind with his wife Sarah. After a couple of days William Foster and one other person, presuming that the couple would be dead, turned back to find the corpses and use them for food. But to their surprise, Sarah Fosdick was still alive, although extremely weak. Remaining faithful to her husband she had stayed by his side, and even after his death a short while later she had abandoned any hope of continuing the journey on her own. Right before Sarah's eyes her husband's corpse was cut up and, after filling the packs with the meat, Foster and Mrs. Fosdick returned to the others who had made a camp to wait for Foster's return.

However, the meat from one very undernourished body did not provide much sustenance for nine people. Among these nine were two Indians, and luckily for the white people they refused to eat any of the human flesh.

William Foster was becoming more and more deranged and started to make plans to kills the two Indians, Luis and Salvadore, to give the remaining party more food. Immediately the two Indians ran away, frightened for their lives. It was easy for the party to follow their tracks though, because their bare feet had become so raw from exposure that the majority of their toes had fallen off, and they were leaving a trail of blood wherever they went. Foster decided that even if the Indians didn't lead them to safety, they could at least find their bodies and use them for food.

Gradually, through lack of food and exposure, the two Indians became weaker and weaker, and eventually the party caught up with them at a small creek. Despite the protests of other members of the party, Foster took out a rifle and shot the two Indians. Even though they were close to death, the others still considered the act to be horrifying.

Armed with more supplies the party reached an Indian village on January 11. There were now two men and five women and the natives offered them clothes, shelter and, more importantly, food. The Indians were well aware that these starving people could easily die from overeating, so they were careful to only feed them small amounts, offering them thin soups made from acorns and venison meat. Despite the constant pleading from the survivors, the Indians would not feed them any more food.

William Foster and the five women were all in a terrible condition, and it was still uncertain whether they would in fact survive. The other man, William Eddy, who was also very sick, knew he had to survive in order to get help to his family who had stayed behind at the lakeside encampment. Whilst the others stayed and rested, Eddy persuaded the Indians to take him to Johnson's Ranch, and a posse of scouts and women led what became known as the First Relief.

Despite being desperately sick, Eddy pushed on through the mountains in a desperate effort to reach his family in the hope that they had survived. However, because he was so weak and holding them back, the First Relief sent him back to Sutter's Fort along with the draft animals.

The First Relief arrived at the camp on Truckee Lake just ten days after Mrs. Eddy had died. The snow was so deep it covered over the top of the cabins and, at first sight, the rescuers feared there were no survivors. All of a sudden, a head popped out of the snow, it was a woman called Lavinah Murphy. She was so pale and gaunt she gave the impression of a ghost, and not sure whether she was dreaming or not she asked the rescuers, 'Do you men come from California, or do you come from God?'

The rescue party managed to take out 21 members of the party left at the lake and Alder Creek, and left enough provisions with the remaining ones that were too weak to leave.

Subsequent rescue efforts brought out the remaining survivors. There were still more deaths at the camp and some died on the torturous trip out of the mountains.

Despite their very weakened state, the survivors had to make the journey on foot because the snow was still too deep for horses or mules to negotiate. The last of the survivors reached Sutter's Fort exactly one year after their original departure from Missouri. In total, of the 87 men, women and children in the Donner party, 46 survived and 41 died.

George Donner and his wife died at the camp, along with his brother Jacob and his wife, and most of the Donner children. James Reed, having safely reached Sutter's Fort actually led one of the rescue parties. Reed's family managed to survive.

The story of the tragedy spread far and wide, and newspapers started to print outrageous stories of men and women who had gone mad by eating human flesh.

The site of the Donner Party encampment is now a State Memorial Park, and there is also a museum to commemorate their suffering.

Werewolves of France

Werewolves (or wolf-men) have been fabled as supernatural legends in numerous cultures throughout the world for centuries

WEREWOLVES WERE ALWAYS associated with a kind of madness that was exacerbated by the appearance of a full moon. The werewolf in literature is the person who acts out the stereotype characteristics of the wolf in the wild, a mental illness known as Lycanthropy. This name derives from the Greek word for wolf, 'lykoi', and for man, 'anthropos'. Quite literally it is the delusion of turning into a wolf, whether through witchcraft or your own will.

In European folklore, a werewolf is a man who transforms himself at night into a wolf, both in form and appetite, and then roams in search of human victims to devour. The werewolf must return to his human form at daybreak by shedding his wolf's skin and concealing it. If this skin should be found and destroyed, then the werewolf would die. A werewolf who is wounded immediately reverts to his human form and can be detected by the corresponding wound on his body.

Belief in 'wer' (or man) animals was common in the Middle Ages, and was probably a relic from early cannibalism. In 16th century France the superstition regarding werewolves seems to have been widespread and prevalent, as is shown by the many trials for murder and cannibalism, all attributed to lycanthropy. However, this belief is now all but extinct.

When werewolves are portrayed in films or books, they show physiological changes including bone structure, skin texture, and the emergence of fangs. Hair grows over the body, the nose protrudes, fangs enlarge, and pointy ears emerge from the head. The difference between the original werewolf and the werewolf of current films is not its behaviour, because that has changed little, but it is the difference in its physical metamorphosis. Perhaps the real horror of the werewolf is the mystery that surrounds it.

In France alone, between the years 1520 and 1630, some 30,000 individuals had the misfortune to be labelled werewolves. Many of these people underwent criminal investigation and torture, confessed, and suffered a vile death at the stake. For those who escaped such a fate, the trauma of interrogation must have left lifetime scars. Here is a collection of some French werewolf trials which have been recorded.

JEAN GRENIER

In the early spring of 1603 fear spread through the St. Sever districts of Gascony, in the extreme south-west of

France. Young children had mysteriously begun to disappear from the hamlets and smaller villages in the area, and no trace was ever found. It seemed no children were safe, and even a baby was stolen from its cradle while its mother went about her work around the cottage where they lived. There was talk in the villages of wolves, but deep down inside the people knew that it was something far more sinister.

Just when fear was at its height, a 13-year-old girl named Marguerite Poitier came forward to tell of an attack by a savage beast, resembling a wolf, on the night of the full moon. The girl told the Judge that she had been watching her cattle, when a wild beast, not unlike a huge dog, had rushed out from the thicket and tore at her skirt with its sharp, fang-like teeth. She said she had been able to ward off the attack by using a pointed staff which she kept with her.

Meanwhile a 14-year-old boy, Jean Grenier, was proudly announcing to his fellow villagers that he was in fact the wolf and had hunted down and eaten many young girls. He claimed he could transform himself into a wolf by means of a 'magic ointment' and a wolfskin cloak that had been given to him by a black man whom he called 'Maître de la Forêt'.

The next girl to come forward with information was 18-year-old Jeanne Gaboriaut. She told the Judge that she had been tending her flock, accompanied by Jean Grenier, both of whom worked for a farmer by the name of Saint-Paul Pierre Combaut. Jean commented that Jeanne was a 'bonnie lass' and he vowed that one day he would like to marry her. When she enquired who his father was, he coarsely replied, 'I am a priest's bastard'. Jeanne remarked that he was both rude and dirty and would never dream of marrying someone like him. To this he replied, that when he wore the wolf-skin it somehow turned him into a beast that prowled the forests by night. He also told the girl that he belonged to a coven of werewolves and that there were nine other members. He claimed that he lusted after the flesh of small children, which he preferred because they were nice and tender. When he took on his wolf's shape and he felt hungry, he told her that he often killed dogs and would lap at their hot blood, but it was not as tasty as the flesh of young boys and girls.

The girl complained to her parents about the behaviour of Jean and told them that he frightened her with his horrible stories. However, her father and mother ignored her accounts until one day she returned home early from watching her flock, and this time she was in a state of complete alarm.

Sobbing uncontrollably she told her parents once more about the terrible stories that Jean had related to her about acquiring the form of a wolf and eating the flesh of young girls. She said she had been watching her sheep as usual, this time without the company of Jean Grenier, when she heard a rustle in the bushes behind her. On turning around a wild beast rushed towards her and tore at her clothes with its sharp fangs. She managed to beat the creature off by using her shepherd's staff. The creature retreated a few paces and seated itself on its hind legs like a dog. She fled in terror from the animal which she said resembled a wolf, although it was a little shorter and stouter. It had red hair, a stumpy tail, and the head was considerably smaller than that of a genuine wolf.

The child's statement caused panic among the parish, as it was well known that several young girls had vanished under mysterious circumstances of late. The case was immediately taken up by the authorities and brought before the Bordeaux parliament.

Jean Grenier was brought to court on June 2, 1603, where he freely confessed of the most hideous and abominable werewolf crimes. It turned out that Jean was the son of a poor labourer from the village of S. Antoine de Pizon, and not the son of a priest as he had so often claimed. Three months before he was arrested he had left home and had been employed by several masters doing odd jobs, or just wandering around the countryside begging. On a couple of occasions he had been hired to look after flocks belonging to farmers, but had been discharged for neglect of his duties.

When he was questioned about the missing children, he openly admitted that he had both killed and eaten as a wolf. He told of the time when he had been overcome by hunger and had entered a cottage where he had found a baby asleep in its cradle. He dragged the baby out of its cradle, carried it into the garden, leaped over the hedge, and devoured it until he had satisfied his hunger. The remainder of the body he fed to a wolf.

When he was asked to explain his actions, he told the court that when he wore the wolf-skin, as commanded by the Lord of the Forest, he would go out hunting for children. Before his transformation, Jean said that he smeared himself with the special salve which he preserved in a small pot, and then hid his normal clothes in the thicket. He said that most of his hunting was carried out during the day when the moon was at its wane, but sometimes his expeditions were at the dead of night by the light of the full moon.

Jean also accused his father of helping him and possessing a wolf-skin. He said that he had accompanied him on more than one occasion, and been present when he had attacked and eaten a young girl in the village of Grilland. He told the Court that his stepmother had left his father, and he believed the reason to be because she had witnessed him regurgitating the paws of a dog and the fingers of a child. He also added that the Lord of the Forest had strictly forbidden him from biting the thumb-nail on his left hand, and warned him never to lose sight of it as long as he was in the disguise of a werewolf.

As a result of his startling proclamations Jean Grenier was deemed by the judges to be mentally ill, and was said to be suffering from lycanthropy which was brought on by the possession of demons. He was incapable of socialization and therefore could not be executed for the crimes he had committed. He was sent off to live in a Franciscan monastery when he stayed for the remainder of his days. However, reports say that as soon as he was admitted to the monastery, he started to run about frantically on all fours and on finding a heap of raw and bloody offal, fell upon it hungrily and devoured it in an incredibly short space of time.

After seven years spent in the monastery, Jean was found to be of considerably small stature, extremely shy, and unwilling to give anyone eye contact. His eyes were deep set and darted about from side to side. His teeth were long and protruding, while his nails were black and worn away in certain places. It seemed his mind was incapable of understanding even the smallest of instructions, and by the age of 20 he was dead.

PIERRE BURGOT AND MICHEL VERDUM

The trial of two French peasants in 1521 received widespread notoriety. The two men convicted of being werewolves were Pierre Burgot and Michel Verdum. Nineteen years before his arrest, when Burgot was desperately trying to gather his frightened sheep together following a violent storm, he came across three mysterious horsemen completely dressed in black. One of the horsemen assured Burgot of the future protection of his flock, and at the same time offered the bewildered shepherd some money. In return the stranger wanted Burgot to obey him as the Lord.

Although a little unsure of the stranger, Burgot agreed to his proposal and arranged to meet him again. In this second meeting his so-called 'Lord' outlined all the conditions and pronounced: 'You must renounce God, the Holy Virgin, the Company of Heaven, His baptism and also His confirmation.'

As more and more time passed by, Burgot became reluctant to stick to the terms of the pact. Then, out of the blue, he was contacted by Michel Verdum, who demanded that he strip naked and rub a magic balm all over his body. Burgot was too scared to disobey and he rubbed the ointment over his skin. As he did so he noticed that his arms and legs were starting to grow long hair, and his hands were changing into the shape of paws. Verdum also started to change shape and together the two men ran through the surrounding countryside.

In their wake they left a scene of carnage. They ripped a seven-year-old boy into pieces, killed a woman and abducted a four-year-old girl. The unfortunate girl was then eaten up by the two ravaging werewolves.

When the pair were finally caught they were duly put to death. Their picture was hung in the local church as a reminder of all the evil deeds that men could commit under the influence of Satan.

JACQUES ROLLET

Jacques Rollet came from Caude in Western France. He murdered and ate several people before he was captured in 1598, while in the process of dismembering yet another one of his victims. At his trial he told the court that he was able to transform himself into a wolf and realizing that the man was clearly mentally subnormal, the judge committed him to life in a mental institution.

GILLES GARNIER

It was during the summer of 1573 that the bodies of several children who had been partially devoured, were discovered in the Dole region of France. Local peasants claimed that they had seen a strange wolf-like beast prowling the area, and that it had a face bearing a resemblance to that of Gilles Garnier.

On November 8, 1573, some peasants from Chastenoy were walking through the forest on their way home from work. Suddenly they heard the screams of a child which was accompanied by the sounds of a wolf baying. They ran in the direction of the sounds, and found a small girl trying to defend herself against a monstrous creature which was attacking her like a mad dog. She had been bitten and scratched in several places, and as the peasants approached her the wolf-like animal fled on all fours into the darkness of the thicket. It was too dark to really see what the creature looked like, but it was certainly very wolf-like, although others said it resembled the hermit, Garnier.

A small boy went missing on November 15, and shortly after this incident two girls and a young boy were also killed. Their bodies had all been ravaged in the same manner, and had been partially eaten.

In the weeks that followed the werewolf's attacks seemed to become more frequent, and the creature also started to seek out adult victims. All the while the locals became more and more suspicious that these attacks were being carried out by the hermit, Gilles Garnier.

Alarmed by the frequency and number of the attacks, the authorities gave permission to the local residents to hunt the monster down. They started to scour the countryside for any sightings of the werewolf. It wasn't long before Gilles Garnier was spotted attacking another one of his victims. Although he was in wolf form at the time, he was easily recognized by the peasants as the lycanthrope who had murdered several children in the area.

They described the hermit as a:

. . . very somber, ill-looking fellow, who walked in a stooping attitude, and whose pale face, livid complexion, and deep-set eyes under a pair of coarse and bushy eyebrows, which met across the forehead, were sufficient to repel any one from seeking his acquaintance. Gilles seldom spoke, and when he did it was in the broadest patois of his country. His long grey beard and retiring habits procured him the name the Hermit of St. Bonnot, though no-one for a moment attributed to him any extraordinary amount of sanctity.

(Sidky, H. – 1997)

Unfortunately the young child died a few days following the attack due to the severity of its injuries. Over 50 witnesses identified the wolf-man to be Gilles Garnier and he was sentenced to appear in court. He willingly confessed to every charge against him and he was sentenced to death.

He was executed on January 8, 1574, which clearly disproves the myth that a werewolf has to be killed with a silver bullet – he was in fact burned to death at the stake!

Survival in Chile

The survivors of a plane crash in the mountains of Chile had to resort to cannibalism in an effort to stay alive

RUGBY HAD ALWAYS been on the curriculum at the Stella Maris school for boys in Carrasco, Uruguay. After leaving the school and moving on to further education, the ex-pupils missed the sport and decided to do something about it. They were passionate about rugby and so in 1964 they organized six other teams from around Montevideo and formed the Rugby Union of Uruguay. The group known as the 'Old Christians' grew in strength as the years went by and in 1971 they were invited to play a match in Santiago, Chile. To keep the costs down the group chartered a plane from the Uruguayan Air Force as their rates were far lower than those of any commercial airline. It was a thoroughly enjoyable trip and so when they were invited back the following year the Old Christians were only too happy to accept.

Again they chartered a plane from the Uruguayan Air Force and this time asked friends and family to join them on their trip to Chile. On the morning of

October 12, 1972, the passengers started to arrive at the small international airport. Apart from the players and their friends and family, their was an independent traveller by the name of Graziela Mariani who had bought her ticket directly from the Air Force so that she could attend her eldest daughter's wedding in Santiago. She had taken the last remaining seat and was consequently travelling on her own.

It was around 7.40 a.m. when the passengers heard the announcement over the loud speaker to start boarding the plane. They all walked across the tarmac to the waiting plane, which was a Fairchild FH-277D. They took off from Carrasco at 8.02 a.m. and on board were 40 passengers and five crew members.

For the first three hours the flight ran smoothly and it was around 11.00 a.m. that the Andes came into view, shrouded in clouds. As the Fairchild could only fly at a height of 22,500 feet it was necessary to fly through the Andes rather than over them, and the pilots, Col. Ferradas and Lt. Col. Lagurara, were used to negotiating the designated gaps between the mountains. Aware that the clouds could signify that there was some bad weather in front of them, Lagurara radioed ahead and their suspicions were confirmed. They decided the safest thing to do would be to land in Mendoza, as it would be too risky flying through the Andes. When they landed they were informed that the weather would not be easing up until the next day, and so the passengers were advised that they would be spending the night in Mendoza.

The passengers and the crew managed to check themselves into hotels, and they were all advised to be back at the airport by noon the following day. Both crew and passengers took advantage of the stopover and purchased several bottles of the local wine.

CRASH IN THE ANDES

The Fairchild aeroplane took off from Mendoza at 2.18 on the afternoon of October 13. They had waited for the bad weather to clear up, and it was decided that it was now safe to negotiate the route through the mountains, known as Planchon Pass. The co-pilot, Lt. Col. Lagurara, had been flying the plane throughout the entire flight and the passengers were quite happy and seemed to be enjoying themselves. At 3.24 p.m. Lagurara radioed to Santiago and informed them that he was flying over Curico. Santiago Control acknowledged this and then told him to turn north and start his descent to 10,000 feet. This would have been alright if the plane had in fact been over Curico, but a headwind had slowed the plane considerably and Lagurara's report was inaccurate – in reality they were just over Planchon which was still within the mountain range. As the plane dropped into the clouds they started to experience turbulence and the 'Fasten Seat Belts' sign was illuminated, while the stewards walked up and down the aisle to make sure the passengers were safely buckled in. Just as the steward took his seat at the back of the cabin, the plane hit two air pockets and sunk into the clouds revealing mountains on all sides. The immediate reaction of the pilots was to put the engines into full throttle and try to pull the plane out of the mountains. However, the air was too thin for the propellers to grab onto and flying at around 14,000 feet the wing on the right-hand side of the plane clipped a jagged mountain peak.

The wing splintered off and smashed down onto the fuselage forcing the tail section of the plane to fall off at the galley. Within a matter of seconds the other wing hit the mountainside and tore off, dropping to the ground in fragments. In the first few minutes of the crash five people at the rear of the cabin actually fell to their deaths through the gaping hole where the tail of the aeroplane had been.

The plane continued to drop rapidly, crashing down onto the mountainside. The fuselage careened down an 80-degree slope just like a toboggan. The sudden decrease in speed caused the passenger seats to come loose from their mountings and to fall forward en masse. As the plane continued its snowy descent the passengers could be heard praying loudly. As the slope began to level off and the snow got deeper the nose of the Fairchild started to crumple, and in so doing, it sandwiched the pilots in the cockpit, before the fuselage finally came to an abrupt halt in a deep bank of snow. Those passengers who were able to move managed to climb out of the hole of the plane where the tail had once been. Back inside the plane a couple of the rugby players were desperately trying to extricate some of the passengers from their trapped seats. When they had freed as many people as they could, they discovered that only three people in the passenger cabin were dead. The team doctor, Dr. Nicola and his wife, Esther, and Eugenia Parrado, who was the mother of one of the rugby players, Nando Parrado.

Many of the survivors of the crash had serious injuries and they realized it was hopeless as they did not have either the knowledge or the medical supplies to treat them. As the cockpit was not accessible from the cabin, one of the passengers, Moncho Sabella, decided to try and access it from the outside. He climbed along the side of the fuselage using seat cushions as snow shoes, and he managed to get inside the cockpit through a foward cabin door that was slightly ajar. Both the pilot and co-pilot were crushed between the instrument panel and the rear bulkhead, and although Ferraras was dead, his co-pilot was still alive, albeit terribly injured. Sabella went for assistance, but despite their brave efforts, Lagurara was beyond their help. The passengers decided the best thing to do was to try and settle down for the night, but without any blankets or anything to stop the arctic air from blowing in, they all found the cold unbearable. They decided they should try and plug the hole at the rear of the plane, and using suitcases, seats, and indeed whatever other debris they could find, they started to build a makeshift wall in the back of the plane.

The following morning, now October 14, the weather conditions were just as bad. During the night four people had died, and Grazeila Mariani died of her injuries later that morning. Of the 45 people who set out from Montevideo two days before, only 27 were left alive.

THE ONLY CHOICE

The survivors of the crash never gave up hope in the following days that they would be rescued and it was on the third day that they heard the sound of a plane flying overhead. They rushed out onto the snow and screamed as loud as they could, waving their hands frantically in the air. They felt sure the plane had seen them, but when no help arrived the truth started to sink in – nobody knew they were there.

There were two medical students among the survivors and they made regular checks of the injured. To help make them more comfortable they devised some simple hammocks by using luggage webbing and some poles that were stowed in the luggage compartment. Another one of the survivors, Fito Strauch, invented a water-making device using a piece of aluminium out of the back of one of the seats. He managed to bend it into a spout, which he filled with snow and wedged between two suitcases. At the bottom of the spout he placed a bottle and when the sun melted the snow, it poured into the bottle. He managed to stockpile quite a few bottles of water by using this method.

Their food supply was very sparse and all that was now left was some chocolate, nougat, crackers and jam. They also had some large bottles of wine and brandy that the pilots had purchased in their stopover at Mendoza. This, however, was not sufficient for the 26 survivors. They rationed the food out as best they could, but it was clear that if they were not rescued soon they would totally run out of supplies. They knew that if they didn't find another source of food they were all destined to die.

The survivors turned to one another with a look of grim resignation on their faces, they knew the only way they were going to survive this ordeal was to eat the flesh of their dead companions. One of the passengers, Canessa, who was one of the first ones to mention the idea, went out into the snow and, using a shard of glass, cut off several slivers of flesh from one of the bodies that had been laid out near the fuselage. He brought the flesh back to the others and, one by one, they forced the meat down their throats, some retching as they took the meat. A few of the passengers actually refused to take part, but as the dwindling supplies of chocolate ran out, even they were forced to eat human flesh.

They had a stock of ten bodies in their makeshift cemetery, and they all agreed that Parrado's mother, sister and Methol's nephew, were not to be used unless they became desperate. Just like the chocolate, the meat was rationed out. As the protein took effect on their weak bodies, the survivors started to grow stronger and they started to make plans on how they could best get out of the mountains.

EXPEDITIONS

The survivors took it in turns to make expeditions through the mountains, mostly in the effort to find the missing tail portion of the plane. They did this for two reasons firstly because they felt that their friends who had fallen out over the mountain may possibly still be alive and living in the wreckage, and secondly because they wanted to get to the batteries. The one remaining crew member, Carlos Roque, who happened to be the mechanic, told them that if they could find the batteries contained in the tail, they would be able to run the plane's radio and thus signal for help.

On their second expedition up the mountain, the survivors managed to find the bodies of the six men who had fallen from the plane, the wreckage of the left wing, but no sign of the missing tail portion. Canessa, Parrado and Vizintin were the ones who eventually found the tail. It was to the east of the fuselage and about 500 feet further down the valley. It took them almost three hours to reach it, but although they successfully located the batteries they were too heavy to transport back to the fuselage. They came back empty-handed but had worked out a plan to take the radio and Roy Harley with them back to the tail, so that he could hook it up. However, their mission was unsuccessful as the transmitter and the batteries were not of the same voltage.

On the 17th night spent on the mountain, the survivors were hit by an avalanche which swept down the valley and covered the whole of the fuselage. The snow even forced its way through their makeshift wall at the back of the cabin, covering all the survivors. All that is, except four – Echavarran, Nogueira and Vinzintin were asleep in their hammocks, and Harley was woken by the noise and managed to stand up before the snow swept over him. They frantically dug in the snow for their friends, but eight of the nineteen survivors had been buried alive in the snow.

One hour later a second avalanche hit the wreckage but, because the entrance was already blocked by snow, it simply swept right over the top of the fuselage. This meant that what remained of the plane was now completely buried in snow. There was very little room left in the cabin, and without their blankets and shoes which were buried in the snow, the remaining survivors struggled to keep warm.

As soon as they spotted the first rays of daylight the group started to burrow through the snow at the front of the fuselage and managed to get through to the pilots' cabin. Because of the tilt of the plane the window in the cockpit was above the level of the snow, but when Roy Harley poked his head out of a hole in the window he discovered that a snowstorm had set in. They had to stay for three days inside their frozen tomb. It wasn't until the morning of November 1 that the snow eased up and they started on the task of digging themselves out. It took them a couple of days, but they managed to make a tunnel out of the rear of the fuselage and up to the surface. They removed as much snow as they could by taking it out through the tunnel, and also removed the bodies of their friends who had died in the avalanche.

RESCUE

On the 62nd day following the crash, Nando Parrado, Roberto Canessa and Antonio Vizintin set out on an expedition to the west, where they hoped they would find Chile. With them they carried a sleeping bag, which they had made up from the plane's insulation, and a ration of food. They knew the journey ahead was going to be arduous as they had to make a steep ascent up the mountains. They climbed and climbed until the last of the sun had disappeared behind the mountain. As dusk fell they set up camp and managed to keep warm throughout the night with their makeshift sleeping arrangements. After three days of climbing they realized that their food rations were not going to last and so they voted and opted for Vizintin to return to the plane. Using a seat cushion for snow shoes it took him only two hours to slide back down the mountain, when it had taken them three days to climb that far. On the fourth day of their expedition the men found that they were starting their descent down the other side of the mountain. It took four more days to reach the bottom where they found green fields and to their delight a rancher who was tending his cattle.

The rancher, Sergio Catalan, saw the dishevelled men trying to attract his attention on the far side of the river. They screamed at him and asked for him to fetch help, but the river almost drowned out the sound of their pleas. The rancher shouted back that he would return the next day. Realizing at last that they were on the verge of being rescued the men set up camp on the side of the river. Catalan managed to throw a rock across the river with a message attached to it which read:

There is a man coming later that I told him to go. Tell me what you need.

Parrado, after reading the message, sent a note back in return which said:

I come from a plane that fell in the mountains I am Uruguayan. We have been walking for ten days. I have a friend up there who is injured. In the plane there are still 14 injured people. We have to get out of here quickly and we don't know how. We don't have any food. We are weak. When are you going to come and fetch us? Please. We can't even walk. Where are we? SOS.

The rancher read the note and pulled some bread out of his pocket which he threw across the river to the survivors. Three hours later another man arrived, this time on their side of the river, and he brought with him some cheese which they grabbed at hungrily. The man, Armando Serda, said he had to go off and see to his cattle but he would return to take them back to his hut, while they waited for the authorities to arrive. They couldn't believe their luck once back at the hut, for they washed, were fed, and were given comfortable beds. It was now December 21, 70 days since the plane had crashed, and as last they were saved.

Meanwhile, back at the plane, they had been listening to the radio news telling them that their friends had been found. At first they couldn't believe what they heard, but when they changed to a different channel and heard the same thing, they were in a state of elation. They rushed around and started to clear up the inside of the plane, and tried to make themselves look as respectable as possible. They did consider burying the remains of their dead companions, but the surface of the snow was rock hard with ice and so they thought better of it.

At around 1.00 p.m. on the 22nd, the remaining survivors heard the joyous sound of helicopters flying overhead. The first rescuer who jumped from the helicopter was greeted with elated cheers and was embraced by those of the survivors who were still able to stand. After a couple of days all the men left at the sight of the crash had been airlifted to a hospital in Santiago.

THE GRUESOME REMAINS

When all the survivors had been safely airlifted away from the site, it was the task of the rescuers to recover the bodies of the 29 people who had died on the mountain. But they soon realized that this was to be no ordinary case. Normally the SAR would have stayed at the site and collected the bodies taking them to Santiago for inspection and eventual release to their next of kin. However, while they discovered 14 intact bodies, only scant, unidentifiable pieces of the remaining 15 could be found. The rescue team decided to leave the remains on the mountain and wait for instructions from a higher authority.

After speaking to the victims' families and considering all the options, it was decided that their remains would be buried on the mountainside where they were discovered. It was felt that this was the best option to avoid the further trauma of their relatives discovering that their loved ones had actually been used for food. Over the course of a few days all the remains were gathered up from inside the fuselage, and outside, were placed in body bags and moved to a shallow grave. This grave was covered in rocks and an iron cross was erected to show the place where they had died.

The wreckage of the fuselage was set on fire, destroying any evidence of the incredible ordeal that had taken place on the side of the mountain in the Andes.

The memorial placed on the grave simply said:

The world to its Uruguayan brothers – 1972
Nearer My God to Thee

Captain Cook

Captain Cook and his crew knew little or nothing of the cultures they were about to encounter, and the islanders knew even less of them

JAMES COOK WAS born on October 27, 1728 in Moreton-in-Cleveland, Yorkshire, the son of a simple farm labourer. It is quite amazing that a man from such humble beginnings became such a prominent character in our history books.

James always had a real yearning for the sea and began an apprenticeship with a ship owner in a nearby fishing village of Whitby. While under this apprenticeship he used his time wisely and studied navigation and mathematics, to help him along his way to one day becoming a captain on his own ship. In 1755, when he was 27, James was offered the command of a north sea trader, but he decided to decline this offer in favour of joining the Navy. He enlisted as an able seaman and within a very short period of time he had earned his Master's Warrant.

James married Elizabeth Batts in 1762 and together they had six children. James Cook was not to spend much time with his family during his lifetime, because throughout the years 1759 to 1767 James was sent by the Navy to chart parts of Newfoundland, Nova Scotia and the St. Lawrence river. The Admiralty were so impressed by the accuracy of his charts that they gave him what was to become one of the most well known voyages in history.

THE FIRST VOYAGE

The first voyage that Captain James Cook undertook was primarily of a scientific nature. Under his command the *Endeavour* sailed to Tahiti in order to observe the path of the planet Venus so that they could calculate the Earth's distance from the Sun. The ship itself was a Whitby Coal ship which weighed around 368 tons, and they set sail in August 1768. Accompanying him on his voyage were Charles Green, an astronomer from the Royal Society, and Joseph Banks, leading a party of botanists.

Cook and his party landed on the South Pacific island in April 1769 and by June of that year they had successfully completed their astronomical observations. Another purpose of this visit was to explore the South Seas to see if there was an inhabitable continent in the mid-latitudes of the Southern Hemisphere.

On leaving Tahiti Captain Cook and the *Endeavour* headed south and reached the coast of New Zealand on October 7, 1769. He made a detailed survey of the coast and established that New Zealand was not part of the Southern Continent.

Cook decided his best route home would be to sail along the then unknown eastern side of Australia (which Cook was to name New South Wales), and they reached the coast of Australia on April 19, 1770. Next the expedition headed north and, despite nearly being shipwrecked twice, they managed to explore the inner shoals of the Great Barrier Reef. As a result of Captain Cook's surveys, both Australia and New Zealand were later annexed by Great Britain. James Cook and the *Endeavour* returned to England in July 1771 with a relatively healthy crew, which was quite an amazing achievement at the time. The combination of his accomplishments brought Cook notoriety and promotion, and he was promoted to Commander, which gave him the opportunity to lead further expeditions.

In 1772 James Cook set sail once more in search of the southern continent. This time his vessel was another coal ship which had been renamed the *Resolution*. On this voyage he was accompanied by Captain Tobias Furneaux in his ship the *Adventurer*. They headed south from the coast of Africa and actually sailed further south than anyone had ever been. They managed to get as far as land known as Enderby Land, but were forced back by solid ice. Cook, who had become separated from the *Adventurer* along the way, returned to New Zealand where he and his crew rested for a couple of months. It was here that he met up again with Captain Furneaux and once more the two ships headed out to sea, this time northwards to Tahiti and Tonga. Once again the two ships were parted when they encountered a powerful gale.

Captain Furneaux had decided to return to England after losing some of his crew to Maori cannibals. Meanwhile Cook continued his search for the southern continent but once more encountered ice. He then charted the Easter Islands, New Hebrides, the Marquesas, discovered New Caledonia, Norfolk Islands, and Palmerston. He then went on to find the Sandwich Islands (Hawaiian Islands), and South Georgia. He returned to England in July of 1775, achieving the testing of the first reliable chronometer. The amazing thing for this era was that in three years at sea only four of his crew members were lost. A tribute to Cook's realisation that a diet including fruit was essential, thus eliminating the problem of scurvy.

FATEFUL JOURNEY

In July of 1776 James Cook set sail on what was to be his final voyage, in search of the northwest passage from Europe to the east. On this voyage his ship the *Resolution* was joined by the *Discovery* which was commanded by Captain Charles Clerke. The two ships headed for the mid-Pacific Islands, discovering some of the Cook Islands, and also the Hawaiian islands. This was the voyage that earned Captain Cook the credit as the first westerner to discover the Hawaiian islands.

When the two British ships sailed past O'ahu to Kaua'i in January 1778, they were met by many canoes filled with islanders who were prepared to do battle. Luckily Cook and his men had managed to pick up several words of Tahitian in an earlier trip, and being close enough to the Hawaiian dialect the natives soon realized that these men had in fact come in peace. The boats were anchored for three days in which time they gave gifts to the natives, and also took advantage of the Hawaiian women's sexual favours. Whilst at anchor the High Chief Kaneoneo boarded the Discovery and met with the two captains before they left the island and headed for Alaska and Canada.

Ten months later, in desperate need of provisions and a safe harbour, Captain Cook decided to return to Hawaii in the Sandwich Islands. But this was to be his last journey as the natives were celebrating victory against the neighbouring Kahekili when they arrived, and mistook the Englishmen for their great god Lono and his immortal company.

Divine honours were offered to Cook and his crew and, strangely enough, the Captain accepted them (probably because he was prepared to accept anything that made for the success of the expedition). However, it wasn't long before the exceedingly expensive and extravagant celebrations turned into a free-for-all. Quarrels broke out, sticks and stones were freely used, and Cook decided to sail away, much to everybody's relief.

However, within a week the *Resolution* had sprung her foremast, and they were back again. Trouble started almost immediately. One of the cutters was stolen, and Captain Cook put ashore to try and settle the matter. Natives crowded the beach, armed and excited. Stones were thrown and there was some firing. Cook turned, and as he did so was stabbed in the back and speared. He fell dead into the water.

Captain Cook died at the age of 51 on February 14, 1779, and will always be remembered as one of the greatest Englishmen of all time.

Just after dark on February 16, 1779, a 'kahuna', or holy man, rode a canoe up to the *Resolution*, still anchored off the coast of Hawaii. The kahuna came aboard with a bundle under his arm. Charles Clerke, the ship's commander, unwrapped the parcel in the presence of his officers. What he found inside was a large piece of flesh which he soon saw to be human. Clerke later wrote in his journal – 'It was clearly a part of the Thigh about 6 or 8 pounds without any bone at all.'

Two days before this, islanders had killed five of the ship's men on the shore of Kealakekua Bay and carried off their bodies. Nothing had been seen of the corpses and Clerke and his men presumed, following their grisly offering, that their fellow men had in fact been consumed in the natives.

James Cook was one of the five men who had died on that shore and there was no way of knowing for certain if that pungent thigh had in fact belonged to him.

However, several days later, the Hawaiians delivered yet another package, this time bundled in a feathered cloak. This parcel contained scorched limbs, a scalp with the ears attached and hair cut short, but what was most distinctive were the two hands that had been scored and salted, in an apparent effort to preserve them. Fifteen years earlier, a powder horn had exploded in Captain Cook's right hand, leaving an ugly gash. When Captain Clerke studied the hands he noticed that this most distinctive cut remained clearly visible on the severed right hand delivered to the ship.

The First Crusade

Deserted and so hungry, followers of the
First Crusade (1095-1099) reportedly
turned to cannibalism

NOW WE ARE travelling back in time to the 11th century to the time of the Crusades. The Crusades were holy wars which were fought by the Europeans who believed that they were upholding the Christian religion against the invasion of the Islamic religion. There were many crusades fought between the 11th and 13th centuries, but it was really only the First Crusade that had a successful outcome.

It was a time when petty disputes between rulers were generally settled by equally petty wars. Although it was not a good time to live if you were a peasant, everyone was at least united by a common religion – Christianity. Everyone, that is, from the nobles in their castles to the peasants living in their ramshackled huts, conformed to their daily form of worship. The Pope, who was the head of the Church, was considered to be God's representative on Earth, and his word was law. He even had enough power to challenge emperors, and this power spread even into the remotest villages. A succession of popes had been constantly fighting wars with the royal houses of Europe in an effort to obtain a unified Christian empire.

In 1095 a fierce band of nomadic warriors known as the Seljuk Turks, who had recently converted to Islam, had advanced sufficiently to establish their own capital within 100 miles of Byzantium (or Istanbul as it is known today). Byzantium, however, was already the capital of the Christian Eastern Roman Empire. A state of panic was declared and Byzantium's Emperor, Alexius, sent a message through to Pope Urban II asking for his assistance.

Pope Urban II dreamed constantly of a united Christian kingdom which would extend from the Atlantic coast into the west Holy Land itself, and all under the jurisdiction of the Pope. So when Alexius asked for his help, Urban was only too pleased to come to his aid. The only problem was that Urban was not content with just defending the capital, he wanted to free the Holy City of Jerusalem itself. Jerusalem had long been occupied by the Muslims, but he saw it as an opportunity to demonstrate his power over the ruler of Europe.

For a long time relations between Christian pilgrims and the Muslims had been peaceful. Muslim traders had provided food, transport and other essential services for the pilgrims, and the income this provided was useful to the local economy. However, with the arrival of the much more aggressive Seljuk Turks, the Christian pilgrimage became a dangerous affair.

All different kinds of people responded to the call from the Pope to go on Crusade. He toured from the south to the west of France recruiting people and spreading the news that there was to be a large convention held in Clermont, a town in central southern France. This meeting was attended by hundreds of clerics, and on the very last day the Pope himself stood up and made a speech. He told of the atrocities committed by the Turks, and pleaded with all the Christians to join forces and make a grand Crusade to liberate Jerusalem.

Many of the war-loving knights of Europe jumped at the opportunity, because they couldn't resist the opportunity to plunder some of the richest cities in the east. Added to that, they could do it with the Pope's blessing. So it was that knights and peasants alike marched from all the corners of Europe towards Byzantium – this was the start of the First Crusade.

THE PEASANTS' CRUSADE

Following Pope Urban II's call for a crusade, Peter the Hermit and a knight called Walter the Penniless led a group that rushed ahead of the official expedition. They were just one of the many. This group became known as the 'Peasants' Crusade' – a band of untrained and undisciplined men. As this motley crew travelled through eastern Europe towards Byzantium, demanding free food and shelter, they slaughtered thousands of people on their way. Wherever they journeyed they left their mark of violence and cruelty. They fell upon the defenceless Jews, murdering thousands in the German towns. Many of Peter's men died before they even reached Asia, while many more were sold as slaves to pay for food. In the end only 7,000 managed to reach Asiatic soil. When they did finally meet the Turks in Nicaea, the ensuing battle was a mismatch. The Christian army was totally routed. About 4,000 of them were killed in the battle. All in all, a total of 300,000 Christians died during this march led by Peter the Hermit.

On the other hand, the force that followed were a far more organized band, led by Godfrey of Bouillon, Raymond of Toulouse, Robert of Flanders, and Bohemond of Taranto. Godfrey of Bouillon alone led a host of 700,000 crusaders. This combined army successfully defeated the Turks at Dorylaeum in 1097, Antioch was captured in 1098, and Jerusalem fell in 1099, thus founding the Christian kingdom of Palestine.

However, while the military campaign was a success, the behaviour of the Christian army certainly did not win them any new converts. When the crusaders were attacking Antioch in northern Syria, they used the heads of slain Turks as ammunition for their primitive cannons. Apart from using the heads as ammunition, about 300 heads were placed on stakes in front of the city to demoralize the defenders of the city. The crusaders finally broke through and slaughtered all the inhabitants. This was possibly the most difficult, and most remembered battle, and it was here that 10,000 or more, were massacred on the first night. After Antioch had been captured, the Crusaders encountered the Turks once more and by the evening of July 3, 1098, the entire city was smeared with blood. Every single Turk was killed. The corpses were left lying where they died, and it wasn't long before the plague caused by the decomposition, killed many more.

Mayhem and desperation ensued, and soon those who were left standing resorted to robbery, rape, and spent their time in a state of constant drunkenness. Then came the inevitable – famine. The crusaders had devastated so much of the country that they even had to resort to eating their own horses, reducing the cavalry from 100,000 to 2,000. Then, when the supply of horsemeat ran out, they resorted to cannibalism.

Their behaviour was even worse during the siege of Marra, where they butchered all the inhabitants, eating their flesh. Pagan adults were boiled in cooking pots, while their children were impaled on spits and consumed after they were grilled over an open fire. The massacre and carnage was seen by many, and there were numerous eye-witness accounts to preserve their evil-doing in the history books.

The crusaders arrived in Jerusalem in the summer of 1099, and recovered the Holy City after six weeks of fighting. Once again the streets ran with blood and the Jews were burned in their synagogue. Ten thousand people perished in the mosque of Omar alone. The old and sick were among the first to meet their grisly end, their bodies were slashed open in search of gold coins they could have swallowed. They were ruthless because the Pope had decreed that any spoils of war were possessions the Christians could keep – and the Christians were greedy. Seventy thousand Muslim inhabitants including men, women, and children where slaughtered. Records show how children were dismembered, babies were put on spits and roasted alive, and then consumed by the voracious crusaders.

It was impossible to look anywhere without seeing the fragments of human bodies, and the ground covered with the blood of the slain. However, as if the spectacle of headless bodies and mutilated limbs strewn in all directions was not bad enough, still more dreadful was the sight of the victors themselves, dripping with blood from head to foot, licking their lips after a meal of human flesh. An estimated one million victims died during the First Crusade, and it is certainly one worthy of being mentioned when it comes to the atrocities of cannibalism.

The Marquis de Sade

The term 'sadism' is derived from the name of a French author who lived from 1740 to 1814, Donatien Alphonse François comte de Sade, better known as the Marquis de Sade

SEXUAL CANNIBALISM IS thought to be a psychosexual disorder, which involves a person sexualizing the consumption of another person's flesh. In simple terms the cannibal does not achieve sexual satisfaction purely from the eating of human flesh, but may also release his frustrations and pent-up anger in other ways. Sexual cannibalism is considered to be a form of sexual sadism and is often associated with the act of necrophilia (sex with corpses). There have been several high profile cases, which have involved sexual cannibalism, including that of Andrei Chikatilo, Edward Gein, Albert Fish, Armin Meiwes and Jeffrey Dahmer, but this story goes back much further to the 1700s.

Donatien Alphonse François comte de Sade was born into nobility in 1740. He was an extremely spoilt child and was raised in various country estates. One of these estates was a remote castle which contained a dank, and dark dungeon, and possibly contributed to the young Donatien's developing psyche. Added to this he attended Catholic school where the pupils were subject to much mental abuse, along with public whippings which were part of the Jesuit daily routine.

It was fair to say that the young boy was already starting to form some very strange characteristics even before he reached manhood.

At the age of 14, Donatien enlisted in the Army and experienced his first real combat in the Seven Years War. The young Donatien did not interact well with the other soldiers, although he did manage to achieve the rank of Captain by virtue of his bloodline. When the war was over he returned to Paris, and immediately enjoyed the privileges which were available to him – the demon drink and female company – which he had previously been denied. A virulent young man he gradually worked his way through the majority of the young female population of the city. When questioned about his somewhat outrageous behaviour the young Marquis simply shrugged his shoulders and said that it was what every healthy young male indulged in.

However his behaviour had not gone unnoticed by his family, and in 1763 he was forced into an arranged marriage with a woman called Renée-Pélagie de Montreuil, the homely daughter of a rich Paris judge. Although she had only met the Marquis several days before the actual ceremony, Montreuil proved to be a loving and devoted wife, especially in the light of his forthcoming activities.

Unfortunately marriage did nothing to curb the Marquis' activities with the working women of the Paris streets. He loved the company of the opposite sex, but it didn't just stop there. Not satisfied with normal sexual practices, he got his thrills from the excitement of orgies, blasphemy and subversion, in whatever way he could get them. So it was hardly surprising that, within months of his marriage, the Marquis de Sade was arrested for combining all of these pleasures. He had invited a prostitute back to his house for what she assumed would be the normal practice, but this soon developed into something far more sordid.

Although his loving wife was prepared to turn a blind eye to his activities, the authorities were not and the Marquis served what was to be the first of many stays in prison. However, thanks to the influence of his family, the incarceration lasted only three weeks. His mother-in-law, Mme. de Montreuil, was a shrewd woman who knew how to handle the judicial bureaucracy. Charmed by her son-in-law, she defended him to his blood relatives and assured them that he would reform soon. He was released after a short incarceration but was exiled to stay outside of Paris, and he was told that he would be kept under close surveillance. This did not deter the Marquis and before long he had returned to his old sordid ways of debauchery.

Over the next few years the Marquis managed to stay out of any major scandal, and satisfied himself with having an affair with his wife's sister. He managed to compile a massive library of pornography, some of which included priests, nuns and monks engaged in various sexual activities.

For the next 15 years the incorrigible de Sade spread his family's shame ever wider and made his own legal situation even worse. On Easter Sunday in 1768 he pretended to hire a woman as a housekeeper; then, after threatening to murder her and bury her in the garden he whipped her and poured hot wax into the lacerations on her back.

Four years later, in Marseilles, he organized a bisexual orgy with his valet, and fed two prostitutes an overdose of Spanish fly* that earned him a conviction for both sodomy and poisoning, but as the authorities were unable to catch him they merely decapitated and burned him in effigy form. Undaunted, after more than two years as a fugitive in France and abroad, the Marquis took five adolescent girls and a boy to his ancestral home of La Coste for a winter of orgies, having them held captive until the marks on their bodies had healed. It was not until August of 1778, following a shooting attempt by the father of one of the adolescents, another arrest, and an escape, that the Marquis de Sade was eventually trapped. He spent the next 12 years behind bars.

During de Sade's 12-year stretch in prison, first in Vincennes and later in the Bastille, his wife bore the brunt of his insults, and she still stuck by him lovingly. She kept him supplied with books, sweets, tailor-made clothes, and the enormous bespoke wooden dildos –

---

*The dried and crushed body of the Spanish fly beetle was earlier used medically as an irritant and diuretic, but was also regarded as a potent aphrodisiac.

which he stipulated had to be made by the same craftsman who supplied the archbishop of Lyons – with which he consoled himself for the lack of sexual partners.

Removed from the world as punishment for his crimes, the Marquis de Sade turned to writing, the result of which would offend society far more than anything else he had done. He continued writing novels and plays and grew more and more crazy as the years went by.

The Marquis de Sade died peacefully in his sleep in 1814, at the age of 74. He will be remembered for his crimes of cannibalism, coprophagy, necrophilia, the rape and murder of children, and countless other perversions. In all, he spent 28 of his 74 years in confinement.

Napoleon's March
on Moscow

Around 400,000 men set out one midsummer's
day in the year 1812, but not one of them could
have imagined the terrors and hardships they
were about to endure

THIS WAS POSSIBLY one of the greatest disasters in
military history. The story really begins with the birth
of Napoleon's heir, the king of Rome, in March 1811.
Paris was in a state of celebration because they assumed,
albeit wrongly, that the establishment of a dynasty
would bring the long awaited peace. But they couldn't
have been more wrong, because Napoleon would not be
happy until he was master of all the capitals of Europe.

In June of 1812, Napoleon began his fatal Russian
campaign. The majority of continental Europe was
already under his control, and the invasion of Russia
was an attempt to force Tsar Alexander I to submit once
again to the terms of a treaty that Napoleon had
imposed upon him four years earlier.

Having gathered nearly 400,000 soldiers, from
France and Europe, Napoleon entered Russia leading
one of the largest armies ever seen.

The Russians, led by Marshal Kutuzov, knew they could not defeat this enormous army with direct confrontation, so they planned a strategic defensive campaign. Instead of advancing towards Napoleon's army they retreated, devastating the land as they went, which caused havoc in the flanks of the French soldiers. Due to the large number of men and the fact that the Russians had made sure they could not get their hands on any further supplies, Napoleon's men started to decline through lack of nourishment. By September, without having even fought one single battle, the French army had been reduced by more than two thirds from fatigue, starvation, desertion and raids carried out by the Russian forces.

Despite their reduced numbers and strength, Marshal Kutuzov knew that unless his army engaged the French in a major battle, Napoleon would take control of Moscow within a couple of weeks. The first confrontation took place on September 7 at Borodino Field. The outcome of the battle was favourable for the Russian army, who had 104,000 men and 627 guns. The French had 124,000 men and 587 guns. The casualties in Napoleon's army ran as high as over 50,000 dead and wounded (28,000 killed), the Russian casualty figures stood at 44,000. The Battle of Borodino heralded a crisis in Napoleon's strategic plan to overcome Moscow. Napoleon failed to totally destroy the Russian army, or indeed make Russia surrender, and the day ended with neither side gaining a decisive victory. Kutuzov, realizing that any further defence of the city would be senseless, withdrew his forces, prompting the citizens of Moscow to begin a massive and panicked exodus.

When Napoleon's army arrived on September 14, they found a city bereft of both people and supplies, which did nothing to lift their spirits due to the onset of winter. To make matters much worse, fires broke out in the city that night, and by the next day the French were lacking shelter as well.

Napoleon waited in vain in Moscow for Tsar Alexander to offer some form of negotiation. Eventually in a state of desperation he ordered his troops to start their march home. Unable to take the easier route south, because this way was blocked by Kutuzov's forces, the French were forced to retrace the long route of the invasion. Having waited until mid-October to leave Moscow, the troops found themselves in the middle of an early and especially cold winter. The temperatures soon dropped below freezing, food was almost non-existent, and the march ahead of them was over 500 miles.

The diminishing band of survivors resorted to cutting chunks of meat out of the living flesh of their horses, who were so numbed by the cold felt very little pain. The one thing the men looked forward to at night as they set up camp was to slit open the stomach of a horse and eat the heart and liver whilst it was still warm. These once proud soldiers had been reduced to desperate men who finally resorted to cannibalism.

By early December the weather had worsened and the

temperature dropped as low as –36°C. By now the men had been reduced to nothing more than savage beasts in an effort to survive. They were quite prepared to kill each other to obtain the coat off a soldier who had died en route, or fight for a piece of fresh meat.

The last lap of their long trek back to Vilnius was the worst part of all. The weakened soldiers had to cross the Berezina River over two extremely frail bridges, and many of the half-dead men waded through icy water to get across. One by one the men dropped like flies into the snow.

Some of the soldiers simply refused to go on, or were captured by the Cossacks, who had harried them throughout their retreat, and had starved the army to death by keeping it to one narrow highway. These prisoners were driven naked all the way back again into Russia.

Finally, the stunned, frozen and starving survivors of Napoleon's Grand Army staggered into Vilnius. There were around 20,000 soldiers remaining of the 400,000 who had originally marched into Russia at the height of summer. They were supposed to rejoin Napoleon, but he had already gone ahead to Paris to give the news of the catastrophe, and to raise new armies. Men could easily be replaced, but not horses. Tens of thousands of soldiers had died in Russia, but it was because of his lack of cavalry that Napoleon was eventually defeated by Austria, Prussia, Sweden and Russia, in 1813.

Dorangel Vargas

An alleged cannibal in Venezuela last month
dished up his favourite recipes of eyeball soup
and tongue stew

FOR A COUNTRY with hardly any history of serial killers, for Venezuela to have a self-confessed cannibal is something that stunned the local press. Dorangel Vargas, dubbed the 'Hannibal Lecter of the Andes' by the local press, claims to have eaten up to ten men in the last two years. He was arrested in February, 1999, in the city of San Cristobal, near to the Colombian border.

Vargas was arrested after police found human remains lying around his home. As they continued the search of his house they turned up more and more gruesome discoveries. More and more human skulls were found and they even stumbled across some fresh entrails. The police were horrified and even more astonishing was that after his arrest Vargas started openly talking about his obsession, without any feeling of guilt.

'Sure I eat people,' the candid cannibal told reporters. 'Anyone can eat human flesh, but you have to wash and garnish it well to avoid diseases . . . I only eat the parts with muscles, particularly thighs and calves which are my favourite . . . I make a very tasty stew with the tongue and I use the eyes to make a nutritious and healthy soup.' When questioned, Vargas told his interrogators that he preferred the taste of men to women and will not eat hands, feet or testicles, 'although I've been on the point of trying them on various occasions'. He also told them that he rejected overweight men because they had too much cholesterol, and the elderly were spared because their flesh was contaminated and very tough.

To add to his already bizarre account, he claimed that he did not kill anyone and that the bodies had been given to him by various different people, including members of the police. However, notwithstanding the large amount of bones that were found buried around his shack of a home, nobody believed his story.

Local press gave a completely different report and claimed that he preyed on homeless men and labourers whom he clubbed to death with a metal tube to satisfy his voracious appetite. It was also speculated that Vargas may have been used as a scapegoat for a ring of human organ traffickers. What was even more disturbing was that Vargas was a former mental hospital patient who was arrested on similar charges several years previously, but was released shortly afterwards due to lack of evidence.

The case of Dorangel Vargas is still undergoing investigation.

The Tupinamba

*The one aspect of Tupi culture that horrified the
Europeans the most was cannibalism*

BRAZIL WAS DISCOVERED by accident when a
Portuguese expedition to India, led by Pedro Alvares
Cabral, swung too far to the west in 1500. It was a land
that was occupied by native indians, but there were a
few forts inhabited by Portuguese and French men.
Although it was the Portuguese who had discovered the
new land, the French decided to form a colony in
Brazil.

Hans Staden was a German soldier who sailed twice
to Brazil on board Portuguese ships. His first voyage
was relatively uneventful, but the second to this New
World in 1549, proved to be disastrous. The convoy of
three vessels was shipwrecked which left Staden
stranded and completely unsure of where he was. He
eventually discovered a Portuguese fort on the coast
which is today known as São Paulo state, where he
served as a gunnery instructor. He was a specialist with
cannons, and it wasn't long before the Portuguese
promoted him to 'Artilleryman' of the Fort of Bertioga.

After working at the Fort for several years, Staden

started to make preparations to return to Europe, where, he was told, he would receive the recognition and gold from the King of Portugal for his work. But, one day, in 1552, he tells the story that he left the Fort for a moment to search for a missing slave. Then, before he was aware of what was happening he was captured by seven Tupinamba indians, who were known to be enemies of the Portuguese. These Tupinambas were families who lived, worked and raised their offspring together, not unlike European families. They shaved their heads into tonsures, played jokes, laughed, and were loyal and genial to their friends. But apart from their friendly façade, there was something very unneighbourly about these Brazilian indians. They were known to be very cruel to their enemies, burying their Portuguese prisoners up to their waists and then throwing darts at their torsos for sport. They spat on them and then challenged them to die a courageous death, and then ritualistically burned them. Next they butchered the corpses of their enemies, cooked them on a wooden barbecue called a 'boucan', ready to be eaten by the whole family.

Believing that Staden was Portuguese, the Tupinamba carried him out to sea in their 'piroga', which was a form of aboriginal canoe. When they arrived at the Tupinamba village of Ubatuba, a festive ritual was waiting for Staden. Suddenly, he became aware that these natives were planning to kill him and cook him for their next meal. Having learned the language of the Tupi during his years in Brazil, Staden was well aware of his very precarious situation. His captors, who had already shaved off his eyebrows using a piece of glass, clearly intended to eat him.

In an effort to survive, Staden tried to convince the indians that he was not Portuguese, but French, and that he was an ally of the Tupinamba. The natives, not believing his story, summoned a Frenchman named Karrwattware from a neighbouring village with whom Staden could converse. Unfortunately for Staden he was unable to understand the man's French, and consequently Karrwattware told the natives to '. . . kill him and eat him, the good-for-nothing, for he is indeed a Portuguese, your enemy and mine'.

As if his situation was not bad enough, things looked even bleaker when the tribal chief of the Tupinamba, Konyan Bebe, announced that he had already helped to '. . . kill and eat five Portuguese who said they were Frenchmen, but had all lied'.

One way or another Staden managed to convince the indians that he was not their enemy and lived for nine months among the Tupinambas. Whether it was the fact that he was very white and blonde, or the fact that he invented that he was a kind of shaman and healer, it is not known, but his luck was with him. Staden become something like a 'Ché remimbaba indé', or a domestic animal, and his 'owner', Great Shark, lead him everywhere just as he would a little dog.

In 1557 Staden was finally received by a captain on his boat (having tried on several occasions before and been refused), in exchange for some merchant, which meant he could return to Europe. On his return Staden compiled a book, Hans Staden: *The True History of his Captivity,* about his capture, including many graphic woodcut prints depicting cannibalism and other elements of the Tupinamba life. It was a fantastic tale and an immediate success which was reprinted several times with translations in Dutch, Latin and French.

Below is an excerpt from Chapter XXVIII of Hans Staden's famous book:

. . . When they first bring home a captive the women and children set upon him and beat him. Then they decorate him with grey feathers and shave off his eyebrows, and dance around him, having first bound him securely so that he cannot escape. They give him a woman who attends to him and has intercourse with him. If the woman conceives, the child is maintained until it is fully grown. Then, when the mood seizes them, they kill and eat it.

. . . When all is ready they fix the day of his death and invite the savages from the neighbouring villages to be present. The drinking vessels are filled a few days in advance, and before the women make the drink, they bring forth the prisoner once or twice to the place where he is to die and dance round him. When the guests have assembled, the chief of the huts bids them welcome and desires that they shall help them to eat their enemy . . .

The Boyd Massacre

The story of the brigantine Boyd, is a horror story of early pioneering.

THE 'BOYD' WAS a ship that had been contracted to carry convicts and free settlers from England to Port Jackson (now known as Sydney), Australia, in the year 1810. The colony had been formed 22 years ago, and it was a fairly straightforward process to transfer their human cargo. The route was well known, and the methods of shipping people on long sea voyages had been successful, without any undue number of deaths.

On its outward journey from the London Docks, the *Boyd* had successfully delivered its human cargo, who were safely secured below deck in irons. Each one of the prisoners had received a sentence from the Court ordering that they immediately be transported to Port Jackson in the British colony of Australia.

The ship, having been cleaned and reprovisioned, was now ready for its return journey. It was a 395-ton vessel which was 106 foot long with a 30-foot beam. On board was a total of 70 people, including some New Zealanders who were returning to their own country, and a son of one of the Maori chiefs of the Kaeo tribe,

Whangaroa, who was called TeAara, or George in English. Other paying customers bound for England were listed as:

Catherine Bourke
Anne Glossop with her two-year-old child
  Betsy Broughton
Mordica Marks
Captain Burnsides
Ann Morley and her baby
James Moore
R. Wrather
John Budden
R & J Thomas
Thomas Martin
William Allen
William Mahoney
Dennis Desmond
John Petty

With everyone on board the *Boyd* set off on its long voyage back to England. From Port Jackson she sailed over the Tasman Sea, around the tip of New Zealand, then down the East coast before entering the harbour of Whangaroa. The Captain, John Thompson, had never been into this harbour before and didn't know what to expect as only two other ships had previously entered this region. It was the Captain's first visit to the Southern Ocean and his first encounter with the native Maori of New Zealand, whom he considered to be savages. Captain Thompson was hoping to use the young Maori boy to act as a negotiator when he reached Whangaroa, as he wished to obtain some kauri spars from the extensive stands of kauri timber which had been noted by Captain Cook during one of his earlier explorations. TeAara, who had asked to work his passage, was ordered to take his turn and work with the other sailors in helping to run the ship. However, he refused, stating that he was in ill health and that the son of a chief should not have to do such menial work. He was ordered in front of the Captain on a couple of occasions, who directed that he be flogged and that his food ration should be taken away. TeAara managed to conceal his resentment of the Captain, that is until they arrived at the harbour of Whangaroa. On seeing the harbour TeAara politely told the Captain the best route in and where to anchor to secure the best cargo.

The *Boyd* dropped anchor close to the entrance of the harbour. It was a little distance from the entrance to the head of this long harbour, where the main tribal 'pa', or village, was situated. TeAara immediately went ashore and wasted no time in telling his father, Piopio, about his treatment and misfortunes at the hands of Captain Thompson. He had great delight in showing Piopio the red weals made by the whip on his back, and the marks and bruises on his wrists where he had been tied to the capstan. The Maori chief was determined to retaliate and get his revenge for the indignities suffered by his son. The ship carried quite an armoury of muskets, gunpowder, axes, knives and iron nails, but the Pakehas on board the *Boyd* had no idea of what was brewing.

The Maori appeared to be very friendly and after three days, Captain Thompson was invited to follow some of the Maori canoes from the harbour mouth and into the forest to find some suitable kauri trees to fell. To be useful as spars they needed to be perfectly straight poles, about 80 feet long by about 20 inches wide. Due to their size and weight, the logs would need to be close to the water so that they could be floated back to the ship and hauled on board with the aid of a windlass. Captain Thompson left his ship accompanied by his chief officer and three other men, while just a few crew members stayed on board preparing the ship for its return journey to England. The Captain and his men were closely followed by the Maori canoes right up to the entrance of the Kaeo River.

The Maori's plan for retaliation started almost as soon as the canoes and longboats lost sight of the *Boyd* lying at anchor. They waited until they had all climbed ashore up the banks of the river before the natives drew out their weapons from underneath their clothing, and then savagely attacked the Captain and his crew members, leaving no-one alive. Then they stripped them naked, and before their bodies had time to get cold, the Maoris donned their jackets, trousers, shoes and frock coats. Meanwhile another group of natives carried their naked bodies back to the village for a tribal feast. The main course being the unfortunate sailors!

Meanwhile, the other natives in their various disguises, waited until dusk before they jumped on board the longboat and headed back towards the harbour. By the time they pulled alongside the *Boyd* it was already nightfall. The lights were shining on board the ship and the passengers were in their cabins relaxing while they waited for their evening meal. Unbeknown to them were the many native canoes surrounding the ship, all waiting for the signal to attack.

The Maoris swarmed up the ladder, their tattooed faces hidden by the disguises. One by one they struck with axes on the unsuspecting heads of the crew of the *Boyd.* They called to the passengers to come up on the main deck, and a woman passenger climbing the companionway to the deck was the first of many to die. In the carnage that ensued, five people managed to climb high into the ship's rigging to hide among the sails, and it was there that they stayed until the light of dawn, bearing witness to the terrible atrocities going on below them. They watched as the natives dismembered the bodies, preparing them to be taken ashore and eaten.

As it grew lighter the people in the rigging spotted a large canoe coming into the harbour and making its way towards the ship. It was Chief TePahi from the Bay of Islands with some of his men, who had come down the coast to trade with the Captain. As he drew level with the ship he was horrified to see the scene of carnage and bloodshed that lay on the decks. Then he heard some English voices shouting down from the rigging, asking for help.

TePahi was in a quandary as to what to do, as his

people did not live in Whangaroa and he felt he couldn't justifiably intervene without risking the safety of his own men. However, he decided he should help the survivors of the *Boyd* and ushered them on board his canoe. The situation immediately became tense and uncertain as they were watched by the remaining bloodthirsty natives who were still in close proximity. TePahi ordered his men to pull swiftly for the shore, but they were immediately pursued by two other canoes containing the previous night's attackers. It seemed they were intent on finishing the job, and wished to slaughter the remaining crew members. As they hit shore the men fled for their lives along the beach. Unable to come to their assistance, TePahi watched helplessly as one by one they were all caught and taken away by the natives. All, that is except Ann Morley and her baby.

Ann Morley had been found hiding in one of the cabins with her baby by TeAara, who apparently decided to spare her life, and she was taken ashore. One other person who was not killed was Thomas Davis, the ship's cabin boy, who had a deformed foot and had managed to hide in the hold during the whole attack. The second mate managed to buy his life for two weeks by making fish hooks from barrel hoops, but when they had enough hooks the natives decided he had no further use and he was killed and eaten.

Anne Glossop's two-year-old daughter, Betsy, was taken by the local chief, who put a feather in the petrified girl's hair, and was held for three weeks until she was finally rescued.

TeAara and his men returned to the *Boyd* and towed it up the harbour towards their own village, until it became grounded in the shallow mudflats and keeled over on one side. Over the next few days the ship was pillaged of her cargo, but the natives saw no use for articles such as flour, salt pork, or even bottles of wine, and they merely threw them overboard. What TeAara and his men wanted were the muskets and gunpowder.

The looting was carried out by TeAara, his father Piopio and around 20 other members of their tribe. They found what they were looking for down in the hold, and brought several barrels of gunpowder up onto the deck. They broke the barrels open while Chief Piopio, who had found several muskets, was trying out one of the flints to see if he could get it to fire. What followed was an explosion that completely levelled the decks of the *Boyd* and killed nearly all the Maori warriors, including Piopio. Those who weren't killed by the blast were soon wounded by the falling debris, as the spars and masts caught in the explosion, crashed down onto the deck.

With no-one able to attend to it, the fire that resulted from the blast, spread rapidly through the ship catching light to the cargo of whale oil that it had been carrying. In a very short time the *Boyd* was reduced to a burnt out hull just above the waterline right down to her copper sheathing. A Maori customary 'tapu' was declared on the ship. The tapu is the strongest force in Maori life, and means that a person, an object or a place, which is tapu, may not be touched by human contact, and in extreme circumstances, even approached.

Back at the village the feasting and sharing out of the spoils lasted for many days. The news of the massacre had reached the Bay of Islands on the return of Chief TePahi. A ship, the *City of Edinburgh*, was loading cargo for her Australian owners at the Bay, and the Captain, Alexander Berry, soon heard about the devastating act. He immediately gathered together his men and arms and went in haste to Whangaroa, and arrived three weeks later.

Armed with muskets three longboats headed up the harbour towards the Maori pah. They passed the burnt-out hull of the *Boyd* on the way and as they approached the landing, Berry handed over his command of the rescue party to a trusted Maori chief by the name of Metenangha.

Metenangha was the first one to go ashore and vanished into the bush near the pah and later returned with two of the principal Whangaroa chiefs and several of the natives who had been involved in the massacre. The natives were dressed in canvas and clothes that had been plundered from the *Boyd*. When asked by Metenangha why they had attacked the ship, one of the chiefs replied, 'Because the Captain was a bad man'. He asked if there had been any survivors and was told that there was a woman, a small baby and a cabin boy back at the pah. Metenangha asked where they were holding them, and summoned the rescue party to follow them back to the main village.

When they arrived at the village a huge crowd had gathered. Several of the native women were wandering around in European dresses that had been taken from the ill-fated passengers of the *Boyd.* The rescuers examined the burnt out remains of the ship, and noticed that nearby were the gruesome remains of flesh and human bones that still bore the teeth marks of their assailants.

The following morning the natives brought out a young woman and her baby, along with a boy who was around 15 years old. These people were Ann Morley, her baby girl, and Thomas Davis, the cabin boy. A Maori woman told them about the second mate, but said she had not seen him for about a week, obviously oblivious to the fact that he had already been slaughtered and eaten. She also spoke about a young girl of no more than two to three years old, and Alexander Berry recognized her description as being that of the infant named Betsy.

Both Berry and Metenangha demanded that the infant be brought to them immediately. They were told that the child was being held by another chief who lived close to the entrance of the harbour. They immediately put the survivors on board their long boats and headed off with the Whangaroa chiefs down the long stretch of the harbour. As they approached the sandy beach, Berry ordered that one of the chiefs go ashore and demand that the child be handed over to him. They waited for a short while before she was brought back to the longboat, crying feebly for her mamma. Her hair had been neatly combed and was adorned with a feather in the Maori fashion. She was quite clean and was dressed only in a white shirt which had once belonged to Captain Thompson.

Having handed over all the hostages, the two Whangaroa chiefs who had been held captive, asked for their release. Through Metenangha, Berry spoke to the chiefs who were clad in irons on board his ship.

'If an Englishman committed a single murder, he would be hanged. You have massacred the whole crew and passengers of a ship, therefore you should be shown no mercy. As you are chiefs you will not be hanged, instead you will both be shot.'

Chief Metenangha pleaded with him to spare their lives. Reluctantly Berry agreed and handed the two chiefs over to Metenangha, and was later thanked for his clemency.

This gruesome tale of slaughter and cannibalism that took place over 200 years ago, is a reminder to us of the differences that existed between the Maori and European cultures during that time.

SECTION TWO

CANNIBALISM
MOST
MACABRE

Alexander 'Sawney' Bean

Alexander Sawney Bean was the head of an incestuous cannibalistic family, who oversaw a 25-year reign of murder and robbery

THE STORY OF Sawney Bean as been recounted over the years and is about a family who lived in a cave in the early part of the 17th century. For 25 years this family, against all standards of human decency and morality, chose murder, cannibalism and incest as their way of life.

Alexander 'Sawney' Bean was born in the late 14th century in East Lothian. He was the son of a ditcher and hedger, and initially Bean followed in his father's footsteps. However, he soon found that hard work and an honest living was not the way he wanted to live, so he fled his family home. So, accompanied by a woman with a similar personality to his own, he went to live in a deep cave at Bennane Head, near Ballantrae in Ayrshire.

The cave itself was enormous and penetrated more than a mile into the solid rock. The entrance into the cave was a dark passageway with many tortuous windings, and just a short way in the tunnel was plunged into complete darkness. Twice a day, at high tide, several hundred yards of this passage would be flooded, which meant that they very rarely got any unwanted visitors, which is probably why they went undiscovered for so many years.

Over the years Bean and his 'wife' had 14 children, and then the 14 children started to mate which produced more children and of course all these mouths needed feeding. Then Bean and his wife came upon the perfect solution, they robbed passers-by on the highland roads. Of course they didn't want to get caught, so they made certain that none of their victims could tell the story by killing them. Then they realized that the people they were robbing and killing had meat on their bones, and meat was food. After they had killed the hapless traveller they would drag the body back to their cave, dismember it, eat some of the human flesh and then pickle the rest. The inside of their cave became like a butcher's shop with the slaughtered bodies hung on hooks around the walls, while the bones were stacked in another part of their home. And this is how their ever-increasing family survived for more than two decades.

LOCAL FEAR

More and more people went missing and soon these abductions created intense fear in the local vicinity. It became an increasing worry that lone travellers seemed to disappear from the quiet country roads without leaving any trace. Although determined efforts were made to try and discover the whereabouts of the bodies, Bean and his family were never found. Their cave was far too deep and complex for anyone to bother to investigate it, and anyway nobody suspected that their murderer could possibly live in such a place that was flooded twice a day with water.

The Bean way of life seemed to settle into a nice pattern. His wife would have more children and, by incest, produced a second generation of eight grandsons and fourteen granddaughters. Soon the killings and cannibalism became just a way of life, a means of surviving. It seems remarkable that with so many children obviously running around near the cave, that the locals did not become suspicious. Perhaps they did and perhaps they themselves were eaten, because it is possible the children regarded any other human being as a source of food.

The Bean children received no form of education and were probably encouraged to join in their parents' 'occupation' as they grew older. Soon the Bean gang swelled to a formidable size and over the years they perfected their art. It appears that although the family was swelling all the time, there was never any shortage of human flesh. Sometimes, despite the salting and pickling process, body pieces had to be disposed of due to the fact that it had gone putrid. Soon pieces of decaying human remains, which had been mysteriously preserved, were being washed up on remote pieces of beach. Since these ghastly objects only consisted of severed limbs or lumps of flesh, they could never be identified, but the authorities realized that they were dealing with something that was far more sinister.

The larger the family grew the more ambitious their attacks became and on occasions as many as six men and women would be attacked by a dozen or more of Sawney's tribe. Their bodies were always dragged back to the cave and prepared for the larder by the women in the family.

No-one ever escaped to give even the slightest clue as to who the attackers were. The Beans had a very strategic plan, whereby they would place guards along the road where the attack took place, to cut down anyone who had the audacity to make a run for it. Although it is not known exactly how long the Beans continued their murderous cannibalistic spree, it is estimated that they killed close to 1,000 people before they were eventually caught.

THE MISTAKE

The existence of the Bean family was never really known, and several of the nearby innkeepers were even wrongly executed after being accused of committing the crimes. It seemed that the problem would never be resolved, that is until the Bean family made a clumsy mistake. For the first time in almost 25 years the Beans, through bad judgement on their part, allowed themselves to be outnumbered.

One night members of the Bean gang attacked a man and his wife who were riding back along a quiet road from a nearby fair. They seized the woman first and while they were still struggling trying to get her husband off his horse, they killed, disembowelled and got her ready to take back to the cave. The same fate would almost certainly have befallen her husband had the Beans not been forced to retreat when a large party of people, also coming back from the fair, arrived unexpectedly on the scene. For the first time in their 'career' the Beans saw themselves at a disadvantage and, after a brief but violent fight, they scurried back to their retreat with their tails between their legs. This was a serious error of tactics as they had left the mutilated body of the woman behind, along with plenty of witnesses.

The man, who was the only person actually to survive a Bean ambush, was taken to the Chief Magistrate of Glasgow to relate his harrowing tale. At last they seemed to be making a breakthrough in the hunt for the attackers who apparently didn't stop at murder. It was obvious they lived in the local vicinity and that they were dealing with quite a large group of people.

Due to the severity of the case the magistrate contacted King James VI, who certainly took the matter seriously. He went in person to Ayrshire along with a small army of 400 armed men and a pack of tracker dogs. With the assistance of local volunteers and his army, the King instigated one of the largest manhunts ever known. They searched the entire Ayrshire countryside and its coastline but with no result. Then one day when they were patrolling the shore they walked past the partially waterlogged entrance to a cave. The dogs, picking up the smell of death and putrefaction, started baying and howling and tried to get into the dark interior.

Cautiously, the pursuers entered the tunnel with flaming torches to help light the way. With their swords at the ready they wound their way down the narrow twisting passages, until at the end of the mile-deep cave they came across the home of the Bean cannibal family.

They were completely sickened by what they saw. All along the damp walls of the cave were human limbs and pieces of flesh, that were hung up like carcasses in a butcher's shop. In various crevices in the cave they found piles of clothing and valuables, including watches, rings and various pieces of jewellery. In another smaller cave they found all the bones that had been collected over the 25 years. When they entered the cave the entire Bean family, all 48 of them, were there in hiding. They knew that there was a large army out looking for them and they had decided to lie low. The Bean crew did try and fight their way out, but this time there was no escape. They were arrested and with the King still in attendance they were marched off to Edinburgh.

They were not offered a trial as the crimes were so horrendous that it was considered they were outside the normal jurisdiction of the law. The prisoners – 27 men and 21 women – all of whom (with the exception of the parents) had been conceived and raised in the cave, were executed the following day.

The men were dismembered, their legs and arms cut off while they were still alive, just as they had done to their victims. Then they were left to bleed to death while the women were made to watch. The women were then burned like witches at the foot of great bonfires. It was a fitting end for a truly monstrous family.

Albert Fish

Albert Fish was a grandfatherly man who specialized in murdering and cannibalizing children - the real life Hannibal Lector

HOW COULD THIS grey-haired little old man be responsible for such atrocities? He molested more than a hundred children, murdered at least 30, and as if things weren't bad enough he ate quite a few of them as well . . .

Hamilton Fish was born on May 10, 1870, in Washington DC. He was the product of a well-respected family and yet if you delve deep into their archives you will find that at least seven of his relatives had severe mental disorders, two of whom died in institutions. When Fish was five years old his father died and his mother placed him in St. John's Orphanage so that she could go out to work and earn herself a living. It was in the orphanage that things started to go badly for him, and in the records he was described as a problem child. It is alleged that Fish was abused while he was at the orphanage and was forced to watch other boys 'doing bad things'. He persistently tried to run away and was known to wet the bed up until the age of 11. As a child Fish had a fall from a cherry tree which caused a head injury severe enough to leave him with permanent problems such as headaches and dizzy spells. This is another factor that may explain why he became a crazed cannibal in later life.

When he was 15 Fish graduated from public school and started to call himself 'Albert'. He discarded the name Hamilton, which he hated, because classmates used to tease him and call him 'Ham and Eggs'.

Albert left the orphanage when he was 18 and started a career as a house painter and decorator, a job which he would keep for the rest of his life. In 1898 he married a woman who was nine years his junior and together they produced six children. However, in January 1917 his wife ran away with a boarder named John Straube, leaving Albert to look after their children. After a short while, Albert's wife returned still with her lover in tow. Albert agreed to take her back as long as she sent her lover packing, but he later discovered that she had stowed Straube away in the attic and, following a stormy argument, she left with Straube never to return to the marital home.

By his own account Albert committed his first murder in 1910, killing a man in Wilmington, Delaware. But it was Albert's own children who noticed a marked difference in their father's behaviour after the departure of their mother. At first he would dance naked in the moonlight chanting, 'I am Christ! I am Christ!' But what became even more disturbing were his strange pastimes – burning himself with pokers, inserting needles into his groin and flagellating himself with a nail-studded paddle. A prison X-ray later in his life revealed that he had at least 29 separate needles in his pelvic region, some of which had eroded over time to mere fragments.

Without a wife to satisfy his sexual desires, Albert decided to answer some 'lonely hearts' adverts from widows who wanted to remarry. He would reply to their adverts with obscene letters and tell them about how he liked to inflict pain on himself and others. Apparently Albert stated that he bigamously married three women whom he met through this form of correspondence.

It was in 1928, when Albert Fish's bizarre fascination with pain, both receiving and inflicting, turned towards children.

THE ABDUCTION OF GRACIE BUDD

Albert Fish looked like every child's favourite grandfather, but behind the gentle facade of silver hair and a moustache lurked a monster who preyed on small children. Albert made friends with a Manhattan family by the name of Budd. It wasn't difficult to earn the trust of the family and he introduced himself as Frank Howard. He soon knew the family well enough to ask them if he could take their ten-year-old daughter, Gracie, to a birthday party. They agreed and foolishly let the daughter go off with the apparently gentle old man. But instead of a party, Albert took the child to an isolated cottage where he strangled her and dismembered her body. When he got back home he unwrapped a package of Gracie's flesh which he cooked up in a stockpot with carrots and onions. The stew he had made lasted Albert for several days which left him in a continual state of sexual excitement.

That evening, with no word from either Mr. Howard or their daughter, the Budds went into a state of panic. The following morning they sent their son Edward to the police station to report his sister's disappearance. The police started a full-scale investigation and it didn't take long for them to realize that Frank Howard was a fraud. The hunt for Gracie lasted for six years and the police had almost given up any hope of finding her body or in fact any clues as to her disappearance.

Two years later, Albert started sending letters to a famous Hollywood producer, offering him large sums of money if he could put him in touch with women who were prepared to indulge in sadomasochistic orgies with Fish. The police were called in and Albert was subsequently confined to a psychiatric hospital. He was kept under constant observation for two months, but was discharged after a report stated that he was not insane but had a psychopathic personality. They did diagnose him as having sexual problems, but they attributed that to dementia and his advancing years. He was therefore deemed to he harmless and released into the custody of his daughter Anna.

On November 11, 1934, a full six years after the kidnapping of Gracie, the police received a slender clue in the form of an anonymous letter written to the Budds. Compelled to gloat about his crimes, Albert had written giving the full gory details of what had happened to their Gracie. The police managed to trace the letter back to the apartment where Albert Fish lived in New York. When they checked the register at the boarding house, they found the signature 'A. H. Smith' to be the same as that in the letter, and they knew they had their man. When they knocked on the door of his room, the police were rather taken aback by his appearance – he was just a harmless-looking, white-haired old man with a rather scruffy moustache. Detective King identified himself and asked Fish if he would accompany him back to police headquarters to answer some questions. Then, without warning, this harmless old man put his hand into his pocket, pulled out a vicious-looking razor blade and lunged at the detective. Luckily the police managed to overpower the little old man and once back at the station, Fish openly admitted to his crimes. He particularly relished recounting of how he had cut off his victim's head, holding her body over a five-gallon paint drum so as not to lose a single drop of her precious blood. As he talked about drinking the virgin's blood, the investigators were appalled to see how his eyes rolled in his head, they could hardly believe the horror that was coming from this old man's mouth.

Fish's confession didn't stop at Gracie, he went on to tell them about 400 child murders that he had committed between 1910 and 1934. Although much of what he told the police in his statements later turned out to be grossly exaggerated or false, he still provided them with enough details of his gruesome past to sicken even the hardened investigators.

As the police began to build up a portfolio on Fish, they weren't really surprised to find out that he had a long criminal record stretching back to 1903, when he had served 16 months in Sing Sing on a grand larceny charge. But what really shocked the police was the fact that he had been arrested six times since the disappearance of Gracie on charges that ranged from petty larceny, to vagrancy, to sending obscene literature through the post.

SENTENCED TO DEATH

At the trial of Albert Fish, the state was desperate to win a death penalty, despite his defence of insanity. The jury were not convinced with his plea and faced with his rambling, obscene confessions they found him both sane and guilty for premeditated murder. Fish was sentenced to die in the electric chair, and he was electrocuted at Sing Sing prison on January 16, 1936. It took two attempts before he died, because on the first attempt the machinery short-circuited due to all the needles that Fish had planted in his body. Albert Fish, monster extraordinary, was, at 65, the oldest prisoner ever to be executed at the New York prison.

Richard Chase

Richard Chase was proud to confess to drinking the blood of his victims and gnawing on pieces of their bodies when he felt hungry

RICHARD TRENTON CHASE became known as the 'Vampire Killer of Sacramento' and for good reason, he loved the taste of blood. He started off by killing animals and then gradually began to kill people to satisfy his bloodlust.

Richard Trenton Case was born on May 23, 1950. His childhood years were not happy as he grew up in a strict and very angry household, where he would frequently receive severe beatings. The darker side of his personality started to emerge even as a young boy, because he seemed to get immense pleasure out of harming, mutilating and killing small animals.

As a teenager Richard developed a liking for alcohol and smoking dope. He had several girlfriends but was unable to form a solid relationship partly due to his impotency. He consulted a psychiatrist about this problem when he was 18, and was informed that it was probably due to the fact that he had repressed anger. Even the doctor considered that he was suffering from a major mental illness it was suggested that he should be institutionalized at that time.

When he moved out of his parents home, his friends and several different roommates noted that his behaviour was becoming more and more weird. He became more dependent on drugs and developed a severe form of hypochondria. He was starting to show even more signs of mental instability which caused him to have an intense fear of disintegrating. In his delusioned state Chase believed that the only way to stop his blood turning into powder was to drink blood. His hypochondria became so bad at one stage that he ran into the emergency room of his local hospital claiming that his pulmonary artery had been stolen, that his bones were protruding out of his neck and that his stomach was backwards. He was put under observation for 72 hours but was allowed to leave whenever he wished.

To satisfy his thirst for blood Chase started to kill and disembowel rabbits. He would put the animals intestines into a blender, liquefy them, and then drink this bloody concoction in an effort to stop his heart from shrinking. On one occasion he was even rushed to hospital due to a severe case of blood poisoning brought on by drinking the blood of one of the rabbits he had killed.

Eventually, in January 1978, Chase was committed to an institution as a schizophrenic who was suffering from somatic delusions. While in the institution, Chase complained that his head kept changing shape, that the Nazis were persecuting him because he was Jewish, and that he was being telepathically contacted by UFOs ordering him to kill to replenish his blood supply. He also earned the nickname 'Dracula' as he was often found to have blood around his mouth.

Chase was placed on strong medication and released when the doctors felt he was no longer a danger to himself or anyone else – or so they believed. Chase's parents were made his official custodians which was to be reviewed on an annual basis. Chase moved into an apartment and it was here that he started to catch and torture domestic animals so that he could drink their blood. Even though he was on medication it appears that at this time we was left completely unsupervised and his mother even helped to wean him off the drugs supplied by the hospital, deciding that he didn't really need them. Also in 1977 the papers giving his parents custody expired, and his parents did nothing to renew them which left Chase totally on his own.

Chase now decided to buy some guns and he started to experiment with them. He paid his mother a visit one day, and on hearing a loud noise she opened the front door to find her son standing in front of her holding up a dead cat. He threw the cat to the ground, tore it open, and then proceeded to smear the animal's blood all over his face and neck. Any normal mother would have immediately taken appropriate actions, but not Mrs. Chase she ignored the incident and failed to do anything about it.

Another strange incident which happened on August 3, was when police officers found Chase's car stuck in some sand near Pyramid Lake in Nevada. There were two rifles lying on the front seat, along with a pile of men's clothing. The inside of the car was smeared with blood and a white bucket contained a bloody object that looked something like a liver. The police spotted Chase through their binoculars and noticed that not only was he naked but his body was covered in blood. As they went to approach him, Chase ran away, but they managed to catch up with him and took him back to his car. They asked him to explain what he was doing there and he told them that the blood was his own and that it had just 'seeped' out of him, while the liver in the bucket turned out to be that of a cow. Again he was not apprehended and left to roam at his own free will.

Chase started to become obsessed by the stories of the Hillside Strangler in the local press. He started to avidly read about all his killings and from animals he soon progressed to far more serious killings. How a man with guns and a very severe mental illness was left un-supervised for so long is still one of life's mysteries.

THE TRAIL OF DEATH

Chase took his first human victim on December 29, 1977. The man's name was Ambrose Griffin, a 51-year-old engineer and the father of two sons. Mr. Griffin had been out on a shopping trip with his wife and was on his way back to their car to pick up another bag of groceries, when he just dropped to the ground. At first his wife thought he had died from a heart attack, even though she had heard two strange popping noises just before he fell. However, soon she was to learn the horrifying truth that her husband had been shot in some sort of random, drive-by attack.

Two other shootings were reported, one by a boy on a bike who claimed that a man with brown hair, possibly in his mid-twenties, had shot at him from his car. The second one was a report from a woman who said that a shot had been fired into her home, just a few blocks down from the Griffin's house. A search of her kitchen produced a bullet that had been fired from the same gun that had killed Ambrose Griffin. But at this stage the police investigations did not lead them anywhere.

Around one month later Chase broke into a house and trashed it whilst looking for money. He urinated in drawers and defecated on the beds, but fled when he was disturbed by the returning owners.

Desperate to satisfy his desire for blood, Chase next broke into the home of Theresa Wallin, who was 22 years old and in the early stages of pregnancy. He found the door unlocked and as he entered the house he saw Theresa with a bag of rubbish in her arms. Chase raised his gun which caused the young woman to drop the bag of rubbish and raise her hands up in defence. One bullet entered her palm and the other through the top part of her skull. As she fell to the ground Chase knelt over her and put another bullet into her head. Not satisfied with just killing Theresa, Chase then dragged her lifeless body into the bedroom. He went into the kitchen and found a knife and retrieved an old yoghurt carton from the rubbish bag that Theresa had dropped.

When David Wallin returned home that evening he screamed out in sheer horror at what he found. His wife's body was lying just inside the bedroom door with her jumper pulled up around her neck and her trousers and underwear still round her ankles. Her knees had been spread apart as if she had been sexually assaulted and her left nipple had been completely cut off. She had been eviscerated and her blood was smeared all over the bedroom and bathroom. The discarded yogurt pot was next to her body, covered in blood, as if he had used it to drink her blood. As if all that wasn't bad enough, Chase had stuffed animal faeces into his victim's mouth. Around the body were strange rings of blood, as if someone had placed a bucket there.

Two days after the attack on Theresa Wallin, a puppy was discovered dead and mutilated not far from the Wallin house. A couple reported that a strange man with rather stringy hair had come to buy a couple of puppies off them, not really caring what sex they were. After he left they discovered that one of the other puppies in the litter was dead.

Chase struck again on January 27. Evelyn Miroth, a 38-year-old woman, was babysitting a neighbour's boy, accompanied by a friend called Danny Meredith. Evelyn's own son, Jason, was going over to play at a friend's house but when he didn't turn up the friend sent her daughter over to see why he hadn't arrived. When the little girl arrived at the house she wasn't able to get any answer, but she told her mother that she had seen movement inside when she looked through the front window. The neighbours were immediately concerned and went round to investigate.

The first thing they saw when they went in the front door was Danny Meredith lying in a pool of blood with a single bullet shot in his head. The six-year-old boy, Jason, had also been shot in the head and was found lying in the bedroom. Evelyn was found lying on her bed, naked, with her legs splayed wide open. She also had a gunshot wound to the head and her abdomen had been cut open and her intestines removed. The bathroom was covered in blood and the bath contained what looked like bloody water, so it would appear that Evelyn had been taking a bath when she was disturbed by her killer. Her attacker had sodomized her, stabbed her through the anus several times, made slashes across her neck and had tried to cut out one of her eyes. Several of her internal organs had also been stabbed, and bloody ring marks around the body again indicated that the killer had used some kind of container to collect his victim's blood.

Around the house Chase had left bloody footprints which matched those the police had found in the Wallin house. Also near the bodies were two large bloodstained knives which he had used to carve up the body. When they questioned people in the neighbourhood a young girl described a man who had been hanging around the area, a man in his mid-twenties with rather unkempt hair. Neighbours reported that

Danny Meredith's car, which had been parked outside the house, was missing. Then the next twist in the story was when Karen Ferreira arrived to pick up her son who Evelyn had been babysitting. No one had seen him, and indeed were not aware that he was in the house. On closer inspection they noticed a bullet hole in a pillow that was in the crib where her son would have been sleeping, and there was also a lot of blood.

It turned out that Chase had drunk Evelyn's blood and then mutilated the baby's body in the bathroom. He opened up the child's head and let pieces of his brain spill into the bathtub. He was, however, interrupted by a knock on the front door and fled with the boy's body. Back at his own home, Chase removed some of the baby's organs and ate them.

CLOSING IN

Chase was probably feeling invincible but little did he realize how close the police were to closing in on their subject. A woman named Nancy Holden, who had known Chase at school, was followed by a man into a car park who then attempted to assault her. She fortunately managed to escape in her car and on arriving at the police station was able to identify her assailant as the man in the police sketch, who they suspected of being the killer. The police started to run a background check on Chase and discovered that he had a history of mental illness, records of drug abuse and also that he had already been arrested on several occasions, so they decided to pay this man a visit.

Detectives managed to trick Chase into coming out of his apartment after he failed to allow them entry. His jacket was heavily stained and the shoes he was wearing were covered in blood and under his arm he was carrying a box. They confiscated a .22 semiautomatic handgun, which was also covered in blood, and when they searched his body they found Danny Meredith's wallet in his back pocket. The box he was carrying contained pieces of bloodstained paper and rags and a pair of latex gloves.

He was taken back to the police station and interrogated, where he admitted to killing several dogs but refused to talk about any murders. While they held him in custody the police obtained a warrant and searched his apartment. When they opened the front door the police were knocked back by the putrid smell. Virtually every article in the flat was bloodstained including food and drinking glasses. In the kitchen were several small pieces of bone and the refrigerator contained various body parts. There was also an electric blender which had a nauseating smell and looked as if it had been used to liquefy body organs. There were photographs of various organs and a calendar marked up with the 'killing days' and an indication of many more to come.

The body of the missing baby was eventually discovered on March 24 when a church janitor reported that he had found a box containing the remains of a baby in a churchyard.

THE TRIAL

The trial of Richard Chase opened on January 2, 1979 and he entered a plea of not guilty to all six murders due to insanity. The lead prosecutor was intent on seeking the death penalty, and the trial dragged on for four months. The jury were subjected to many theories on his desire for blood, but finally, on May 8, the jury came back with a guilty verdict on all six murder charges.

Chase was sentenced to death and sent to San Quentin to await his punishment. Since his arrest Chase had been prescribed a daily dose of a drug called Sinequan to treat both depression and hallucinations. But, unbeknown to the guards, Chase had not been taking his tablets and he had been hoarding them for future use. On Boxing Day in 1980 the guard looked into Chase's cell and noticed that something wasn't quite right. He was lying on his stomach with both legs hanging off his bunk with his feet just touching the floor. His head was against the mattress and both his arms were extended towards the pillow. The guard called out but Chase failed to respond. When he entered the cell and pulled Chase's body off the bed it was obvious that he was dead. He had died from taking an overdose of Sinequan.

He had certainly been psychotic since the time he entered San Quentin prison, but no one had really bothered to do anything about it, and just ignored his bizarre pleadings for blood.

Ed Kemper

*Ed Kemper had death fantasies since
early in his childhood and he fulfilled
these in his adult years*

EVEN AS A child Ed Kemper had fantasies about death.
What his mother's friend didn't realize was quite what
they would be eating when Ed invited her round for a
surprise dinner . . .

Delving in Ed Kemper's past exposes many clues as to
why he would become a killer. His parents Clarnell and
Ed Kemper Jr. had an extremely stormy marriage and
they eventually split up when Ed was only nine. Ed
missed his father terribly and his mother subjected him to
severe discipline. Although Ed was to have a succession of
stepfathers he never succeeded in forming a close
relationship with any of them. Ed was constantly belittled
by his mother and his two sisters, and when he reached
puberty his mother started to lock him in the basement
for fear of him scaring his sisters. Ed spent many hours on
his own in the dark, damp cellar, and thought about
murdering his mother for making his life such a misery.

With very little human contact Ed became withdrawn
and he started to entertain fantasies which combined sex

and violence. In his early teens he killed two of the family cats, and his mother discovered the remains of one in a dustbin, minus the head, while other dismembered pieces were found in Ed's cupboard. He combined his animal mutilations with his sexual fantasies and his behaviour really started to worry his mother.

Clarnell was starting to find her adolescent son unmanageable, and at his own request Ed was sent to live with his father and stepmother in Los Angeles. However they found his behaviour just as disturbing as his mother had and they were at their wits end as to what to do with the boy. Ed's father decided that he should go and live under the strict discipline of his grandparents, Ed and Maude Kemper. The Kempers had a 17-acre farm in California and Ed arrived to stay with them during the Christmas holidays of 1963. His grandmother wasn't happy about having to look after a problem child, and little did she know that it would be for such a short time.

For a while Ed seemed to settle down and made reasonable progress at his new school, Sierra Joint Union High School. His teachers found him co-operative, and said he never drew any attention to himself apart from his unusual size. The situation at home was a little tense and his grandparents found the young lad rather disconcerting. His grandfather gave him a .22 rifle and to keep out of their way Ed would go off with his dog and shoot rabbits, gophers and birds.

When his school year finished he went back to stay with his mother and stepfather, allegedly for the rest of the summer, but this stay was to only last for two weeks. He returned to his grandparents' farm where Maude noticed that he had regressed and seemed more sullen and ominous than when he was at school. Ed found his grandfather boring and his grandmother's nagging was starting to get on his nerves. Once again he started to fantasize, with more and more violent visions of how he would like to kill her. All summer long the tension got worse and worse and Ed got more and more broody.

HIS FIRST MURDERS

On August 27, 1964, Maude Kemper sat at her kitchen table reading through some proofs of a children's book she was in the process of writing. She looked across at her grandson and noticed that he had a strange expression on his face, an expression which unnerved her. She warned him to stop looking at her like that, and with that he picked up his gun, whistled his dog and said that he was going out hunting. Maude warned him not to shoot any birds while he was out, and this was enough to tip him over the edge. As Ed reached the back door of the farmhouse, he turned round, levelled the rifle at her head and fired. He fired twice more hitting Maude in the back, and then came back into the house. He wrapped Maude's head in a towel and dragged her body into the bedroom. Then he grabbed a knife and started to slice the woman's body into pieces, also stabbing it repeatedly to try and relieve his anger.

After a few minutes Ed heard the sound of his grandfather's truck in the driveway. As his grandfather began to unload the truck, Ed raised his rifle, took aim and shot Ed Snr. in the head.

As soon as he had fired the rifle Ed felt perturbed, not so much for the evil he had just carried out, but because he knew he would get caught. His grandparents were not the sort of people who would go off on a holiday on a whim and they would soon be missed. Worried and upset the 15-year-old killer phoned his mother back in Montana, who advised him to ring the sheriff and tell him what he had done. This is exactly what he did.

Ed Kemper was taken in for questioning and when he was asked why he had killed them he responded by telling them that he had often fantasized about killing his grandmother, but he had killed his grandfather out of mercy so that he wouldn't have to see his dead wife. The courts appointed a psychiatrist to study Ed and he was diagnosed as being paranoid and psychotic, and the Youth Authority committed him to Atascadero State Hospital. So, still only 15, Ed entered the institution on December 6, 1964, and stayed there for a total of five years. While at Atascadero Ed was under the watchful eye of Dr. Frank Vanasek and he became a trusted inmate amongst the rest of the staff.

Ed quickly learned to say exactly what the doctors wanted to hear, not what he was actually thinking, and consequently he managed to fool them into believing he was a reformed boy. He also loved to listen to other serial sex offenders who would spend many nights fantasizing about their crimes and saying that the only reason they were caught was because their victim's identified them. Kemper made a firm resolution that any future victims of his would not be allowed to live.

After five years the doctors at Atascadero no longer believed Ed was a threat to society, although they did agree that his violence may come to the surface again if provoked. By the time Ed left the hospital he had grown to a full 6 ft 9 in and weighed 300 lbs. He was now an angry young man of 21, and just his appearance was enough to frighten anyone.

BACK HOME WITH MUM

Although the doctors had felt that his domineering mother may have been responsible for Ed's simmering rage and it was best that they be kept apart, he returned to live with his mother. Clarnell was now working at the University of California. Ed's time in the hospital had made him rather envious of anyone who was in authority and he had a desire to join the police force. Unfortunately for him his height made him ineligible, but this did not stop him hanging around with the local police in a bar called the Jury Room. He was well liked and became known as 'Big Eddie' the gentle giant. He managed to get a job as a flagman on the highways, and this meant that, now he was earning a living, he could move out of his mother's apartment.

He moved in with a friend in an apartment in Alameda and bought himself a car. Ed started to fantasize once more about picking up women hitch-hikers and what he would do to them. He cruised around the highways and with the aid of a sticker from his mother's job at the University, soon gained the trust of the hitch-hikers as they felt it was safe to accept a lift from a fellow student. After he had picked up around 150 hitch-hikers, Ed felt he was ready for the next step in his gruesome plan.

It was Sunday, May 7, 1972, and Ed Kemper was preparing for murder. He stashed away under his car seat a hunting knife, some rope, a plastic bag, a pair of handcuffs and a Browning 9 mm automatic pistol, then he set out to find his victims. Just after 4.00 p.m. he came across two teenage girls thumbing a lift. They were May Ann Pesce and Anita Luchessa, and they happily accepted Ed's offer of a lift. They told him that they were on their way to see a friend at Stanford University but were unsure of the way. Ed used this information to his advantage, and unaware that they were being driven in the wrong direction, the girls were taken down a side road. Suddenly Mary sensed something was wrong and she asked Ed what he wanted. Ed immediately stopped the car, pointed the pistol at the two frightened girls and replied, 'You know what I want!'

Mary tried to keep her wits about her and endeavoured to keep her attacker talking, but Ed was too astute and realized what she was up to. He forced the petrified Anita into the boot of his car and then returned to give Mary his full attention. He handcuffed her hands behind her and then tried to suffocate her with the plastic bag. But Mary was not prepared to give in without a fight and she bit holes through the plastic so that she could still breathe. Kemper got more and more angry and soon overpowered her by stabbing her twice in the back and once more in the chest. Then Ed grabbed Mary by the chin and slashed her throat.

Realizing that Anita would have heard the struggle from her position in the car's boot, Ed knew he had to kill her too. So he got out of the car, opened the boot and began stabbing Anita all the while trying to subdue her screams of terror.

Ed decided to take the two bodies back to his apartment as he knew his flatmate wouldn't be at home. Once back in his room he stripped both the girls naked and started to take Polaroid photos of the various stages of dissection before finally decapitating his prey. He wrote down all their details from their student ID cards and then destroyed all the possessions they had with them. Then he buried the body parts in the bush around Santa Cruz, but kept the two heads as trophies on his shelf. He later returned to the buried parts and threw them into a ravine, in the hope that they would be even harder to identify when they were eventually found.

However, Ed need not have worried because the two girls had not been reported as missing. Their colleagues at the University just assumed that they had gone off travelling as students so often did.

For a few months it seemed that the photographs he had taken were enough to satisfy Ed's sexual fantasies. He had also suffered a broken arm in a motorcycle accident shortly after his last killings, but by September of that year Ed's homicidal urges were starting to surface again.

It was 14 September, 1972, late in the afternoon, and Aiko Koo, a 15-year-old dancer from Korea, was thumbing a lift on University Avenue Berkeley. When the friendly-looking man offered her a lift she was delighted, that was until she realized they were heading off in the wrong direction. She started screaming, and in an effort to shut her up Ed produced his gun and shoved it into the girl's ribs. He pretended that he was feeling suicidal and needed someone to talk to, and for a while this ruse seemed to work. Once they reached a secluded spot Ed suffocated the small girl until she was unconscious, and then proceeded to rape and finally strangle her. Ed placed the body of Aiko into the boot of his car and then drove to a nearby bar where he sat and enjoyed a beer, all the time savouring the delights of his slaughter.

Later that evening he took the body, bundled up in a blanket, back to his room. Once again he dissected the corpse, and then scattered the remains around the Santa Cruz woods. This time he kept the head of little Aiko in the boot of his car.

Ed Kemper had a follow-up evaluation on September 15 by the board of juvenile psychiatrists. By now he was expert at fooling his doctors and he was declared mentally stable. Little did they know that all the while they were interviewing their patient, Aiko Koo's head lay in the boot of his car! Ed, with his slate now wiped clean, felt he was invincible. It also meant that now he had no-one looking over his shoulder he could go out and buy a gun of his own. The only real problem he could see was that his broken arm prevented him from working and earning the money he needed to live on his own, so back he went to live with Mum.

FROM BAD TO WORSE

There is no doubt that Clarnell tried to get along with her 'freak' of a son, but the quarrelling went from bad to worse. With each confrontation, Ed's mother became more and more nervous and maybe she was just too scared to do anything about it.

Ed went out and bought himself a .22 Reuger automatic gun and he desperately wanted to try it out. It was now January 1973, and because the weather had been so bad it meant that there were very few young women out on the highways thumbing a lift. He was getting more and more frustrated but his luck was to change on January 8.

Ed's next victim was an 18-year-old girl called Cindy Schall who was on her way to an evening class at her nearby college. He drove her into the hills above Watsonville, where he bound and gagged her and placed her in the boot of his car. Then he lovingly handled his new toy and felt excitement rise in his groins as the bullet hit Cindy's head. Still buzzing from the thrill of his actions, Ed drove back to his mother's house and took the body of the young girl inside. Clarnell was out so he was free to carry out his fantasies.

He laid Cindy's body out on the bed and had sex with her and then the following morning, with some difficulty, due to the fact that his arm was still in a cast, he carried the body into his bathroom. He cut it into pieces and then placed the body parts into plastic bags and tossed the grisly remains into the ravine. This time he kept her shirt and ring as trophies, and put her head in the back of his wardrobe.

The next day there were reports buzzing around about the dismembered body of a girl being found. Ed decided that the safest thing to do was to bury Cindy's head in the front garden.

About a month after the killing of Cindy Schall, the mother and son had another blazing row. Ed stormed out of the house taking his gun with him. He had an evil glint in his eyes and he drove down the road in a rage. Rosalind Thorpe was just coming out of a lecture and wondering how she was going to get home, when a kind young man stopped and offered her a lift. Seeing the student sticker in his window she accepted his kind offer and they chatted away like old friends. A little further down the road they spotted Alice Lui hitch-hiking, and she too jumped into the back of the car. However, the joviality of the situation was soon to change because as they went over the brow of a hill, Ed pulled his gun out of his jacket and instantly fired it into Rosalind's temple. Alice starting screaming in terror as Ed leaned over the seat and shot her in the head. Although Alice was no longer moving she started to make a strange guttural moan, which got on Ed's nerves. He was starting to feel rather weak and nauseous – perhaps the reality of his actions was starting to hit home. He decided to stop the car and finish off Alice for good before heading off for home.

It was about 11.00 p.m. when Ed arrived home, but seeing that his mother was still up decided he would come back later and drove off to buy some cigarettes. He drove off to a secluded spot, grabbed his hunting knife and promptly decapitated both the girls.

The following morning, back at home, Ed was lying in his bed when he felt all his sexual frustrations rising up within him. He went down to the car and brought Alice's headless body into his room where he had sex with the corpse after ritually cutting off both her hands. As for Rosalind, he left the body where it was but brought her head back to his room where he desperately tried to remove the bullet that was lodged in her skull. He did not want to be traced through the bullet, and when he had finished he stuffed everything back in the car and drove out of town to dispose of the bodies. This time he dumped the torsos in the ravine but threw the heads and hands into a nearby canyon called Devil's Slide.

At the time of Ed's killing rampage two other maniacs were wreaking havoc – John Lindley Frazier and Herbert Mullin. Police were baffled by the amount of bodies that were turning up on their normal peaceful patch. Ed, who had always wanted to be a policeman, took great interest in their investigations and he used to frequent their favourite haunts so that he could hear all the grisly details.

By April 1973, Ed felt like his life was falling apart and decided to pack up all the evidence of his murders in one case, together with his gun, and toss it into the ocean. He felt that the stress of killing was becoming too much and he was also constantly in discomfort from stomach ulcers.

THE ULTIMATE KILL

On Good Friday, April 20, Ed sat drinking beer with his mother, pondering about what he should do with his life. Suddenly he came to a decision. He had always hated his mother, after all she had locked him in a black cellar full of evil spirits that were trying to harm him when he was only a child. Now he knew it was time for revenge.

Later that day Ed crept into his mother's bedroom. She was still awake and, feeling that something was really troubling her son, asked him if he needed to talk. He said no he was okay, but returned shortly afterwards carrying a hammer and a knife in his hands.

By this time she was asleep and Ed brought the hammer down full force onto her skull. With anger racing through his veins he turned his mother onto her back and started to saw into her throat until she was decapitated. Cutting off his mother's head gave him a lot of satisfaction but he wasn't finished yet. The part of her that he hated the most was the area around her vocal cords, because this was the part that had given him the most misery. He removed her larynx and angrily tried to push it into the waste disposal, but it jammed. When the waste disposal started to spit pieces of tissue back at him, Ed wasn't surprised. He felt that she had bitched and screamed at him for years and even in death she wasn't going to stop.

Ed Kemper was now totally out of control, the killing had not calmed him in the way he had hoped. Still on a sexual high, Ed had sex with his headless mother. He then decided he would go out for some beers before coming back home and deciding what to do next. He called a friend of his mother's, Sara Hallett, and told her that he was doing a surprise dinner for his mum and would she like to come as well.

Back at home he propped his mother's head onto a hatbox and used it as a dartboard, all the while she just sat there staring at her deranged son – between them they were not a pretty sight.

Sara Hallett had been delighted by the invitation to come round for dinner, after all the old friends had a lot of gossip to catch up on. She arrived all dressed up for dinner and slumped down in a chair innocently saying, 'Let's sit down. I'm dead.' And what do you know, within a few minutes she was. Ed killed the poor woman by placing his enormous hands around her throat, squeezing all the life out of her. A little later on that evening, with the initial excitement of the kill over, Ed started to feel bored. So he stripped the now headless Sara Hallett, dragged her to his bed, committed necrophilia and then went to sleep in his mother's bed.

ENOUGH'S ENOUGH

Ed Kemper now felt that enough was enough and that he didn't want to kill any more. He drove away from his last two murders leaving a note behind him, and then reflected on all his previous murders. He had been nicknamed the 'Co-Ed Murderer' by the press and he had murdered six pretty hitchhikers. They were shot, stabbed, strangled, decapitated and he had even cooked and eaten their flesh, and he still hadn't been caught. Due to his immense size Ed decided to dump the small car he was driving and opted for a larger one that would afford him more comfort. He drove for 18 hours arriving at Pueblo, Colorado, where he set about finding some digs. The town was buzzing with tourists and it was easy for the big man to go unnoticed. He scanned the newspapers and listened to the radio to hear the reports of the 'Co-Ed Killer' and of his two latest victims. But there were no reports and this made Ed really angry. He felt like running out into the streets and shouting at the top of his voice that he was the one they were looking for. He was the evil behind all those killings.

He was even more incensed when he got stopped for speeding and, having given his correct name and details, still wasn't recognized. He paid his fine, drove away, and suddenly decided it was all too much. Feeling totally desperate he reached for a phone and called the Santa Cruz police headquarters:

It's me . . . Ed Kemper. K-e-m-p-e-r . . . I'm the guy you're looking for. I am the Co-Ed Killer. If you want me I'm here in Pueblo.

He gave his address and waited. However, back at the busy police station the policeman who took the call simply slammed the receiver back into place and muttered something about it being another damned crank. Frustration rising in his body, Kemper tried again, almost pleading with them to arrest him. He told them they couldn't miss the great hulk of a man who was 6 ft 9 in tall. This time someone was prepared to listen. An officer who knew about Ed Kemper sent a fleet of squad cars with their sirens blaring to go and pick up the man from the telephone booth.

Ed's confession to the police was long, articulate and detailed – after all he had spent many many hours fantasizing about each and every minute of his killings. The details were horrendous even down to the slaying of his mother and her friend. He confessed to eight murders and gave details of cannibalism. The more Kemper revealed to the police the more and more relaxed he became, he seemed to be basking in the attention.

He was charged on eight counts of first degree murder on October 25, 1973 and on November 8 he was found guilty on all counts. He was sentenced to life imprisonment in California Medical Facility in Vacaville. Although his crimes were serious enough to receive the death penalty this was not available at the time in California.

When Ed was asked what he thought would be a fitting punishment for his crimes, he replied, 'Death by Torture'. Edmund Emil Kemper was definitely a misfit from the moment he was born.

The Team From Hell

Henry Lucas was to meet his lover and friend Ottis Toole in a soup kitchen in Florida and they were soon to become the 'Team from Hell'

HENRY LEE LUCAS and Ottis Toole were indeed the team from hell. No one can be sure how many people they actually killed – it has been said as many as 600 – but whatever the number they certainly left a wake of destruction wherever they went. Toole openly admitted to being a cannibal whereas Lucas abstained because he said 'he didn't like the taste'.

Henry Lee Lucas was the epitome of a child who would grow up to be a killer. Born on August 23, 1936 in the back woods of Virginia, he lived with his family in a two-room log cabin with dirt floors. He had eight brothers and sisters who were all either placed in institutions, looked after by relatives or put into foster care, but for some reason Henry stayed at home with his parents. His mother, Viola appears to have hated Henry right from the start and would seize every moment to make his life a living hell. He was constantly subjected to abuse and was thoroughly mistreated. He was undernourished, uneducated and forced to watch his mother, Viola, carrying out the tricks of her trade as a prostitute. His father was an alcoholic and was known by the name of 'No Legs' due to an unfortunate incident involving a train earlier in his life. His father eventually committed suicide to escape the repeated humiliation he received at the hands of his wife.

Once, when little Henry was playing with one of his brothers with a knife he accidentally sliced his own eye. His uncaring mother, probably preoccupied in another direction, declined from taking the poor lad to a doctor and his eye simply withered away and eventually had to be removed and replaced with prosthetic glass. He was beaten so badly by his mother on one occasion that it left him in a semi-conscious state for three days. Viola's boyfriend at the time, 'Uncle Bernie', eventually showed some compassion for the lad and took him to the local hospital where he received treatment. Finally, as if all this was not enough for a young boy, his mother often sent him to school barefoot, wearing a dress and with curlers in his hair. Obviously he became the subject of ridicule and dropped out by fifth grade, which left him semi-literate for the remainder of his life. Henry was lonely and when he turned to animals to receive the affection he craved, his mother would simply kill the animal and consequently Henry grew up thinking that life – just like sex – was cheap.

Subjected to such untold horrors as a young child, Lucas began indulging in sadistic depravity. By thirteen, he was having sexual relations with his older half-brother, who also introduced him to the excitement of bestiality and animal torture. One of their favourite games was to slit the throat of a small animal and then sexually violate the corpse.

At the age of 15 Lucas became desperate to have sex with a girl and he picked up 17-year-old Laura Burnley near Lynchburg, strangled her when she refused his clumsy advances, and then buried her body in the woods. Her disappearance would remain unsolved until Lucas confessed to the murder in 1983.

As Lucas grew older he became bitter and distant, with little food and education he never really managed to put any real value to his life. His teenage years were spent in and out of correctional institutions, starting in 1954 when he carried out a string of burglaries in and around Richmond. He was sentenced to six years, but managed to escape and fled to his older sister's home in Tecumseh. He was captured three months later and returned to Virginia, where he tried to escape again one month later. This time he was recaptured on the same day, but, despite the two escapes, was released on September 2, 1959. He went back to live with his sister in Tecumseh where he received numerous calls from his mother ordering him to go back and live with her. He ignored her pleas, and so Viola followed him to Michigan.

REVENGE IS SWEET

On the evening of January 11, 1960 Lucas and his mother went out for a drink together at a local bar. They both got very drunk and Lucas was getting tired of Viola's incessant nagging for him to return to Virginia with her. Lucas kept refusing and eventually told her that he really didn't want anything further to do with her. When they got back home later that night they were still arguing, which continued until the early hours of the morning. At one point the dispute got so heated that Viola hit her son over the head with a broom, but he had had enough and he struck back – with a knife.

The next day, 74-year-old-Viola was found dead on the bedroom floor with a fatal stab wound to her neck. Lucas, who everyone immediately suspected, was nowhere to be found.

Lucas was picked up five days later in Toledo, Ohio. When questioned about the death of his mother he openly admitted that not only had he killed her but he had also committed necrophilia. The pocket knife that was consistent with his mother's wounds was found in his pocket, and that was all the evidence they needed to prosecute him.

The trial was held in the nearby town of Adrian, Michigan in March 1960. Since Lucas had already confessed to the crime the main issue at his trial was the degree of sentencing. He was convicted of second degree murder and given a 40-year sentence to be served at Jackson State Penitentiary in southern Michigan. After two attempts at suicide, Lucas was transferred to a state psychiatric facility for the criminally insane, where he was diagnosed as a suicidal psychopath, sadist and sexual deviant.

Despite his own admission that he was not ready to be released, Lucas was paroled in 1970 after having served only ten years. This was to be a very big mistake on the part of the authorities, because this dangerous and sick man had in no way reformed.

GETTING WORSE

Following his release things certainly didn't improve. Lucas had an unsuccessful marriage which ended when his wife found out that he was having sex with her two young girls. Next he went to live with his sister, Wanda, but she also asked him to leave after accusing him of abusing her young daughter.

In December 1971, Lucs was back in prison, this time on a charge of molesting two teenage girls. The charge was reduced to kidnapping at his trial and he was sent back to the Jackson State Penitentiary. He was released in August 1975, once again protesting with the authorities that he was not ready to be released and that he knew he would kill again. For a short time Lucas found employment on a mushroom farm in Pennsylvania. In December 1975 Lucas again tried his hand at marriage, this time to Betty, the widow of his cousin. After three months they moved to Maryland but the marriage only lasted until the summer of 1977, due to the fact that Lucas had been sexually abusing her daughters from a previous marriage.

LUCAS MEETS TOOLE

Following his second failed marriage, Lucas became a drifter. Lucas met Ottis Toole in 1978 after a chance meeting in a Jacksonville soup kitchen. The pair shared a meal together and as they got talking Lucas discovered that his new-found friend, a part-time transvestite and a vicious psychopath, was erotically stimulated by arson and had a penchant for human flesh. They started to exchange grisly stories about their homicidal adventures and thrived on each other's excitement. They soon became friends and part-time lovers and Lucas went to live with Toole at his mother's house. Toole's ten-year-old niece, Becky Powell, and her brother Frank lived at the same house. Becky was of unsound mind and she found in Lucas the affection she so desperately craved. In return her love for him helped him feel special for the first time in his life and they formed a very intimate relationship.

In 1981, Toole's mother died and shortly after his sister, and the family were forced to break up. Becky and Frank wre placed in juvenile homes, but with the help of Lucas managed to run away. The four of them took to the road, drifting around the country surviving on the proceeds of robberies. They satisfied their lust for blood by picking up random hitchhikers and they just went from killing to killing, sometimes enlisting the help of the juvenile Becky and Frank.

In 1982 the authorities came looking for Becky, and Lucas thought it was wise for the murderous partnership to split up and so he and Becky headed west. They took jobs as hired hands with a couple named Jack and O'Bere Smart who lived in California. After they had been with the family for four months, O'Bere suggested that the couple should go to Texas to take care of her 80-year-old mother, Kate Rich. They arrived on May 14, but after only four days it was discovered that the couple had cashed two $50 cheques on Mrs. Rich's account and were subsequently asked to leave.

RELIGIOUS INTERLUDE

As the couple thumbed for a lift out of town, they were picked up by a man named Ruben Moore who invited them to join his religious commune – the 'All People's House of Prayer'. An abandoned old chicken ranch provided shelter for many 'lost souls' and Lucas and Becky settled there posing as husband and wife. One day Becky unfortunately lost her temper with Lucas and slapped him in the face. Lucas was incensed and grabbed a large carving knife and stabbed her in the heart. She died instantly and, after raping her corpse, he dismembered her, stuffed her body parts into a pillow-case and then left her remains spread over a field. Back at the commune Lucas told Ruben Moore that his wife had left him and had accepted a ride by a passing truck. Then Lucas resumed his life in the commune as if nothing had happened.

Three weeks later, on September 16, the elderly Kate Rich went missing. The police became very suspicious when Lucas left town the next day and his car was found abandoned in Needles, California. Lucas was tracked down by the police and apprehended. He denied any involvement in the killing of Kate Rich and was later released when charges of car theft couldn't be upheld.

THE TRUTH COMES OUT

Lucas was arrested again in June 1983 on a weapons charge and was held in the Montague County jail. After several days and being deprived of his craving for cigarettes, Lucas was ready to talk. He confessed to killing Kate Rich and then over the next 18 months confessed to a seemingly endless number of murders. All the time the numbers were increasing, until eventually he had admitted to killing around 500 people.

Ottis Toole, who was serving time in Florida on an arson charge, was also implicated in many of the crimes. Lucas got great pleasure in describing the heinous acts and went on to say that Toole sometimes ate the flesh of the victims they had killed. When the investigators asked Lucas why he hadn't joined him, he gave the reason that he didn't like the taste of the sauce he put on the meat. When Lucas had finished his statement, he told investigators that there was something he needed to get off his chest and told them about the murder of Becky Powell. The police were quite amazed by this confession because by all intent and purposes they believed that she was still alive.

They found enough evidence at The House of Prayer

– human bone fragments in the stove and Rich's eyeglasses in the yard – that meant Lucas could be charged with first-degree murder. Meanwhile he gave details on the Powell murder and took investigators to the scene of the crime. They found the remains of a white girl around the same age and height of Becky Powell, and Lucas was charged with murder number two.

Due to the number of people that Lucas had claimed to have killed over the years, a task force was set up to handle all the inquiries that were coming in from around the country. Lucas was revelling in the fact that he was becoming the centre of attention and for once could be useful in the daily business affairs of the task force. Before long, Lucas was touring the country as a 'star killer' uncovering evidence of his so-called handiwork. I suppose in his warped mind Lucas felt that he had become someone of importance.

Day by day his stories became more and more outrageous making claims that were soon proved to be untrue. He said he was the hitman for a Satanic cult named the 'Hand of Death' and that he had committed murders in Spain and Japan, even though he had never even been out of the country. He also claimed to have killed a Virginia schoolteacher who the police later discovered to be still alive. Many investigators still believe that Lucas was in fact only responsible for a couple of murders and that officers just fed him information on unresolved crimes. Although his outlandish confessions have drawn a certain amount of scepticism, it is still believed that Lucas was a prolific serial killer.

Lucas stood trial in 1985 and was convicted of ten homicides, which was more than enough to get him the death sentence. He was granted a stay of execution in September 1995 so that his claims of false confessions could be investigated, but this stay was to be lifted one year later. On June 27, 1998, Governor George W. Bush spared Lucas's life because of overwhelming evidence that he did not kill one of the victims that he had been charged with. He is undoubtedly guilty of other despicable crimes and he has been sentenced to spend the rest of his life in prison.

OTTIS TOOLE

While Ottis Toole was waiting for his trial on an arson murder in 1983, he confessed to the murder of six-year-old Adam Walsh. Ottis was diagnosed as a paranoid schizophrenic and was therefore not given a death sentence. Ottis Toole died of cirrhosis of the liver in the autumn of 1996.

Toole had a very bad start to life, just like his partner in crime. As a young child he would dress as a girl and even into his adult years he still preferred to dressed as a woman and solicited sex as a prostitute. He openly admitted that he did not enjoy having sex with women and always considered himself as a homosexual. His background was one of poverty, alcoholism and under-nourishment and he never found his place in society. He had suffered both frontal and limbic brain damage which resulted in him having numerous seizures. He had a tendency to black out which resulted in confusion about the details of his crimes. His awareness of reality was hazed due to years of drug and alcohol abuse and his excuse for his actions was:

If I was in my right mind at the time, it wouldn't have never happened. I was on dope, strung out, just wild and crazy, you know?

Jeffrey Dahmer

*A cannibalistic serial killer who tried it, liked it,
and did it again and again*

IT WILL BE HARD for the residents of Milwaukee to
forget the name of Jeffrey Dahmer due to the sheer
horror of his killings and the gruesome discoveries
found in his house.

Jeffrey Dahmer was born on May 21, 1960 in an
Evangelical hospital in Milwaukee. Unlike most of the
killers we have discussed so far Jeffrey had a decent upbringing and was loved and well-cared for by his
parents. His father was a student at the local university
studying chemistry and spent many hours working
away in his laboratory. His mother worked as a teletype
machine operator.

At the age of four Jeffrey had to undergo an operation
for a hernia and for some reason this had a catastrophic
effect on his developing personality. He became more
and more withdrawn and would sit for long periods of
time staring into space, with his face somehow
motionless. In April 1967 the family moved to Ohio
and it seemed to have a good effect on the young
Jeffrey. He adjusted well to the change and formed a

close relationship with another boy named Lee. At school he was considered to be intelligent, but rather than pay attention he would disrupt the rest of the class with his clowning around.

In 1968 Jeffrey was sexually molested by another boy in the neighbourhood and, although the incident was not reported, this may have played quite a big part in the boy's developing fetishes. Time and time again in his young life Jeffrey would show signs that something was seriously wrong. His father remembers a time when he swept some animal bones out from beneath the house, and he noticed how delighted his son was by the sound they made. The small child dug his hands deep into the pile of bones, but his father just put it down to a passing fascination at the time.

By the age of ten Jeffrey was starting to experiment with dead animals. He decapitated rodents, bleached chicken bones with acid, nailed a dog's carcass to a tree and mounted its severed head on the end of a stake. As Jeffrey reached puberty his shyness and isolation were to return and he pushed away what few friends he had. At a time in his life when he should have been enjoying the company of other boys of his age, Jeffrey Dahmer simply withdrew into himself and became very secretive.

At the age of eighteen, Jeffrey had to experience the bitter divorce of his parents and he lived with his mother in Bath Township, Ohio, that is until she ran off with the younger brother of Jeffrey's father. Feeling totally deserted and alone Jeffrey resorted to alcohol to try and take away the pain. When he was sober Jeffrey was a quiet, gentle person, but with alcohol as his prop he changed completely and a violent rage would build up inside waiting to erupt.

HIS FIRST VICTIM

After graduating from high school and dropping out of university, Jeffrey decided to join the Army which he seemed to enjoy until his constant drinking became a problem and he was discharged. It was now obvious that Jeffrey had a real problem with alcohol addiction, but still he would not seek help. His father had almost given up on him by now and Jeffrey moved in with his grandmother and he managed to get himself a job, at least until he got arrested for drunkenness and disorderly conduct.

On June 18, 1978, Jeffrey went to see his father to ask him if he could borrow his car so that he could go to the cinema. His father agreed, but instead of going to the cinema as planned he just drove around the countryside. He spotted a young, bare-chested hitchhiker who was thumbing for a lift, and Jeffrey offered him a ride into town. The hitchhiker was 19-year-old Steven Hicks and Jeffrey's wrath began when he took the man back to his grandmother's house. It was here that he beat the poor man with a barbell then strangled him to death. Next he stripped the corpse down to the bone, then pulverized them with a sledgehammer and threw them into the bushland behind his grandmother's house. The remainder of the body he buried in a shallow grave underneath the house.

After this vicious murder Jeffrey Dahmer did not strike again for another nine years, but he eventually went on to kill 16 more young men. During the nine-year period Jeffrey was arrested on many minor offences, including assault of a young boy, indecent exposure, disorderly conduct and drunken behaviour. He eventually managed to get a job working at a chocolate factory in Milwaukee, and although a little confused by his homosexuality, Jeffrey found much pleasure in the gay bars in and around that vicinity.

THE KILLING SPREE

On September 15, 1987, Jeffrey picked up Stephen Tuomi, aged 24, at a gay club called Club 219. After talking for a while they decided to go to the adjoining hotel for sex. Jeffrey recalled that due to the amount of alcohol he had drunk that evening he does not have any recollection of the events, but remembers waking the next morning to find Tuomi dead with blood coming out of his mouth. Jeffrey panicked and rushed out to the nearest store to buy a large trunk, which is where he placed the dismembered carcass of Tuomi. Then he took the trunk back to his grandmother's house and put it into the basement where he could continue to further mutilate the body. When he had finished he placed the remains in a plastic bag and threw it out into the rubbish. The remains of Steven Tuomi were never discovered.

The murder of his second victim seemed to open the

floodgates to Jeffrey's homicidal tendencies and it gradually spiralled out of control until he was claiming around one victim a week by 1991. His killing spree over the next three years is as follows:

January 1988, Jeffrey picked up James Doxtator, who was only 14 years old, in West Allis and enticed him back to his grandmother's house. He first drugged his victim and then strangled him. Then he removed the flesh from the body with acid and, as before, the bones were pulverized.

March 1988 he picked up Richard Guerrero, aged 23, and once again lured him back to his grandmother's house. After having oral sex with the man, Jeffrey spiked his drink with sleeping pills and then strangled him. He dismembered the corpse and then put the remains into the rubbish.

The following day the victim was 26-year-old Anthony Sears and again he was invited back to Jeffrey's grandmother's house. He was strangled, the body dismembered and this time he kept the head and genitals as trophies. Lastly he painted the skull grey and disposed of the other remains in the rubbish.

The more he killed, the more he got the taste for flesh, and Jeffrey started to put muscles and various other body parts in the freezer so that he could eat them later. Meanwhile, his grandmother, who was completely unaware of the grotesque things that were happening in her basement, she was fully aware of the noise and drunkenness of Jeffrey and his male friends. Finally the odd hours and the stench of her grandson's experiments was too much for his grandmother and she asked him to leave.

Jeffrey took an apartment on North 24th Street in Milwaukee and the very next day he got himself into trouble. He offered a 13-year-old Laotian boy named Sinthasomphone, $50 to come to his apartment and pose for some photographs. Jeffrey drugged the boy and then fondled him, but the boy escaped unharmed. When the boy returned home his parents realized that there was something wrong with him and after being checked out at the local hospital, discovered that he had been drugged. The boy was able to give a full description of Jeffrey and the address where he had been taken, and they arrested Dahmer on charges of indecent assault and enticing a child for immoral purposes.

While Dahmer was waiting for his sentencing he once again went to live with his grandmother.

In 1989 Jeffrey went for a drink at a gay bar called 'La Cage' and was approached by a man named Anthony Sears towards the end of the evening. Anthony's friend, Jeffrey Connor, offered to drive the couple to Jeffrey's grandmother's house. He dropped them off in West Allis and Anthony Sears was never seen again, but his skull, scalp and penis were found in Jeffrey Dahmer's apartment when he was arrested over two years later.

At his trial for the assault on the young Sinthasomphone, Jeffrey plays the part a true psychopath and manages to convince the judge that he is a reformed character and is determined to turn his life around. Dahmer was put on probation for five years and was ordered to spend a year in the House of Correction under 'work release' which meant that he could go to work during the day but had to return to the jail at night. After only ten months, and despite requests from Jeffrey's father that he remain inside until he receives treatment, he is released back into an unsuspecting society.

On his release Jeffrey went to stay with his grand-mother for a short while but on May 14, 1990, he moves to an apartment on North 25th Street. It was then that his killing spree began in earnest. Over a period of 15 months, 13 men lost their lives.

June 1990 Raymond Smith
June 1990 Edward Smith
July 1990 Ricky Lee Beeks
Sep 1990 Ernest Miller
Sep 1990 David Thomas
Feb 1991 Curtis Straughter
April 1991 Errol Lindsey
May 1991 Anthony Hughes
May 1991 Konerak Sinthasomphone
(the younger brother of the boy assaulted in September 1988)
June 1991 Matt Turner
July 1991 Jeremiah Weinberger
July 1991 Oliver Lacey
July 1991 Joseph Bradehoft

Dahmer's normal practice was to pick up young homosexual or bisexual men at a bar and then either offer them money to pose for photographs or just to invite them back to his apartment for a drink. His unsuspecting victims would then fall into a drugged sleep after a couple of spiked drinks and would then be either strangled or stabbed to death, before being dismembered with a hacksaw. He frequently had sex with the corpse and often masturbated over it later on. The remainder of the body would be boiled down using chemicals and acids and then disposed of down the drain. He used a Polaroid camera to capture the entire experience so that he could remember every one. He was apparently fascinated by the colour of the viscera and would become sexually aroused by the heat of the freshly-mutilated body. Certain parts would be retained as trophies, usually the head and genitalia. The genitals would be preserved in formaldehyde, while the heads were boiled to remove all the flesh. Once the skull was clean he would paint it with grey paint to make it look like plastic.

It is very common for a necrophiliac to also be a cannibal, and that was the case with Jeffrey Dahmer. He believed that if he ate the flesh of his victims they would come alive again within his own body. He tried various seasonings and meat tenderizers to make the flesh more palatable, and he later told his doctors that eating human flesh gave him an erection. He said he had also tried human blood, but he could not get the taste for it.

HIS BIG MISTAKE

Three police officers were called to a rundown suburb

of Milwaukee on May 27, 1991. Two black teenage girls had come a cross a young Asian boy who was running around without any clothes on and rambling in an incoherent way. The two cousins, Sandra Smith and Nicole Childress, who were both 18, were convinced that the young boy was scared of the tall white man who had followed him out into the street and was trying to convince him to follow him back inside. However, when the police arrived on the scene they paid far more attention to the tall white man than the two young black girls, and they believed the man's story when he told them that the boy was his 19-year-old lover and they had simply had an argument.

Unwittingly the police actually escorted the Asian boy back into Dahmer's apartment, despite the protests of the two teenage girls. It was to prove a very costly mistake for the police as this proved to the black Milwaukee community that the police force was inherently racist.

The Asian boy in question was 14-year-old Konerak Sinthasomphone, and as soon as the officers left he was strangled by Dahmer. Next he abused his lifeless body and then proceeded to dismember it. Had the police bothered to check to see whether the white man had a record, they would have discovered that Jeffrey Dahmer was already a convicted child molester. Instead they chose to believe the word of a 31-year-old man over that of two teenagers and that cost the young Asian lad his life – and indeed four other young males before he was finally caught.

THE ONE THAT GOT AWAY

Tracey Edwards accepted the offer by Jeffrey to go back to his apartment and watch some pornographic videos. Tracey was a homosexual who enjoyed that sort of thing and couldn't see anything wrong with his new friend's offer. However, once inside Jeffrey's apartment, Tracey realized that he was about to become a player in some sort of homosexual perversion. Tracey was given a 'cocktail' which made him drowsy, and then Jeffrey made sexual advances towards him. As Jeffrey tried to slip handcuffs on his victim, Tracey started to struggle which made Dahmer go for a knife. With that Tracey made a grab for the door handle of apartment number 213. He knew he had to escape the mad man who only moments before had threatened him with death. Dahmer tried to drag him back inside the apartment, but a fight broke out and Jeffrey was hit on the side of his head causing him to drop to the floor. Tracey managed to escape and ran into the street where he managed to flag down a patrolling police car.

After listening to his fantastical story, the officers decided to accompany Tracey back to the apartment where the alleged attack had taken place.

Dahmer answered the knock on the door and when he saw that it was the police tried to bluff his way out of the situation. He told them that he had just lost his job at the chocolate factory (which was true) and that he had lost his temper after getting rather drunk. He offered to go and get the key to the handcuffs from his bedroom, but as one of the officers followed him into the room he noticed the photographs. There were dozens of Polaroid pictures of bodies in various states of dismemberment and human skulls in a refrigerator.

Becoming increasingly worried about what he had stumbled across, the police officer walked into the kitchen and noticed that the refrigerator was the same as the one in the photographs. When he opened the door to the refrigerator he literally screamed out loud at what he saw, as a human head lay on the shelf and was staring out blankly at him. Also inside the refrigerator were three bags containing a heart, flesh and portions of muscle. Inside the freezer were three heads, a human torso, a bag containing human flesh and some internal organs. A cupboard in the kitchen contained various chemicals and two bleached human skulls. On the floor there was a large kettle containing two hands, a penis and testicles.

In the other rooms, three more skulls were discovered in a filing cabinet, while a wardrobe contained a whole skeleton, dried human scalp and more genitalia. In a box there were two more skulls, and next to this was a 260-litre vat of acid. Finally the police found three human torsos in various stages of decomposition. Everywhere the stench of death and rotting flesh was making the officers retch.

Dahmer's calm exterior soon disappeared and he started to squeal and struggle as the three police officers attempted to overpower him. Tracey Edwards just stood aghast, with his mouth open, realizing that the threats by Jeffrey to cut out his heart and eat it, had probably been true.

THE END

Dahmer entered a plea of guilty but insane on July 13, 1992. During the trial he was protected by an 18-foot high barrier because of the intense reaction created by his crimes. The trial was short and the jury found Jeffrey Dahmer to be guilty but sane. He was sentenced to serve 15 life sentences, or 957 years.

Dahmer was sent to Columbia Correctional Institution, in Portage, Wisconsin. On November 28, 1994 Dahmer was ordered to clean the shower block by the prison warders, along with another inmate. As the warders turned a blind eye, the pair of inmates were clubbed to death by fellow prisoners carrying broom shanks. The leader of the rebel gang was a man named Christopher Scarver. Scarver was a convicted killer on antipsychotic medication, who claimed to be Christ because he was a carpenter and his mother's name was Mary. Scarver was hailed as a hero for killing the cannibal and said that he was acting out his 'father's' commands to kill Dahmer.

Ironically this was only the second time that Jeffrey Dahmer had been allowed to associate with fellow inmates, and the previous occasion had also resulted in him being seriously injured. Jeffrey Dahmer was convinced that he would be killed while he was in jail, and as it happened he was right.

Hoping to lay to rest the grisly ghosts which haunted Milwaukee, the city elders purchased all the gruesome memorabilia and incinerated the lot.

Andrei Chikatilo

Chikatilo – The Ripper of Rostov – was a former teacher, who preyed on adolescent boys and girls

ALTHOUGH THE SOVIET Union liked to think they didn't have any serial killers, Andrei Chikatilo soon disproved this theory. He was a self-described 'mad beast' and 'mistake of nature' who confessed to occasionally nibbling on internal organs.

Born on October 16, 1936, Andrei Chikatilo was a native of the Ukraine. His background gives certain clues as to why he developed into a depraved killer. Andrei's family had suffered greatly in the 1930s due to Stalin's forced collectivization. Collectivization meant the destruction of a centuries-old way of life, and alienation from control of the land and its produce. Collectivization also meant a drastic drop in living standards for many peasants, and it faced widespread and often violent resistance among the peasantry. Apart from the poverty and hunger that Andrei experienced, he also lost an older brother, Stepan, who was allegedly murdered and cannibalized by neighbours during the famine that spread across the country. People, desperate for food, would remove meat from corpses just in an effort to survive. Human flesh was bought, sold, or even just hoarded. Children saw the terribly disfigured corpses, heard terrible tales, and Andrei's mother warned the young lad to stay in his own yard or he might get eaten as well. All this must have had a terrible effect on a growing boy, and indeed he was to carry this memory with him for the rest of his life.

Most of his childhood was spent alone and he used to live in his own world of fantasy. The other children in his neighbourhood often mocked him for being 'strange' and he developed a rage which would build up inside him. His first sexual experience was when he struggled with a ten-year-old friend of his sister's and the experience excited him to such an extent that it caused him to ejaculate. To keep himself amused in his many hours of solitude he would dream up images of torture, and this was to be a major part of his killings in his adult life.

After Andrei left school he joined the army for a while and when he returned home tried to have a girlfriend. However, he was unable to perform the sexual act and the girl made a fool out of him by spreading rumours of his lack of manhood. Andrei had visions of catching the girl and ripping her body to pieces, which caused him to become sexually excited – then he knew there was something very wrong inside him.

Ironically, Andrei became a teacher and did get married to a local girl named Fayina, even though it was arranged by his sister. Andrei was painfully shy sexually and Fayina realized he had no real interest in conventional sex. She did manage, however, to coax him into providing her with two children, and to the outside world he presented himself as a meek family man. But beyond this facade there were dark and sinister urges brewing.

Andrei's mother died in 1973 when he was 37, and it wasn't long before he realized that he loved the feeling of power when he molested young girls. He knew that to get real satisfaction he needed to get violent, and this is why this pervert turned into a cold-blooded killer.

FIRST MURDER

On December 22, 1978, in the town of Shakhty, Andrei Chikatilo followed nine-year-old Lena Zakotnova and managed to lure her back to his house. He used his teaching skills and kind manner to befriend the little girl, but behind the closed doors of his home Andrei turned into a monster. He jumped on top of the frightened girl, covered her mouth to suppress her screams, and began tearing at her clothes. He tore at her underwear and rubbed his genitals against her body. His inability to achieve an erection made Andrei angry, and his attack became more and more violent. The moment he saw blood trickling from her body he achieved the orgasm he was so desperate for, and from that moment on he knew that fondling and rape would not be enough for him, he needed the sight of his victim's blood.

Still in a state of frenzy he thrust a knife into the girl's stomach and tore open her chest cavity to get at her blood and organs. This inflamed his pleasure even further and when he was satiated he put his hands round young Lena's throat and simply squeezed the remaining breath out of her body.

Coming out of his crazed state Andrei suddenly realized exactly what he had done. He looked down and saw the severely mutilated body of the young girl. There was blood all over the room and indeed all over his own body. He covered her body with what was left of her clothes and then carried her to the nearby Grushevka River. Her body was discovered two days later.

Many men were questioned over the attack on Lena, and Chikatilo was one of them. However, his wife gave him an alibi and a man named Aleksandr Kravchenko was charged and later executed for her murder in 1984. Only when Chikatilo confessed to the girl's murder in 1990 did the authorities realize that they had killed the wrong man.

THREE YEARS LATER

Chikatilo managed to control his violent urges for another three years. However, in 1981, he was fired from his teaching job due to allegations that he had molested some of the male students and, unable to get another teaching job due to his reputation, was forced to take a job as as a supply clerk at the Rostovnerud factory. This new position meant he had to travel to and from his place of work by bus or train. Turning this situation to his advantage, Andrei started looking for victims to satisfy his sexual cravings at the local bus and train stations.

On the evening of September 3, 1981, Andrei was out looking for his next victim. He watched everyone as they walked past him, fantasizing what he would like to do with them. Soon he saw someone who took his fancy, 17-year-old Larisa Tkanchenko who was sitting at a bus stop. She was a girl who was well known locally for her loose morals and when Andrei approached her, Larisa was quite willing to accept the older man's invitation to go for a walk. Once Chikatilo and Larisa reached a secluded spot, he instantly starting tearing at her clothes, his extreme desires taking complete control of his actions. As the young girl started to scream and fight off her attacker, Chikatilo's pleasure heightened. He pushed Larisa onto the ground and pushed dirt into her mouth to suppress her screams, then he punched her in the face and chest and finally strangled her into unconsciousness. As Larisa gasped her last breath Chikatilo, at the height of his frenzy, ejaculated over her body and bit off one of her nipples. Unlike his first murder which had left him frustrated and confused, this time he felt elated and actually 'danced with joy' around the body. With his sexual appetite satisfied he threw the body in the River Don, where it was discovered the very next day.

The murder of Larisa must have satiated his desires for a while because Chikatilo did not kill again until the following June. On June 12, 1982 Chikatilo was in

Zaplavskaya on a business trip, when he came across 13-year-old Lyubov Biryuk who was walking along a quiet, wooded path to Donskoi Village. Chikatilo attempted to rape the young girl before stabbing her to death. Her body was discovered on June 27 and, although parts of it had been eaten away by animals, the medical examiner managed to find 22 separate stab wounds. Most of the wounds had been to the breasts and genitals, but even more disturbing was the fact that Lyubov had been stabbed in both eye sockets.

Chikatilo took his fourth victim just two days before the discovery of the body of Lyubov Biryuk. Lyuba Volubuyeva was 14 years old and once again Chikatilo satisfied his sexual urges by repeated stabbing of the chest and the eyes.

Then, for some reason, Chikatilo changed his usual pattern of killing as his next victim was a young male. Nine-year-old Oleg Pozhidayev was killed on August 13, 1982, although his body was never recovered.

Again and again Chikatilo murdered young male and females and every time a body was discovered they had been severely mutilated around the genital area. On the girls he would gouge the breasts and destroy the vagina, uterus and bladder or abdomen. On the boys he would mutilate the penis, scrotum and anus.

THE INVESTIGATION

An experienced detective, Major Mikhail Fetisov, from the Moscow militia, was sent to Rostov in September

1983 to head the investigation. He immediately criticized the incompetence of the local police and told them that the killings were the work of a single sex-crazed man. He even went as far as to use the words 'serial killer' which was unheard of in the Soviet Union at the time and was still seen as a purely western concept.

The police started to study the criminal profiles on their records in the hope that they might find someone who had a mental health background.

The Rostov police placed patrols at the bus and train stations, having realized that this was where their killer picked up most of his victims. One day when Inspector Aleksandr Zanosovsky was on duty he noticed a middle-aged man in glasses who seemed to be paying a lot of attention to young girls. The detective approached the man and asked to see his identification papers. The man produced his documents which identified him as Andrei Chikatilo, a freelance employee of the Department of Internal Affairs, which was a wing of the KGB. He was allowed to go about his business but several weeks later, Sanosovsky noticed the same man acting suspiciously.

This time the detective did not approach him but kept a watch on him for several hours. Chikatilo didn't seem to be going anywhere in particular but he just rode bus after bus around the local district. During these bus rides he would approach young women and try to engage them in conversation. After numerous rejections Chikatilo eventually found a young girl who had had too much to drink and he persuaded her to put her head in his lap while he fondled her. Zanosovsky decided it was time to make a move and he approached Chikatilo who immediately started to perspire profusely. The detective demanded that he open the briefcase he was carrying and inside they discovered a jar of Vaseline, a piece of rope, some dirty towels and a kitchen knife.

On arriving back at the police headquarters, Zanosovsky learned that the culprit was already under investigation for stealing a car battery from the factory where he worked. This was enough to keep him in custody while they made further investigations to connect him with the 'Forest Strip Killer' as he had become known. However, when they checked Chikatilo's blood group it did not appear to match and to make matters even worse an incompetent policeman allowed the contents of the briefcase to be returned to their owner. Of course Chikatilo took no time at all in destroying this evidence. With no other evidence to hold him on, the police could only prosecute him with the theft of the battery and he served three months in prison. This time the police had let their man slip through their fingers.

As a result of his conviction Chikatilo lost his job at the factory, but in January 1985 he managed to get a new one, this time working as a travelling buyer for a locomotive factory in Novocherkassk. Whether his three months incarceration had had any effect on Chikatilo is a matter of opinion, but for six months he resisted any urge to kill again. That was until August 1985 when he killed 18-year-old Natalya Pokhilstova and dumped her body near Domodyedovo Airport.

On August 27 Chikatilo murdered 18-year-old Irina Gulyayeva and police once again stepped up their investigations to apprehend the Rostov killer. It is believed that, for some reason, Chikatilo did not murder again until May 1987, a long period which leaves many questions unanswered. On May 16, 1987, 13-year-old Oleg Makerenkov was murdered near the village of Revda and the remains were not discovered until after the arrest of Chikatilo.

From this point Chikatilo's killing spree seems to have spiralled out of control. In 1988 he claimed eight lives and in his last year of freedom, 1990, he killed another nine people.

A new man, Issa Kostoyev, who was director of the Central Department for Violent Crime, had now taken over the investigation and started very carefully going over all the evidence they had gathered. After the body of 16-year-old Vadim Tishchenko was discovered near the railway station in Rostov, Kostoyev decided to inundate the area with undercover agents, many of them equipped with night vision goggles. However despite this increase in patrol, Chikatilo still managed to claim his very last victim – 22-year-old Svetlana Korostik.

After Chikatilo had killed her he cut off parts of her body and ate them before covering the remains with leaves and returning to the station. One of the plain-clothes officers on patrol noticed the middle-aged man who was sweating heavily, and also that he had spot of blood on his cheek and earlobe. He checked his papers, but unaware of Svetlana's murder, he felt he had no reason to hold the man and let him go on his way.

Korostik's body was discovered on November 13 and when Kostoyev came across the report of a man being stopped in the vicinity of the railway station on the night of the murder he decided to look further into the background of Chikatilo. When he discovered that Chikatilo's work records showed him in the vicinity of many of the murders, Kostoyev decided to have his suspect followed.

On November 20 Chikatilo left work to get treatment for a broken finger which, unbeknown to the doctor, had been bitten by one of his victims. Then he picked up his briefcase and went off in the search for a young boy. He spotted one but was distracted when the boy's mother called him away. Annoyed at being interrupted, Chikatilo carried on further down the street and was promptly approached by three men who identified themselves as police officers. They demanded that he opened up his briefcase and again the contents were a knife, a length of rope, a jar of Vaseline, and a few dirty rags. Andrei was searched and they found there was a cut on his finger and abrasions on his genitals, but he denied any knowledge of how they had got there. He was arrested and the police arranged for a search of his home. Here they found another 23 knives, a hammer and a pair of shoes that matched a footprint found at one of the crime scenes.

A leading Russian psychologist was called in and,

after eight days of interrogation, Chikatilo confessed to a total of 55 murders. He led the police to several corpses that had not yet been discovered. Chikatilo told the psychologist that he got sexual gratification from murdering and mutilation, and he also told him how he reached an even higher level of satisfaction from cannibalism. He seemed to delight in recounting his stories and played the part of a lunatic with an enormous bloodlust.

Chikatilo faced trial in April 1992, throughout which he was transported to and from the court in a large metal cage. This was for two reasons, firstly to keep the revenge-seeking public out but also to keep Chikatilo in. He remained locked inside the cage during the trial and he lived up to the image of a caged animal. He rattled the bars, beat himself against them and ranted and raved like a madman. He screamed insults and obscenities at the judge and his poor wife, Fayina, was understandably both shocked and horrified by her husband's behaviour.

The court was not convinced by his lunatic ravings and he was found legally sane and sentenced to die for the 53 murders he was known to have committed. To loud cheers from the public section of the courtroom, the judge pronounced 52 death sentences – one of the charges had been dropped due to insufficient evidence.

After losing an appeal, on February 21, 1994, Chikatilo was taken from his prison and marched to the execution room. He was made to kneel while his sentence was read, and then the executioner drew a gun and fired a single shot into the back of the serial killer's head. Unlike his victims, many of whom were still alive when they were mutilated, Andrei Chikatilo was killed quickly and compassionately.

Ed Gein

'Weird old Eddie' as the local community knew him, told the police that he just had a compulsion to do it!

ED GEIN IS seen as one of the most weird and bizarre serial killers of the 20th century. He became a grave robber, a necrophiliac, a cannibal and his crimes were such that he inspired movies like *Psycho*, *The Texas Chainsaw Massacre* and *Silence of the Lambs*.

Ed Gein was born in August 1906 into the small farming community of Plainfield, Wisconsin. Gein lived a solitary life on his family's 160-acre farm with his ineffectual brother, Henry, his alcoholic father, George, and his very domineering mother, Augusta. Augusta was a powerful woman with a puritanical view of life, and she drummed into her two sons the immorality of sex. This view clashed with with Ed's natural attraction towards girls and probably contributed to his sexual confusion in adolescence. Augusta discouraged her sons from having any contact with women and kept them busy with work on the farm.

Ed's father, George, died in 1940 and a few years later in 1944, his brother, Henry, died whilst fighting a forest fire. Shortly after Henry's death Augusta suffered a stroke, followed by another one in 1945, from which she never recovered. This left Ed, who was now 39 years old, traumatized and alone and still very much enslaved to the mother-figure who had dominated his life. Left to his own devices Ed did his own sort of house decorating. He started off by sealing off the upstairs, the parlour and his mother's bedroom by boarding it up and decided to make his own living quarters in the remaining bedroom, the kitchen and a shed in grounds of the farmhouse. He was able to stop working the farm due to a subsidy provided by a government soil-conservation programme, and so he left the farmland untouched and did odd jobs for the residents of Plainfield, to earn a little extra cash.

Ed remained on his own in the big old rambling farmhouse, uncertain about his masculinity and even considering amputation of his penis from time to time. He also considered having transsexual surgery because he had read so much about it in the newspapers, but he realized that the operation would not only be costly but it also frightened him. He tried to think of other ways in which he could turn himself into a woman. He began to develop a very unhealthy interest in the intimate anatomy of the female body – an interest which he fed by reading books and pornographic magazines. He became interested in the atrocities committed by the Nazis during the Second World War and in particular the experiments they carried out on the Jewish people contained in their concentration camps.

All alone, with hardly any friends, Ed thought endlessly about sex and then one day he knew what he had to do when he read about a woman who had been buried that very day.

Ed decided to enlist the help of an old friend named Gus, who, like Ed, was a very weird loner. However, Gus was Ed's trusted buddy and he agreed to help his friend open up a newly-dug grave to obtain a body for experimental purposes. The first corpse came from the cemetery where Ed's own mother was buried and over the next ten years Ed would do the same thing again and again. First he checked the newspaper for fresh bodies, then always visiting the graveyard during a full moon, would dig up a female corpse or just the parts he wanted, fill in the grave and take his pickings home with him.

The experiments he carried out on these corpses were bizarre to say the least. He would dissect the body, and keep some parts like the head, sex organs, liver, heart and intestines. Next he would remove the skin from the body, draping it over a tailor's dummy. On some occasions he would actually wear the skin himself and dance around the farm, a practice which apparently gave him intense satisfaction. On other occasions Ed would simply take the body parts that particularly interested him, especially the excised female genitalia. He loved to fondle them and would sometimes stuff them into a pair of women's panties which he would wear around the house. This was the closest he could get to being a woman, and soon he made a full body suit from human skin, complete with a mask and breasts. Soon, and not surprisingly, he became a total recluse, discouraging anyone from calling on him at the farm.

As his collection of trophies grew, so did his range of experiments and obsessions. Then his trusted friend Gus was taken away to an asylum and once more Ed was on his own.

TURNING TO MURDER

Ed started to tire of his lifeless corpses and he decided he needed much fresher flesh, and this is when he turned to murder. Mary Hogan was a 51-year-old divorcee who ran the local Hogan's Tavern at Pine Grove, around six miles from the farm. Ed liked women who were around his deceased mother's age, and Mary fitted the description of what he needed. She was on her own at the tavern when Ed turned up on cold afternoon in December 1954. He shot her in the head with his revolver, placed her body in the back of his truck and then took her back to his lair.

Mary's disappearance was discovered when a customer dropped into the tavern and found the place deserted. When they saw a large bloodstain on the floor and a spent cartridge beside it, they realized that something was very wrong. The bloodstains ran all across the floor and out of the back door into the parking lot where they stopped beside some tyre tracks. The police were unable to find any clues as to Mary's disappearance, but a few weeks later when a sawmill owner named Elmo Ueeck was talking to Ed about the missing woman, Ed replied that she wasn't missing, she was up at his farm right now. Ueeck, realizing that Ed was an oddball, didn't even bother to ask him what he meant. Even thought the police considered Ed Gein to be a suspect in the case, no charges were ever made and the files were left open.

There may have been other victims between the years 1954 and 1957, but there is no definite evidence – that is until November 16, 1957. Bernice Worden was a woman in her late fifties who ran the local hardware store. Ed shot Bernice with a .22 rifle that he stole from a display rack within the store, and then he drove the body home in the store's own truck. Ed also took the cash register containing $41, but not because he wanted the money, he later explained, but because he wanted to see how it worked.

Bernice's son, Frank, was a deputy sheriff who also often helped his mother out in the store. On the Saturday morning his mother was shot, Frank had gone deer hunting. When he got back to the store in the afternoon, he found the place closed with the lights still on, his mother missing and blood on the floor. He also noticed that the cash register was missing. When he asked the neighbours if they had seen anything, some-body mentioned that they had seen the store truck drive away at around 9.30 that morning. Frank immediately called the Sheriff, Art Schley, and told him what had happened. They checked the record of sales that had been made that morning, and one of them was for a half gallon of antifreeze. Frank remembered that Ed Gein had stopped by the previous evening just before they were closing and said that he would be back in the morning to pick up some antifreeze. Frank also remembered that Ed had taken an interest in the fact that he was going hunting in the morning.

Very suspicious that the peculiar Ed Gein had been spotted in the town that morning, the sheriff and his deputy decided to go and check the farmhouse, which the local children had nicknamed the 'Haunted House'.

GRUESOME DISCOVERIES

The farmhouse was in darkness when they arrived, and Ed Gein was nowhere to be found. Acting on a hunch, they drove to a store in West Plainfield where Ed normally did his grocery shopping and it paid off. Ed had just had lunch with the proprietor and his wife and as Frank and the Sheriff arrived Ed was about to leave in his truck. The sheriff called him over and asked if he would mind sitting in the police car while they asked him a few questions. Ed told the Sheriff that he thought someone was trying to frame him for Bernice Worden's death. The Sheriff decided immediately to take Ed Gein into custody – he hadn't even mentioned the death of Bernice!

With Ed safely locked up, Sheriff Schley and Captain Schoephoester returned to the house with some other officers. The doors to the farmhouse itself were locked, but the door to the side shed at the rear of the house opened when Schley pushed it with his foot. By now it was dark, and as the farmhouse had no electricity, so they had to carry out their search by torchlight. It was then that the gruesome evidence of Gein's bizarre obsessions was uncovered. In the woodshed they found a naked, headless body hanging upside down from a meat hook, the legs spread wide apart and a long slit running from the genitals up to the throat. Like the head, the genitals and anus were missing – Bernice Worden had been disembowelled just like a deer.

Already sickened by what they had seen, the sheriff and his men moved on to the main house. Again they had to use torches and oil lamps to light the rooms. As they broke into the farmhouse they noticed that it obviously hadn't been cleaned for years, there were piles of rubbish everywhere and the stench was over-powering. The few remaining rooms that hadn't been nailed up were littered with books and magazines, various utensils, old tin cans and loads of other old junk. But the mess was nothing compared to what else they found in the jumbled old farmhouse – two shin bones, four human noses, a quart can converted into a drum by human skin stretched over both the top and bottom, a bowl made from the inverted half of a human skull, nine 'death masks', ten female heads with the tops sawn off above the eyebrows, bracelets made from human skin, a purse with a handle made from human skin, a sheath for a knife made from human skin, a pair of leggings made from human skin, four chairs with the seats being replaced by strips of human skin, a shoe box containing nine salted vulvas of which his mother's was painted silver, a hanging human head, a lampshade made from human skin, a shirt made of human skin, a number of shrunken heads, two skulls for Ed Gein's bedposts, a pair of human lips hanging from string, Ed's full woman body suit constructed with human skin and complete with mask and breasts, Bernice Worden's heart in a pan on the stove, and a refrigerator full of human internal organs.

The scattered remains of an estimated 15 bodies were discovered at the Gein farmhouse, but Ed himself was unable to remember how many murders he had actually committed. Neighbours reported to the Sheriff that Ed had often bought them gifts of fresh venison and yet he had never been hunting or indeed shot a deer in his life.

BY REASON OF INSANITY

On January 16, 1958, a judge found Ed Gein insane and had him committed to the Central State Hospital at Waupon. After ten years Ed was considered to be competent to stand trial and although he was found guilty he was also pronounced to be criminally insane. He was returned to the Central State Hospital and then moved in 1978 to the Mendota Mental Health Institute. Ed Gein died of cancer on July 26 1984, at the age of 78.

Gein was considered to be a model prisoner, always polite, gentle and discreet, spending his long, lonely hours doing occupational therapy, rug making and stone polishing.

Ed Gein ended up achieving immortality thanks to a horror writer named Robert Bloch. Ed Gein had inspired the fictional character Norman Bates, originally in a book and then it was transformed into a film by Alfred Hitchcock in 1960 called Psycho. But it didn't stop there because Ed Gein is often considered to have been the inspiration of quite a few other spine-chilling masterpieces.

THE HOUSE OF HORRORS

When Ed was committed to the mental hospital, the people of Plainfield were able to take out their revenge on the Gein farmhouse. They had come to think of it as a monument of evil in their community. On the morning of March 20, 1958, firefighters were called out to a blaze at the farm but they were unable to save it from being razed to the ground. It had almost certainly been started on purpose and when Ed was told about it, he simply said: 'Just as well.'

Some of the possessions which survived the fire, like his 1949 Ford sedan, were later sold off at auction. The car was bought by a businessman who showed if off at state fairs with a banner attached to it saying:

Come and see the Ghoul Car in which Ed Gein transported his victims

HENRY GEIN

We will end this story with the mystery surrounding Ed's brother, Henry. It has been rumoured that Ed killed his own brother so that he could have the sole attention of his mother. Some reports say that he was found dead in the Gein barn and others say that he was killed whilst trying to put out a forest fire. There is nothing to substantiate the story that Ed killed Henry, but it does seem feasible seeing as Ed was totally obsessed with his mother. He killed women who were around her age and who had similar looks, so why indeed wouldn't he kill his brother to get all the attention himself?

Gary Heidnik

Neighbours had not only reported tales of orgies, screams and the buzz of a power saw late at night, but also that they couldn't stand the smell of burning flesh ...

GARY MICHAEL HEIDNIK did not have the best start to his life. He was born in November 1943 in Eastlake which is a suburb of Cleveland, Ohio. His brother Terry was born 18 months later and shortly after the Heidnik's marriage broke up and ended in divorce. For a while the boys lived with their mother and her new husband. However, she was an alcoholic and, feeling she was unable to look after her two young boys, packed them off to live with their father and his new wife. They were not happy times, for their father was a true disciplinarian and also a heavy drinker which was not helped by their constant arguing with their stepmother. Gary started to wet the bed and became the subject of his father's ridicule, even to the point that his stained sheets would be hung out of the window so that everyone could see what he had done.

Gary also received ridicule from school due to the fact that his head was somewhat misshapen following a fall out of a tree. It was possibly this fall that was the root to Gary's bizarre behaviour later in his life.

When Gary left school he was desperate to join the army, an ambition that was so strong that his father arranged for him to study at the Staunton Military Academy in Virginia. Gary stayed at Staunton for the next two years and managed to achieve excellent grades. Living back with his father again, Gary found it hard to settle into another school and eventually, at the age of eighteen he was allowed to join the regular army.

Gary soon adapted to army life which he loved and once again did very well in his training receiving excellent grades. He made few friends and, although he was refused for the Military Police, eventually got a posting in San Antonio, Texas, to train as a medic. Once again Gary took to the training like a duck to water and even managed to build up a thriving business by lending money to other students at exorbitant rates. However, this good fortune was all to come to an end when he was transferred to a field hospital in Germany. In August 1962 he was taken to the sick bay and was diagnosed with gastroenteritis. During his examinations a neurologist also reported that he was showing signs of mental illness which meant the end of his career in Germany. He was prescribed heavy tranquillizers and was transported back to the United States. Within three months he had been discharged from the Army on medical grounds and was given a 100 per cent disability pension – the official diagnosis being 'Schizoid Personality Disorder'.

After being discharged from the Army Gary settled in Philadelphia and qualified as a nurse. He managed to get a job in the University Hospital in Philadelphia but was later fired due to a poor standard of work. From there he enrolled at the Veterans Administration Hospital to train as a psychiatric nurse, but was asked to leave because they did not like his attitude.

THE DECLINE

From then on Gary Heidnik's life went from bad to worse and he spent much of his time in and out of mental institutions. In 1970, his mother, Ellen, committed suicide by drinking poison, and this only added to his already disturbed state of mind. Gary himself attempted suicide on numerous occasions which meant more and more time in hospital, and so the vicious circle continued. With each admission into hospital, Gary's behaviour became more and more bizarre, and most of his days were spent in complete silence. Refusing to communicate verbally, Gary's only form of contact was by writing notes. His personal hygiene became virtually non-existent and also around this time he developed very peculiar habits and mannerisms.

Gary's world outside of institutions revolved around the Elwyn Institute for the Retarded. He became the father-figure to the mostly black or Hispanic female inmates, most of whom were extremely gullible and desperate for some form of affection. In 1971 Gary came up with the brainwave that he would like to start his own church and he joined the United Church of the Ministers of God and appointed himself as the 'Bishop'. The church at the time only had eight members, one of these was Gary's mentally handicapped girlfriend, and the remainder were from the under-privileged at the Elwyn Institute.

There were strange goings-on at the United Church of the Ministers of God and especially at night, and it wasn't long before the neighbours were complaining to the police. Gary didn't want them to start snooping around and so he decided it was time to move on. He sold the premises and when the new owner moved in they founds piles of pornographic magazines, rubbish was strewn throughout the house and there were boxes and boxes of battery-operated sex toys.

In 1977 Heidnik invested $35,000 in shares at Merrill Lynch, and over a period of 12 years managed to acquire a fortune of half a million dollars. He spent the money lavishly and bought himself a fleet of luxury cars including a Rolls Royce, a Lincoln Convertible and a customized van. Using his assumed title of Bishop of the United Church of the Ministers of God, Gein was able to avoid paying tax on any of the cars he purchased. His greatest possession was his Cadillac and he spent a lot of money buying extras for it and making it his pride and joy.

Now relocated Heidnik carried on various relation-ships with women, most of whom were black and some of them even with serious mental problems. His aim at this time was to try to father a child and indeed his very first black partner bore him a daughter, but left shortly after the baby was born. Gary would simply bring women off the streets to have sex with him, including his own girlfriend's sister. The sister lived in a mental institution and on one occasion Heidnik and his girlfriend drove up to Harrisburg to take her out to dinner on a special 12-hour pass. However, they never went out to dinner. He took the 34-year-old woman, who only had the mentality of a baby, back to his cellar where he raped and sodomized her while his girlfriend looked on. When the girl failed to turn up at the institute, the police were called and they turned up at Heidnik's house and took the girl back. They arrested Gary on June 6 and he was charged with kidnapping, rape, deviant sexual intercourse using the handle of a hammer, unlawful restraint and interfering with the custody of an illiterate and committed person. The case went to trail in November 1978, and Heidnik took the stand in his own defence pleading that he was not guilty. Heidnik was given a psychological examination and he was diagnosed as being 'manipulative and psycho-sexually immature'. He was found guilty and sentenced to serve between three and seven years in jail. He ended up serving four years, three of which were spent in various mental institutions, after three attempted suicides in prison. On one of the occasions he nearly succeeded when he swallowed a light bulb.

HOUSE OF HORRORS

Once back on the streets Heidnik's next purchase was a rundown house at 3520 North Marshall Street in Franklinville, Philadelphia which later became known as the 'House of Horrors'. Heidnik made this house his headquarters of the United Church for the Ministers of God. Feeling lonely, Heidnik decided to put an advertisement in the newspaper for a wife. His require-ments were quite simple – he wanted an oriental virgin. This advertisement caught the eye of a beautiful Filipina girl by the name of Betty Disto.

For the first couple of years Heidnik and Betty started corresponding by mail and the occasional phone call. Then Gary proposed marriage telling Betty that he was a minister of religion and she immediately accepted. Despite the objections of her parents Betty boarded a plane to Philadelphia on September 29, 1985. Heidnik met her at the airport and then took her home to North Marshall Street where he showed her her room. She was taken aback to find a mentally disturbed black woman asleep in her bed, but Heidnik explained that she was a paying tenant. Despite her misgivings Betty married Heidnik in a 'quickie' ceremony on October 3 and then went straight back to the house. For the first week Heidnik treated her well and even talked about starting a family, but her happiness was to be short-lived. They had been married for less than a month when she arrived back home one day to find her husband in bed with three black women. He asked if she would join them, but horrified Betty burst into tears and asked for him to give her the money so that she could return home. He categorically refused and said that as he was the master it was his right to have numerous sexual partners.

From then on life was hell for Betty and her husband always had several women in the house to act as his sex toys, sometimes forcing his wife to watch. If she dared to complain he would beat her and as the days went by he became progressively more and more violent. Eventually she couldn't take any more and she turned to some fellow Filipinos for advice. When she told them about the macabre details of her marriage they told her she must leave him at once, even if he had threatened to kill her. So one day having plucked up the courage and on the pretence of going shopping she left and went to stay in a home for battered women.

Two weeks later Gary Heidnik was picked up and charged with assault, indecent assault, spousal rape and involuntary sexual intercourse. However, Betty failed to turn up for the preliminary hearing and the charges had to be dropped. What Gary didn't realize was that Betty was pregnant at the time with his child, and in 1987 she took him to court to try to win financial support for her son. As the case progressed the judge became aware of Heidnik's medical history and ordered that he undergo a series of psychological tests. What the judge didn't know, however, was that two of the girls that Heidnik had held captive in his basement were already dead.

JOSEFINA RIVERA

Josefina Rivera will never forget November 26, 1986. Josefina was a prostitute and on this particular night she was on her way to work following a violent argument with her boyfriend. It was raining and bitterly cold and she walked up and down the streets waiting for a likely punter. She was just about to give up for the night when a car drove slowly passed and then stopped. The car was a silver and white Cadillac and as she put her head in through the window a bearded man asked her if she was 'hustling' for business. The man introduced himself as Gary and he told Josefina that he had a call to make before they got down to business. Josefina introduced herself as Nicole and together they drove to a local McDonald's, drank coffee together and then went back to North Marshall Street.

When they went inside the house Josefina was startled by the shabbiness of the surroundings, but still went upstairs and got into bed. Heidnik stripped off, passed her a $20 bill and then slipped into the bed next to her. Sex that evening was very quick and, thinking that she had fulfilled her obligation, Josefina got out of bed and started to get dressed. Suddenly Heidnik leapt up and clamped his hands around her throat and forced her downstairs and into the concrete cellar. The room was cold and damp and Josefina, only wearing a thin blouse, started to shiver uncontrollably. She pleaded with her captor to let her go, but he just told her to be quiet and threatened to hit her if she didn't comply.

Deciding that it would be wise to go along with his wishes, Josefina was dragged onto a soiled mattress and then her ankles were manacled to an iron pipe. She looked around her in desperation to see if there was any way she could escape. When Heidnik had finished he told Josefina to sit up and he laid his head in her lap and fell into a deep sleep. During the night Josefina herself drifted off to sleep and woke up with a start later to find that she was on her own. She looked around her cell and realized that the only light penetrating the cellar came from a boarded up window. She realized that the man was obviously a complete psycho but she shuddered and tried to remain calm. The basement itself was bare except for a freezer, a pool table and a rusty old washer-dryer. In the middle of the room she noticed that a small area of concrete had been removed and that a shallow pit had been dug into the ground underneath.

Later Heidnik returned and offered her some food, but even though she was really hungry, Josefina refused his offer because she was frightened that it was either drugged or poisoned. Heidnik took the food away and then came back with some digging implements. Josefina watched as he set to work making the hole in the middle of the room wider and deeper, wondering if that was where she was going to end up.

When Heidnik had finished his excavating, he came over to Josefina and demanded sex, after which he went back up upstairs. Left on her own again she managed to loosen one of her ankle clamps and with the chain stretched to its limit managed to reach the boarded window. Stretching up as high as she could she managed to pry open one of the boards and she started screaming at the top of her voice. Rivera's plan to escape attracted the attention of her captor, and it brought swift punishment. She was viciously beaten with a plastic rod and then forced into the hole he had dug in the middle of the cellar. He forced her to curl up into a ball and then covered the hole with a piece of board and weighted it down. It was cold and damp and her cramped limbs started to ache, which made it impossible for Josefina to fall asleep. Heidnik had left the radio on at a high volume to cover the noise of any screams and as she lay waiting to die, she mentally ticked off each hour as listened to the radio news.

It was twenty-seven hours later that Heidnik came back to the basement and this time he was not alone. She could hear the sound of chains being dragged along the floor and also a whimpering noise. When Heidnik lifted the board Josefina had to blink to adjust her eyes to the light, and then she noticed that the whimpering had come from another girl. The girl was 25-year-old Sandra Lindsay, who had been chained to the same iron pipe. Sandra appeared to be mentally disturbed and walked with a limp and she told Josefina to call her Sandy.

After Heidnik had had a snack he had sex with both women and threatened them not to cause any trouble while he was away. Although Sandy's speech was slow she told Josefina that she had known Heidnik for a long time and she knew that she had to play by his rules otherwise she would receive a beating and be confined to the pit. They were just his sex toys which he liked to play with several times every day and night.

It was nearly Christmas and Heidnik was out looking for more young women to add to his 'harem'. He picked up a young 19-year-old black girl called Lisa Thomas and brought her back to the house, but not before he bought Lisa a meal and some new clothes at Sears. Perhaps there was a human side to this monster, or perhaps he had just got into the spirit of Christmas. Lisa was drowsy from the wine she had drunk at dinner, and when she woke up she found herself naked in Heidnik's bed. She started to protest but the more she complained the tighter Heidnik's grip became on her throat, until eventually she submitted and allowed him to have his wicked way. His erstwhile charm and compassion had vanished.

When he was sexually satisfied Heidnik handcuffed Lisa and led her down to the basement to meet his other two slaves. Crawling out of their pit they immediately saw the horror on the new girl's face, but they could do nothing to comfort her. Just like the other two, Lisa would become the object of his severe and frequent beatings. Their bodies became marked with the bloody weals left by a strap or a stick, and the more they screamed the more excited Heidnik became.

As if things weren't bad enough the women received very sparse portions of food and there was a complete lack of toilet facilities. If they pleaded for more food Heidnik would bring down tins of dog food which they would devour ravenously, basically life was completely unbearable.

The next woman to arrive was Deborah Dudley who struggled like mad when Heidnik applied the chains. However, she was no match to his strength and eventually the 23-year-old was virtually beaten senseless.

January 18 saw yet another victim arrive in the chamber of horrors, this time it was 18-year-old Jacqueline Askins. She was very slight in stature and she was only allowed to wear her panties and nothing else. The only creatures that were allowed to roam free in that already overcrowded chamber were Heidnik's two dogs, who often shared the cellar with the other prisoners.

The first of the girls to die was Sandy. She had been hung from a beam by her wrists for committing something that Heidnik disapproved of, and when she was let down she was simply thrown into the pit as a warning to the others. When she stopped breathing Heidnik got angry and dragged her body out of the pit. He proceeded to cut it up using an electric saw, the noise of which put the fear of God into the other women.

The next meal the girls were dished up was not just dog food, it also contained ground up human flesh!

As each day went by Heidnik became more and more deranged. The girls prayed daily to let there be an end to their suffering but things were to become even worse. As the stench of death hung around the cellar, Heidnik hung each girl from a beam by the wrists and then forced a screwdriver into their ears, piercing the eardrum and thus blocking out any sound.

The only one to survive from this ordeal was Josefina who feigned affection for Heidnik, telling him that she needed him as her partner. Heidnik started to trust her and expected her to beat the other girls and to tell him if any of them misbehaved. As for Deborah Dudley, who was still constantly trying to fight off his attacks, he led her shuffling in her chains into the kitchen, where he pointed to a large pot on the stove which contained Sandra Lindsay's head.

Totally dumbstruck by what she had seen she was led back to the basement and simply sank to the floor in despair. Shortly after she recovered her composure and started to scream at the top of her voice, which made Heidnik even more angry. He tried to subdue her by using electric shocks. He stripped the flex from a cable, pressed the wires into her chains, and then watched her violently jolt as the current passed through her body. The other girls watched in complete horror, this madman just went from one crazed act to another. He threatened them that if any of them misbehaved they would receive the same punishment, already demoralized and weak the girls just sank to the floor.

Heidnik was getting the taste for killing and it didn't take long before he decided to make his next move. Askins, Thomas and Dudley, who were all tightly bound, were pushed into the pit which was covered by the plywood board through which Heidnik had drilled several holes. Next he ordered Josefina to fill the pit with water using a garden hose. Convinced that they were about to be drowned, the three women clawed at the board and begged with Josefina to help them. Next, two bare wires were poked through the holes and as soon as they touched the chains there were frantic screams from inside the pit. The next time the wires were poked through the holes, one of them touched Deborah's flesh which caused her heart to stop beating. She dropped face down into the murky water, dead. Her body was dragged to the freezer and later buried in New Jersey State Park. It was Josefina Rivera who later led the police to the place where she was buried.

Totally unconcerned by the death of his slave, Heidnik decided to go cruising for a replacement. This time Rivera went with him, always hopeful for the chance to escape the nightmare. Together they picked up a girl called Agnes Adams, and made a deal with her for sex. They took her back to the House of Horrors where she soon found herself chained, along with the remaining girls, down in the basement.

Josefina's chance to escape came on March 24. She persuaded him to take her cruising in his favourite Cadillac so that she could find him a 'sexy, beautiful girl'. She promised she would be back by midnight, and she kept her promise she did return, but this time it was in a police patrol car. The officers, having seen the scars on her ankles, decided to take the matter seriously and accompanied her back to 3520 North Marshall Street.

NUMBER 3520

The rundown house at North Marshall Street had in fact been under suspicion for several weeks, due to complaints from the neighbours. They had not only complained of screaming and the noise of orgies going on late at night, but they said there was a stench of burning flesh and the sound of a buzzing power saw. By now it was five o'clock in the morning and they wasted no time in gaining entry by smashing down the barred and bolted front door. Only then was the full extent of the horror revealed, when Josefina led them down to the dark and grimy basement.

Two women, heavily scarred and trembling, lay cowering beneath a filthy blanket. They had red weals around their wrists and ankles where they were both chained together. A third girl lay completely naked in chains, and curled up like a child in the filthy 'punishment pit'. The hole was about 4 ft deep and was covered by a plywood board held down by heavy bags. The girls, who were all black, once freed from their bondage were able to give their names as Jacqueline Askins and Lisa Thomas, and Agnes Adams, who was the girl who had been lying in the pit.

While the three women managed to stagger out to a waiting ambulance, Homicide Lieutenant James Hansen and his men continued their gruesome search. When they opened the refrigerator in the filthy kitchen, they found a human arm and beside it, labelled 'Dog

Food', were 24 lbs of frozen human limbs packed into polythene bags. They consisted of two forearms, one upper arm, two knees and pieces of thigh, and all still had skin, muscle and soft tissue clinging to the bone. They had been cut from the body using an electric saw. A food processor on one of the bloodstained worktops contained traces of human flesh, while an oven dish had what looked like the burnt remains of human ribs. On top of the cooker was a pot which contained a foul-smelling fatty substance – it was the boiled remains of a human head.

Hansen and his men were totally nauseated, never in their life had they come across such atrocities. There was a dog wandering around the house chewing on a human leg bone. With their noses covered with hand-kerchiefs to try and block out the sickening stench, the police went from room to room only to discover more blood and bits of flesh and bone scattered everywhere. This was indeed a house of horror, a human abattoir that had been witness to the most unspeakable actions – murder, rape, torture, electrocution, savage beatings and cannibalism.

While the grisly search took place, Gary Heidnik was back at the police headquarters facing stiff questioning. Tall, broad-shouldered and somewhat broody, this man with the dark moustache and beard was the epitome of pious hypocrisy, claiming to be a self-styled 'Bishop'. He had been conned by his trusty captive, Josefina, and while the police checked her fantastic story all he could do was sit and wait. Mind you, he didn't have to wait for long because back at the house was all the over-whelming evidence they needed to back up her story.

THE TRIAL

Josefina Rivera told the horror-struck courtroom every-thing that had happened to the girls at the house in North Marshall Street. She told the jury that Heidnik had forced her to write a confession admitting that she had killed Deborah Dudley. She said that at no time did she consider disobeying his orders as she knew what the consequences would be.

However, as the trial continued Thomas took the stand and said that she felt Rivera had started to enjoy the grotesque tortures that she was forced to carry out on the other girls. She even nicknamed her the 'boss of the basement' and said that it had been her idea to use the electric shock punishment. Askins also corroborated this story, and went on to add that Rivera would warn Heidnik if any of the girls made plans to jump him and attempt an escape. She added that Rivera would be re-warded with a night out with Heidnik at a fancy restaurant and when they came back she would brag about the lovely time they had had and the delicious food they had eaten. However, the jury decided that Rivera really had no choice than to play up to her captor if she wanted to stay alive, and under the circum-stances there wasn't much else she could do. The three remaining captives all testified that Heidnik was desperate to get them pregnant so that he would have a load of his own children playing in the basement.

The already horrified courtroom then had to listen to the testimony of Dr. Paul Hoyer, who told them that he had found several bags of white meat in the freezer compartment of Heidnik's refrigerator. In the oven itself there were several body parts that had been dressed up like roasts and assorted chops, which made it obvious that Heidnik was planning, and had indeed, committed cannibalism.

On April 6, while Gary Heidnik was waiting for his case to come to trial, he tried to hang himself in his cell. Meanwhile, the gruesome details of his killings had been so widely publicized in the press that the judge deemed it would prevent Heidnik from receiving a fair trial. They set a new venue for June 13, three hundred miles away in Pittsburgh. An unbiased jury was selected and as the case unravelled, the people of Pittsburgh could not believe their ears. The jurors sat pale-faced as they heard all the gory details and soon a picture of a deranged madman emerged. In fact at one point the whole courtroom sat transfixed as they learned of how Heidnik had dismembered Sandra, cooked her head, feet and hands and then fed her to the other girls.

In his defence, Philadelphia lawyer, Charles Peruto, stated that although his client was undoubtedly guilty of everything that had been outlined to the court, he had never in fact intentionally killed anyone. The deaths of the two women were an accident, and besides anyone who commits such heinous acts could certainly not be right in the head and he put in a plea of insanity.

In his own defence Heidnik claimed that the women were already living in the house when he first moved in – but for some reason the judge didn't believe him!

The jury started their deliberations on June 29, 1988 and on Saturday morning, July 2, The Inquirer ran the headline – HEIDNIK IS CONVICTED OF MURDER. Heidnik stood convicted on 18 separate counts which ranged from murder, rape and kidnapping, to aggravated assault and deviant sexual intercourse. Gary Heidnik was sentenced to death.

After his sentence was read out, Peruto told reporters that he felt that Heidnik would kill himself, before they actually managed to carry out the execution, and his prediction almost came true. A guard found Heidnik unconscious on New Year's morning, January 1, 1989, following an overdose of Thorazine, an anti-psychotic drug that he had been prescribed by the prison doctors. However, the doctors acted swiftly and he was saved for the executioner.

Heidnik spent 11 years on death row and on July 6, 1999, at 10.29 p.m. after a final meal of pizza and black coffee, he was executed by lethal injection at the Graterford Prison at Rockview. Not one member of his family came forward to claim his body, and his victims started civil proceedings to release the funds from his Merrill Lynch account. His $550,000 stock market fortune was divided between his victims, the taxman and his lawyer.

Issei Sagawa

Issei Sagawa was dubbed the 'Godfather of Cannibals' but due to a legal loophole this monster was released back into our society and still walks free today

---

ISSEI SAGAWA IS just under 5 ft tall and considered to be a very intelligent Japanese man. He walks with a limp and, many say, talks with the voice of a girl. He has never considered himself to be an attractive man, and was always very self-conscious of his shortcomings. When he was a child, Issei had a dream about himself and his brother being boiled alive in a pot, to be served up as someone's dinner. It appears that ever since he had that dream he has fantasized about being a cannibal himself. He had pictures in his mind of eating a large, blonde woman, with beautiful white skin. He was very attracted to Nordic women, tall and beautiful, in fact everything that he was not.

TURNING DREAMS INTO REALITY

Soon Issei's obsession with tall women was not enough and he decided to turn his fantasy into reality. He was studying for a degree in English literature at Wako University in Tokyo, when he became attracted to one of his teachers, a tall German woman. He started to fantasize about eating her, and one summer's day he crawled through her apartment window with the intention of killing her. To his sheer delight he discovered her asleep, wearing very little clothing. He became very excited and looked around for something to either knock her out or stab her with, when he spotted an umbrella in the corner of the room. Luckily, for her, the woman woke up and saw him in her room. She screamed so loudly, it frightened the young Issei and he fled quickly from her apartment.

The sight of this lovely white woman haunted him and he knew that he had to prepare himself better if he was to fulfil his fantasy. He started to make plans and looked around for his next victim. However, it wasn't until he went to Paris several years later, in 1981, that he actually found the woman of his dreams.

RENEE HARTEVELT

Issei could not get 25-year-old Renee Hartevelt out of his mind. He thought she was the most beautiful woman he had ever seen, with her white skin, her fleshy buttocks and her beautiful features. When he sat next to her in his class he knew instinctively that she was the perfect woman for what he wanted to do. This time he would go more slowly; he knew he had to be really careful if he wanted to succeed.

Renee was extremely intelligent and spoke three different languages, she had a very bright future ahead of her. Issei approached her and asked if she would be prepared to teach him German. He told her that his father was wealthy and would pay her for her tuition, and so she agreed. She was impressed by his intelligence and ability to talk knowledgeably on most subjects. Issei started to write her love letters and invited her out to concerts and exhibitions.

Before long he had completely gained her trust and respect and he invited Renee over to his apartment for a Japanese dinner. After they had eaten, Issei asked Renee to read him his favourite German Expressionist poem, and as she spoke he found he could not take his eyes of her – he was totally obsessed. After she left he could still smell her body where she had sat on the bed sheets reading the poem, and he started to lick the chopsticks and the dishes she had used to eat her meal. With the taste on his lips his passion heightened and he knew then and there that he just had to eat her.

On the evening of June 11, 1981, he invited her over again for dinner. This time he asked if he could record her reading his favourite poem and she agreed. When she arrived the recorder was already positioned and Issei prepared himself to carry out his ultimate fantasy. When Issei had first arrived in Paris he had bought a .22 calibre rifle, and this he placed beside a chest of drawers. He asked Renee to sit on the floor, Japanese-style, so that they could partake in the oriental tradition of drinking tea. He poured some whisky into her tea to make her relax, and while he waited for the alcohol to have its effect they sat and chatted as two old friends. When he noticed that Renee was starting to relax he told her that he loved her and that he wanted to take her to bed. She answered by saying that although she found him very good company she was not sexually attracted to him and only wanted to be his friend.

Issei said that he understood and got up from the floor to get the book of poetry. He handed the book to Renee and started the tape recorder so that she could read the poem in her native language. As he listened to her perfect German, Issei reached for the rifle that stood beside the chest of drawers. Issei came up behind her and shot her in the back of the head, and her body immediately slumped from the chair onto the floor. He tried to talk to her and seemed a little bemused when she didn't answer. There was blood pouring from the wound in her head and Issei tried in vain to clear up the ever-increasing pool of blood on the floor. Soon he realized that there was no point and the silence of death surrounded him.

Next Issei tried to undress her, but he found it hard to take the clothes off a dead body. Finally when she was laying completely naked he marvelled at the beauty of her body. He had waited so long for this moment and he couldn't resist touching her amazing white skin. He was desperate to eat her but didn't really know where to start. He went to the kitchen and got a knife and cut off the tip of her left breast and a piece of her nose and put it into his mouth. Next he chose her right buttock, but found it difficult to bite into it, so he stabbed deeper into her skin. He watched with great delight as the fat oozed out of the wound. Underneath the sallow fat he managed to find the red meat and he scooped it out of her body and placed it into his mouth. The first thing he noticed was that it didn't have any real taste or smell and he later stated that it 'melts in my mouth like a perfect piece of tuna'.

Issei thought she was totally delicious and he looked into Renee's unseeing eyes and told her so. He was ecstatic, he had her beautiful body all to himself. Then he got down to the real business of carving her body using an electric carving knife. He laid out pieces of her flesh to store for later consumption, while he nibbled pieces of her meat again and again.

Next he took a photograph of her white body with its deep wounds, and then had sex with her mutilated corpse. He later recalled that as he hugged her she let out a breath as if she was still alive, and a little frightened he kissed her and told her how much he loved her.

Then Issei dragged the remains of Renee's body into the bathroom. By this time he was totally exhausted and decided that he needed more of her flesh to give him strength. He cut into her hip and put the meat into a roasting pan. When it was cooked he turned on the tape recorder so that he could listen to her reciting the poem, and then sat down to enjoy his meal. He was a little disappointed that it didn't seem to have much taste and so he added some salt and mustard which he said made it absolutely delicious.

Having enjoyed the meal so much he returned to the bathroom where he cuts off her breast and baked it. Again he roasts the meat and served it up on a plate. He started to eat it with a knife and fork but decided it didn't taste so good, it was too greasy. He returned to the body and repeated the exercise with a piece of her thighs – the thighs were delicious and he considered it to be the best meal he had ever tasted. With his appetite now satisfied, and feeling totally exhausted, he took what was left of the corpse to his bed where he spent the night.

The next morning he woke and realized that he would have to do something about destroying the evidence. He decided he would take it into the bathroom, finish cutting it up and then put the pieces into a suitcase and take them to the lake. While he was busy cutting into her calf he was overwhelmed once again with the desire to eat her flesh. The wonderful taste started to lift his spirits again and he ate more and more pieces, discarding several pieces that he didn't like the smell of.

By now Issei had noticed that there were several flies starting to settle on the corpse, and he decided that the time had come to say goodbye to his beloved Renee. He took a hatchet and chopped the remainder of her body into pieces. He had already bought two suitcases to dispose of the pieces, but as he started to dismember her he became sexually aroused and he used her hand to masturbate himself. Wanting to keep a memento of his experience he decided to remove her lips and put them by for his later pleasures.

By the time he had finished tasting and bagging the remaining pieces of Renee's body it was midnight of the second day. He locked the suitcases and then called for a cab.

He asked the cab to take him to the Bois de Boulogne, and then dragged the suitcases into the park, intending to push them into the pond. However, being of small stature he struggled under the weight of the large suitcases. He got scared when he saw two people watching him, and so he just abandoned the cases and ran. The couple were suspicious and so they went over to have a closer look and were horrified to see a blood-stained hand hanging from the side of one of the cases. They immediately called the police. When the cases were opened the police were horrified to find the human remains and started the job of trying to find the person who had purchased the suitcases.

Meanwhile Issei had returned to his apartment to enjoy the remaining pieces of Renee Hartevelt that he had put into his refrigerator. Each day he ate a little more and each day he found the pleasure greater and greater and the taste became more sweet and delicious.

ALLOWED TO GO FREE

Eventually the suitcases were traced back to Issei Sagawa and the authorities obtained a warrant to search his apartment. When they entered his flat they soon found Renee's lips, her left breast, and both buttocks which Issei had stored in the refrigerator. He was immediately arrested for the murder of Renee Hartevelt.

Issei was placed under psychiatric care at the Henri Colin institute in Villejuif to be assessed for his competency to stand trial. He was studied by three separate psychiatrists and they all agreed that he could never be cured of his cannibalistic fantasies. The authorities considered that the cost of maintaining Sagawa in a French sanitorium for the remainder of his life was too expensive and so they arranged for him to be deported back to his native Japan in 1985. Arriving back in Japan Sagawa was swarmed by the media who all wanted to meet the famous cannibal in person. He was taken to the Matsuzawa hospital in Tokyo where he was diagnosed as being sane and guilty of murder. It was therefore decided that he should be tried and imprisoned for his crime. However, thanks to his very wealthy father, Akira Sagawa, who was the president of Kurita Water Industries in Tokyo, Issei was released from the hospital after only 15 months. It seems unbelievable that a man as sick as Issei Sagawa who, after killing a woman and eating her remains, was allowed to walk about freely in society only five years after the crime. What was even more absurd was that he was invited to go on television and radio where he freely talked about his crime and seemed to revel in the attention he was receiving. He has appeared in several Japanese pornographic movies and has written four novels. It is very obvious that this sick little man finds all the attention he received very amusing and yet he still doesn't feel that he did anything wrong.

Of course only time will tell whether Issei Sagawa will kill again, but would you feel happy with a man like that living in your street?

Karl Denke

Karl Denke pickled the flesh of his
victims and sold it on the market
in Wroclaw as 'pork'...

KARL DENKE WAS born on December 8, 1870, the son
of a wealthy farmer from Oberkunzendorf in Poland.
The records show that Karl was quite a difficult child to
raise and at school he was one of the worst students. He
tried to run away from home for the first time at the age
of 12.

When he eventually graduated from elementary
school he started an apprenticeship as a gardener. Karl's
father died when he was 25, and the farm was taken
over by Karl's elder brother. Karl himself inherited a
sum of money which enabled him to purchase his own
farm and garden in the town of Ziebice. However, his
career as a farmer was not very successful so he decided
to sell the land and buy a house instead. He purchased
a two-storey house with an accompanying shed in
Ziebice, but after World War I, due to inflation, he lost
his savings and was forced to sell once again. However,
although he sold his house he did stay on as a tenant
and rented an apartment on the ground floor.

Karl Denke was well respected in the town of 8,000 inhabitants. He was pious, refrained from alcohol and did not have relations with women. He led an honest, lower to middle class lifestyle and was known to give assistance to beggars, even as far as giving them a bed for the night in his small apartment. It was not surprising, therefore, that this devout, peaceful and charitable man was offered a vending licence when he applied to the police to sell goods on the market. He set up a small shop and sold leather suspenders, belts, shoe laces and on Wroclaw market he also offered boneless pickled 'pork'. Nobody thought anything of it and he traded unhindered, that is until one particular day . . .

THE VAGRANT

It was Sunday, December 21, 1924, at around 1.00 p.m. when a man entered the Ziebice police station covered in blood. He was rambling but managed to say how he had barely escaped death in Karl Denke's apartment. At first the police did not believe this story, they were surprised that a vagrant like Vincenz Olivier could possibly be accusing such an upstanding citizen as Mr. Denke. The police decided that he was worthy of having a medical examination and the doctor confirmed that he had indeed been seriously wounded. Again they questioned Vincenz but he would not change his testimony and the police were obliged to arrest Karl Denke. During his interrogation Denke told the police that the vagrant had attempted to rob him after receiving a handout, and he had been forced to retaliate to save his belongings. As a result of this Denke was locked up in a holding cell for the night. That very same night, around 11.30 p.m., when Sergeant Palke looked in on him, he discovered that Karl Denke was dead. He had managed to hang himself using a noose made from a handkerchief.

The police waited until his corpse had been handed over to his relatives and then they went and searched his apartment. It was Christmas Eve and the country was in the middle of an economic crisis. Polish money was losing its value from day to day, and most families were struggling to put any decent food on their tables. So the already despondent police, were even more dismayed when they arrived at the house and made some horrifying discoveries. What the police found in his apartment and shed made their bodies literally tremble with terror.

In the apartment, hanging in the closet were several items of bloodstained clothing, along with one skirt. On the windowsill lay various documents containing the names of people who had been released from either prisons or hospitals. They found several containers filled with pickled meat, and the laboratory analysis carried out later showed that it was of human origin. There was an apparatus for making soup along with human bones that had been placed ready for processing. On the walls were hanging dozens of belts, suspenders and shoelaces all of which had been made from human skin.

From the evidence they recovered from Denke's house and shed the police were able to identify 20 victims of the Ziebice cannibal. Realistically, though, it is believed that Karl Denke killed, cut up, pickled and probably ate more than 40 people.

For now the local celebrity only has a small exhibit of bloody knives and axes in the museum in Ziebice but as his memory draws more crowds who's to say that it won't be enlarged.

Robin Gecht

*During the 1980s Robin Gecht
led a group of three other men known
as the Chicago Rippers*

IN 1981 AND 1982 Chicago was besieged with a string of gruesome killings that was believed to be the work of the Chicago Rippers, led by Robin Gecht. In some sort of sick cult ritual the killers would cut off their victim's right breast and later eat it . . .

During the 1980s, Robin Gecht led a group of three other men – Ed Spreitzer and Andrew and Thomas Kokoraleis – who became known as the Ripper Crew or the Chicago Rippers. They are estimated to have killed around 18 women. Their modus operandi was to kill a woman, sever her left breast with a thin wire, clean it out to use for sexual gratification, and then cut it into pieces for consumption. Their claim was that they were worshipping Satan and that eating the flesh of a fellow human being was a form of devilish communion.

BRIEF BACKGROUND

For some reason Robin Gecht had inherited a bizarre

obsession with breasts and when asked about it he claimed that it went back as far as his great grandfather. He went on to say that all the male members of his family had gone on to marry women with large breasts, and indeed his own wife had a very fine pair of size 39Ds.

Gecht had the ability to attract people like magnets and seemed have a strong influence over their actions. It didn't seem to matter how sick or perverse his requests became, his followers were only too pleased to carry out his instructions.

The first sign of any maladjustment came when he molested his own sister and was subsequently sent to live with his grandparents. Even in adolescence Gecht developed a keen interest in Satanism and he believed that its secret rituals offered some form of power over others.

Gecht met the other three members of the gang when he was 30 and, being the oldest member of the gang, naturally assumed the role of both mentor and leader. Spreitzer was 21 while the two Kokoraleis brothers were only in their teens. All three young men were hypnotized by the powerful charisma of Gecht's personality, and together they would drive around at night in Gecht's old van looking for female victims.

THE BEGINNING

The Chicago Rippers found their first victim on May 23, 1981. Twenty-eight-year-old Linda Sutton was abducted from Elmhurst, a suburb of Chicago and ten days later her mutilated body was recovered from a field in Villa Park. The young woman had been stabbed to death and her left breast had been removed by using a sliver of wire. The evidence suggested that the woman had been used in some sort of sadistic ritual, but the police had nothing in the way of solid clues. The gang had apparently taken the amputated breast, scooped out the inside and then used it for sexual gratification before being eaten by the gang as part of the Satanic worship.

A year went by before the gang would claim their next victim. Twenty-one-year-old Lorraine Borowski was reported missing on May 15, 1982, when she failed to turn up to open the Elmhurst realtor's office where she was working. When the employees turned up for work that morning they found the office door still locked, and Borowski's shoes and the contents of her handbag strewn across the pavement outside the office. They called the police immediately, but it was five months before they managed to find her body. It was discovered in a cemetery on the south side of Villa Park on October 10, but advanced decomposition left the cause of her death a mystery.

Two weeks later on May 29, 1982, a woman called Shui Mak was reported missing from her home in Hanover Park, Cook County. Her mutilated body was recovered at Barrington on September 30. Just like the other two victims, the killers had removed her breast and had sex with the open wound. The removed breast was then taken home by the men and the flesh scooped out and eaten.

On June 13, the same year, prostitute Angel York was picked up by a man in a van, subsequently handcuffed, her breast slashed open before being dumped on the roadside, still alive. She survived the attack and was able to give the police a good description of her attackers. Unfortunately her descriptions did not lead the police anywhere, and the gang struck again on August 28. Sandra Delaware, a teenage prostitute, was found stabbed and strangled to death on the banks of the Chicago River. Once again the killers had left their hallmark – amputation of the left breast.

Thirty-year-old Rose Davis was found in an identical condition in a Chicago alley on September 8. Three days later, 42-year-old Carole Pappas, who was the wife of the Chicago Cubs' pitcher, vanished without any trace from a department store in nearby Wheaton, Illinois.

THE BREAK THEY NEEDED

The police had been making no headway in their investigations until October 6, 1982, when they got the break they needed. Twenty-year-old prostitute Beverly Washington was picked up by the Chicago Rippers and dragged into their van. She was stripped naked, raped, had her left breast sliced from her body and her right breast partially removed. Then her attackers throw her out of the van leaving her to die on the side of the road. However, even with the severity of her wounds, Beverly survived the attack and was picked up and taken to hospital where she received emergency treatment.

When she was well enough she was able to give the police a really good description of the men and the type of van they drove.

Several hours later, in a seemingly unrelated incident, a drug dealer named Rafael Torado was killed and his male companion was wounded when the occupants of a van opened fire on the two men in a phone booth.

Two weeks later the police picked up Robin Gecht and charged him with the violent assault on Beverly Washington. He was also suspected of wounding prostitute Cynthia Smith before she managed to escape his van. Gecht was certainly an odd character, but the police had no real evidence to convict him and he made bail on October 26.

Continuing with their investigations on Robin Gecht the police learned that he was in fact one of four men who had rented adjoining rooms at Villa Park's Rip Van Winkle Motel just a few months before Linda Sutton was found murdered nearby. The manager of the motel remembered them well, and described them as party animals who loved to bring women back to their rooms. Another piece of information he came forward with also surprised the investigators, as he said they were possibly some sort of cultists, or even devil worshippers. The two Kokoraleis brothers had left a forwarding address for their mail and when the police called round they found 23-year-old Thomas at home. When he failed to answer their questions with any consistency, the police decided to take him down to the police station for further interrogation. Thomas failed a polygraph examination and eventually cracked under the stiff interrogation. He described how Gecht had set up some sort of Satanic chapel in his bedroom, where captive women were taken and tortured with knives and ice picks. Then the victim would be gang-raped and finally sacrificed to Satan by members of the four-strong cult. He described in detail how their rituals included the severing of one or both of the women's breasts with a thin wire garrote. Next each participant of the ritual would take 'communion' by eating a piece of the flesh before it was placed inside Gecht's trophy box. Thomas went on to tell the police that he remembered seeing as many as fifteen breasts inside the box. He also told his interrogators that other women had been killed out in Villa Park and he was able to pick out Lorraine Borowski from police records as the woman they had picked up for a one-way ride to the motel.

The police now had enough evidence and they swooped on Robin Gecht, Ed Spreitzer and 20-year-old Andrew Kokoraleis on November 5. When the police searched Gecht's apartment they found the Satanic chapel that Thomas had told them about, and they also discovered the rifle that had been used in the recent phone booth shooting. When the police searched the apartment occupied by Andrew Kokoraleis they discovered a considerable amount of Satanic literature. They now had enough evidence to charge their suspects and it was thought that the gang may have murdered as many as eighteen women in as many months.

Thomas Kokoraleis was charged with the killing of Lorraine Borowski on November 12, and was formally indicted by a grand jury four days later. His brother Andrew, along with Edward Spreitzer, was charged on November 14 with the rape and murder of Rose Davis.

Robin Gecht, who had been assessed as being mentally competent to stand trial, faced charges of attempted murder, rape and aggravated battery. His trial opened on September 20, 1983, and Gecht took the witness stand the very next day confessing to the attack on Beverly Washington. He was convicted on all counts and received a prison sentence of 120 years.

On April 2, 1984, Ed Spreitzer pleaded guilty on four counts of murder which included victims Davis, Delaware, Mak and Torado. He was sentenced to life on each count and received additional time on convictions of rape, deviant sexual assault and attempted murder.

Thomas Kokoraleis was convicted of the murder of Lorraine Borowski on May 18, 1984, but while he was waiting to be sentenced he led police to a field where Carole Pappas was allegedly buried, but her remains were never found. However, on September 7, due to his helpful attitude Thomas was rewarded with a sentence of life imprisonment. Eighteen days later his brother, Andrew and Ed Spreitzer were both sentenced to death for their roles in the murders. Andrew Kokoraleis was subsequently executed on March 17, 1999. Edward Spreitzer was convicted of murdering Linda Sutton and was formally sentenced to death on March 20.

INJUSTICE

The charges of kidnapping and rape have since been dropped against Robin Gecht and he is still trying desperately to obtain DNA testing that he is certain will clear him of all charges. So far he has been unsuccessful and the authorities refuse to comply with his request.

He is reported to have said that each day he sits in jail he loses hope. He admitted that although he is no angel he would never intentionally kill or indeed hurt someone unless it was to protect his own family. There is no hard evidence to prove that Robin Gecht is guilty of anything except the attempted murder of the gang's last victim. Gecht's family have supported him all the way and are looking forward to the day when he will be eligible for parole in 2022.

One other small point worth remembering about this man is that he used to work for the serial killer John Wayne Gacy.

Alferd Packer

Judge Melville B. Gerry pronounced that
Packer 'be hanged by the neck until
you are dead, dead, dead ...'

ALFERD PACKER IS probably best known as the only American ever to be convicted of cannibalism. At his trial Packer admitted to 'eating the flesh of his fellow man' knowing that he was on the brink of death from starvation.

Alferd Packer was born on January 21, 1842 in Allegheny County, Pennsylvania. He was a shoemaker by trade, but at the age of 20 was enlisted in the Union Army at Winona, Minnesota. He was honourably discharged on December 29, 1862, at Fort Ontario, New York, due to a disability so he decided to go west and continue in his trade and have a go at prospecting.

JOURNEY TO HELL

On November 8, 1873, Packer was enlisted as a guide for a party of 21 men who wanted to go prospecting. They left Bingham Canyon, Utah to go to the gold fields of the Colorado Territory. Part of their food supply was accidentally lost when they did a particularly difficult river crossing by raft, and their journey was further hampered by very severe winter conditions. Eventually the party completely ran out of food and in late January 1874 they were forced to take shelter at Chief Ouray's camp near Montrose, Colorado.

The men recovered their strength and stamina and, contrary to the advice of Ouray, Alferd Packer along with five other men, left the camp on February 9, 1874. While the original party had been considerably larger, only Packer (still acting as their guide), Israel Swan, Shannon Wilson Bell, George Noon, James Humphrey and Frank Miller dared risk the brutal Colorado winter to continue their search for riches. When they left Ouray's camp the men had about seven days supply of food sufficient for one man. The weather was indeed brutal, and only two or three days into their journey the group was totally engulfed by a violent blizzard. They struggled on and came across a mount, managed to cross a gulch and then found the snow so deep that they had to climb upwards. After the fourth day the only food they had left in their packs was about a pint of flour. They continued to follow the line of the mountain until they came to the main range which took them around ten days, and all the while they were living off rosebuds and pine gum. The men were becoming desperate, and even broke down in prayer for the Lord to save them from their plight. When they eventually came across the main mountain range the party made camp on a stream which ran into a big lake.

After taking a brief rest the men crossed the lake and cut holes into the ice in an endeavour to catch fish. However, their attempts were to no avail and some of the men ended up falling into the icy water where the ice was rather thin.

The men were becoming more and more angry and they sent Packer, who was supposed to be their leader, off in the search of food. All he managed to find was a few rosebuds and when he returned to their camp a day later, he found his red-headed colleague, Bell, sitting by the camp fire roasting a piece of meat. Bell, who had been acting rather crazy over the past couple of days, had apparently cut the piece of meat out of the German butcher's leg. The man in question, Frank Miller, was lying further down by the banks of the stream, his skull had been crushed with a hatchet.

Packer immediately noticed that the other three members of the party were lying near the fire and they too had several cuts in their foreheads made by the hatchet. As Packer started to approach the fire, Bell spotted him and immediately jumped up wielding the hatchet, and in self-defence Packer shot him sideways through the stomach. Bell immediately fell forwards, whereupon Packer grabbed the hatchet and hit him in the top of the head.

That night Packer stayed awake sitting by the fire and when morning broke he followed his tracks from the day before back up the mountain. However, the snow was too deep for him to continue and he was forced to return to the camp. He decided the best thing he could do for protection was to build himself a shelter and using some pieces of timber and pine boughs that were lying around, he made himself a rough cabin. Next he went and covered the bodies of the men who were lying around the camp and then set about rebuilding the camp fire. Packer was literally starving and getting increasingly weaker, so he decided to cook the piece of meat that was lying by the fire and had his first real meal for days.

Time and time again he tried to leave the camp, but the weather always forced him back. So for a period of around sixty days Packer lived off the flesh of his travelling companions. Then the weather started to change and he noticed that the snow was starting to form a crust and he decided it was time to leave. He cooked up some more meat which he carried with him, along with a blanket, the money he had taken from his colleagues packs and his gun.

ACCORDING TO PACKER

Packer arrived at the Los Pinos Indian Agency in Colorado on April 16, 1874. Despite the fact that Packer had been stranded for some considerable time his appearance was of someone who had been well fed, and when he started to spend quite a considerable amount of money at the nearby saloon, the locals became suspicious of his story. He had told them that his party had been hit by a storm and while he set up camp the other members of his party had gone off in search of food, but not one of them ever made it back to the camp. However, unluckily for Packer there were several men from the original Provo group who were dubious about his version of the story.

Indian Agent Charles Adams took Packer in for questioning and on May 8, 1874, managed to extract the first of two conflicting confessions. According to Packer, Israel Swan had died and the others, being without food, had eaten him in order to survive. Subsequently, the other three had died from exposure and starvation. Packer admitted to killing Shannon Bell, but he claimed it was in self-defence.

Packer was sent to Saguache jail, which was just outside the town. In August Packer managed to escape and was not seen again until March 1883, when Frenchy Cabazon, who was one of the original prospecting party, bumped into him purely by chance in Douglas, Wyoming.

On the day that Packer escaped, the remains of the missing prospectors were discovered in a valley. There was certainly evidence of a struggle and the authorities were convinced that there had been foul play.

After his recapture, Packer was taken to Denver, Colorado and once again questioned about the incident. In his second confession, Packer stuck to his original claim that he had killed Bell in self-defence, but this time admitted to stealing a rifle and around $70 in cash from the bodies of the dead men. Packer was charged with the murder of Israel Swan, who was the first man to die, and was taken to Lake City to stand trial.

Packer faced a jury of 12 honest citizens, who took no time in finding him guilty of willful and premeditated murder. Judge Melville B. Gerry, who resided over the case gave his final summing up as follows:

'Alferd Packer, the judgement of this Court is that you be removed from hence to the jail of Hinsdale County, and there be confined until the 19th day of May, A.D. 1883, and that on said 19th day of May, 1883, you be taken from thence by the Sheriff of Hinsdale County, to a place of execution prepared for this purpose, at some point within the corporate limits of the town of Lake City, in the said County of Hinsdale, and between the hours of 10.00 a.m. and 3.00 p.m. of said day, you then and there, by the said Sheriff, be hung by the neck until you are dead, dead, dead, and may God have mercy upon your soul.'

Packer appealed against his conviction to the Colorado Supreme Court, where the verdict was indeed reversed. He was tried again and this time fount guilty of manslaughter and sentenced to 40 years in the state penitentiary.

Packer served 17 years of his 40 year sentence and in 1901, Governor Charles S. Thomas granted Packer's parole request. Packer moved to Littleton, Colorado, where, if the story is true, he became a model citizen who was well liked by all of his neighbours.

Alferd Packer died of natural causes on April 23, 1907, and was buried in military style in Littleton

Cemetery. Alferd Packer's memory lives on in The Ballad of Alferd Packer written by Phil Ochs in 1964. Below is just one verse from this ballad:

Two cold months went slowly by;
Packer came back alone.
'My comrades they all froze to death,
I'm starving,' he did moan.
The Indian chief knew how he lied,
He spat upon the ground,
For Packer's belly hung out all over his belt:
He'd gained some thirty pounds.

Fritz Haarmann

*Haarmann saw killing as a business
opportunity not to be missed*

HAARMANN BECAME KNOWN as the 'Butcher of
Hanover' and was thought to have been responsible for
the deaths of as many as 27 young men. He was a lust
slayer who would experience an orgasm as he chewed
his way through his victim's flesh.

Freidrich Heinrich Karl Haarmann was born on
October 25, 1879, and was the youngest of six children.
His mother, who was 41 when he was born, adored him
and pampered him continually. She encouraged him to
play with dolls rather than the more masculine games,
and even as a young child loved to dress him up like a
girl. In contrast, the young Fritz loathed his father,
something that would not change even when he was an
adult. This hatred most probably stemmed from the
fact that his father was both a drunkard and a
womanizer, and Fritz could not stand the way it upset
his adoring mother.

The birth of Fritz had left his mother very weak and
most of her remaining 12 years were spent in bed. Fritz
always felt a very strong bond with his mother and

always spoke of her with warmth and compassion.

Fritz started to show some strange traits that were apparent all through his school years. The first was his noticeable femininity (bordering on being a transvestite) and the second was the apparent pleasure he showed when he inflicted fear or horror. One trick that really pleased the young Fritz was to tie his sisters up and then frighten them in the dead of night with stories of werewoves and ghosts.

Fritz failed his exams to become a locksmith and was sent to a training school for non-commissioned officers at Neu-Breisach in April 1895. He was an obedient soldier and developed a talent for gymnastics. However, he suffered concussion when one of his moves went wrong and afterwards suffered periodic lapses in consciousness and epileptic fits. He discharged himself from the school in November 1895 saying that he didn't like it there anymore, and returned home and started to work for his father.

Although Fritz was a rather lethargic and lazy person, in contrast to that was his rapidly developing sexual appetite. Sexual offences against children seemed to be happening on a regular basis and soon the finger pointed at Fritz. He was studied by the town doctor who prescribed him as being deranged and shortly after his 18th birthday he was sent to an asylum. It was while he was there that he suffered some kind of trauma which left him with an intense fear of the asylum. He begged and pleaded to be released, and then one day he managed to escape and fled to Switzerland.

When he was 20, Fritz returned to Hanover and for a while managed to lead a fairly normal existence. He seduced and eventually married a very pretty girl by the name of Erna Loewert and both sets of parents were very pleased by the news and hoped that this would prove to be the making of the young Fritz Haarmann. Unfortunately, this was not to be the case, and before long he deserted his wife and their unborn child and went into military service.

Fritz seemed to thrive in the routine of army life and became a soldier of high merit. He was later to refer to that time as the happiest in his entire life but everything was to change once again. After approximately a year in service Fritz collapsed whilst taking part in a military exercise. He was admitted to the military hospital and remained there for another four months. He was diagnosed as having a 'mental deficiency' and therefore considered unsuitable to remain in the service.

Despondent and down-hearted Fritz returned to his family and the life-long battle he had with his father. His father tried to have him committed to an asylum but the town doctor did not consider he was ill enough to be interned and was left to his own resources.

Fritz turned to a life of petty crime and committed burglaries and minor confidence scams and, after 1904, spent the majority of the next 20 years either in custody or inside a prison cell. In the year 1914 he was arrested for theft from a warehouse and sentenced to five years imprisonment. On his release in 1918 he joined a smuggling ring and managed to conduct quite a prosperous business. He also became an informer for the police thinking that if he was helping them they wouldn't look too closely into his other activities. For someone who was supposed to be mentally insecure he certainly had quite an acumen for planning his criminal life. His sexual crimes continued during this period but he was rarely convicted as his partners were too ashamed to report the assaults to the police. But soon his crimes were of a more serious nature.

THE KILLING PHASE

Haarmann's criminal career really took off in September 1918, a time when Germany was suffering the effects of economic depression. A young boy by the name of Friedel Roth had run away from home on September 25, leaving a letter for his mother saying that he would not return home again until she learned to be nice to him. Friends of the boy were able to give the police information about his whereabouts and eventually this information led them to number 27 Cellerstrasse. When the police arrived they found Fritz Haarmann in bed with a young boy and he was arrested and later sentenced to nine months in prison for seducing a juvenile. For some reason his rooms were not searched at the time, and five years later Fritz was to admit that a murdered boy's head had been wrapped in newspaper and stuffed behind the stove in the kitchen.

On his release in 1919, Fritz met the young Hans Grans at the Hanover railway station. Hans had run away from home and was living on the streets surviving on the profits of his stealing. Seeing the obviously homosexual Fritz, the boy offered himself for money. They formed a strong bond and the young boy moved in with Fritz. Together they formed a deadly partnership. Hans was the dominant one in the partnership, and it appeared that he treated Haarmann little better than a servant. It was always Hans who selected their victims, but he always made sure it was his partner who took all the risks.

In early 1922 the two men moved in a district known as the 'haunted area' and took lodgings at number 8 Neuestrasse. Their killing rampage really took off in February 1923 when Haarmann approached two youths at Hanover station. He pretended to be a police officer who was inspecting the waiting rooms. He sent the less attractive lad on his way but Fritz Franke accompanied the bogus policeman back to his home.

From then on the murders gained pace and in the next nine months 12 more young men lost their lives. The modus operandi was always the same, they would lure the young refugees with the promise of food and shelter. Once back in the house at Neuestrasse, Haarmann would sexually assault his victims before biting them through their throats to kill them. Many times Haarmann would achieve an orgasm as he was chewing on their flesh. After the attack the bodies would be chopped up and their flesh would be sold on the black market as 'beef'. Nothing went to waste, they sold the boys' clothes and any part of the body that wasn't worth eating was dumped into a river.

The murders continued unabated until early 1924. A woman who had bought some of Haarmann's beef believed it to be human flesh. She gave a portion of the meat to the police, but the analyst who studied the meat said that it was pork!

On May 17, 1924, some children playing at the edge of the river near the Herrenhausen Castle came across a human skull. On May 29 another one was washed up on the riverbank and the town went into panic when two more were found in the river's silt. An autopsy showed that all the skulls found belonged to young boys and, in all the cases, a sharp instrument had been used to separate the skulls from the torso and the flesh had been completely removed.

The killers' reign ended with the disappearance of Erich de Vries on June 14, 1924. It is estimated that by this time Fritz Haarmann had murdered as many as 27 boys in less than 16 months, which worked out at an average of two a month. The city was gripped by sheer terror and the police stepped up their enormous hunt for this human 'werewolf'.

Every thief and sexual deviant in Hanover was called in for questioning and, by a series of strange coincidences, a suspect by the name of Fritz Haarmann had been taken to the court prison. The man was already known to the police and as they started to question him they noticed his pleasant manner changed drastically. His hands became restless and he plucked nervously at his long fingers. Suspicious of this effeminate man, the police decided to search his home. This time the police did not miss all the blood, and blood-stained clothes that littered the rooms. At the same time a more extensive search of the river revealed a sack of bones as well as a sack full of human skulls.

With all the evidence they needed they backed Haarmann into a tight corner where he gave in and confessed to the murder of some 50 young men. He also implicated his partner in crime Hans Grans. He described to the police that he would grab the young boys off the street, sodomize them and while doing so would chew through their throats until the head was practically severed from the body. As he tasted their blood oozing into his mouth, he would achieve a sexual climax. Next he would cut the flesh off the bodies, consume his favourite parts and then sell the rest on the open market as butchered meat.

Fritz Haarmann was sentenced to death and while he was in prison awaiting his punishment he made an even more lengthy confession and blamed his lust for killing on his sexual perversions. He was finally decapitated on December 20, 1924, within the walls of Hanover Prison.

Hans Grans was originally sentenced to death for his part in the murders, but when a letter was discovered written by Fritz Haarmann claiming his innocence, they cut Hans' sentence to 12 years imprisonment. As to what happened to him after his release there is no mention.

Joachim Kroll

*Joachim Kroll was known as the 'Ruhr Hunter'
and for nearly 20 years the police of West
Germany hunted a sex-killer with a very unpleasant trademark*

ON APRIL 17, 1933 Joachim Georg Kroll was born in
Hindenburg, Oberschlesien, near the Polish border.
Sometime during 1947, the Kroll family fled to the
West. Kroll's father was taken prisoner by the Russians
during World War II, and he never returned home to
his family.

Kroll was only 21 when he committed his first
murder, just three weeks after the death of his mother
on January 21, 1955. On February 8, Kroll stabbed to
death Irmgard Strehl, after raping her in a barn near
Lüdinghausen. The following year, Erika Schuleter was
raped and became Kroll's second victim in Kirchellen.

In 1957 Kroll moved to Duisburg, which was a heavy
industrial city in the middle of 'Ruhrpott', and it was
this area that will became his hunting ground for the
next 20 years.

On March 24, 1959, Kroll attacked another woman,
known only as Erika, near the Moerser Straße in Rhein-

weisen. A second attack on the same spot took place on June 16, 1959, and this time Kroll was more successful, having raped and strangled Klara Frieda Tesmer.

His next attack took place on July 26, 1959, and the body of 16-year-old Manuela Knodt was found near the village of Bredeney, south of Essen. Medical evidence revealed that she had been a virgin before her killer strangled her into unconsciousness and raped her. There were no bruises or scratch marks around her genital area, which suggested that she had made no resistance to the rape. This time Kroll had left a trademark – he had taken slices of flesh from her buttocks and thighs. A man named Horst Otto was later arrested for this murder, and after initially confessing, received eight years imprisonment for the crime.

Sometime in 1962 Kroll made a journey south to Burscheid, near Köln, where he raped and strangled Barbara Bruder.

On April 23, 1962, 13-year-old Petra Giese went to a carnival at the village of Rees, near Walsum. She had gone to the carnival with a friend, but during the course of the day had become separated, and Petra's friend had returned home without her. The following day Petra's body was found in a forest about a mile away from the carnival. The red dress she had been wearing had been ripped from her body, and it appeared as though the killer had been in a state of frenzy. After raping her, he had removed both of her buttocks, her left forearm and a hand, and had taken them away with him.

Two months later on June 4, another 13-year-old girl, Monika Tafel, was on her way back home from school in Walsum. She met a similar fate to Petra, and her body was dragged into a rye field. Once again the killer had cut steaks from her buttocks and the back of her thighs, which indicated that the killer was possibly a cannibal, as these were the meatiest parts of the body.

The police were desperate to track down this perverse killer and arrested a steel-worker for the murder of Petra Giese. However, due to lack of evidence against him they were forced to release him without charge. The man's neighbours were convinced that he was the killer, his wife divorced him, and he ended up by committing suicide. Fourteen years later, a confession would reveal that he had been completely innocent.

LOVER'S LANE

On August 22, 1965 a young couple parked their car in Lover's Lane in Grossenbaum-Duisburg, but unbeknown to them they were being watched. As Kroll watched the young couple having sex in the Volkswagen, he became sexually aroused and decided he needed to rape the girl, but somehow had to get rid of her boyfriend first. He decided to slash the tyre on the front left of the car and, uncertain of what was happening the boy got out of the car. Kroll immediately jumped on him and stabbed him to death. Meanwhile, the petrified girl jumped into the driver's seat and managed to drive off almost hitting Kroll in the process. Kroll managed to escape into the nearby woods unnoticed, and this was the only occasion that he actually killed a male as opposed to a female.

Ursula Rohling was Kroll's next victim on September 13, 1966, and her body was found strangled in Foersterbusch Park. Ursula's boyfriend, Adolf Schickel, was falsely accused of her murder and subsequently drowned himself in the Main river in Wiesbaden.

Kroll, who had been given the nickname the 'Ruhr Hunter' by the police, abducted five-year-old Ilona Harke on December 22, 1966. First Kroll took her on a train to Wuppertal, and then on a bus to Remscheid or Hueckeswage, but somewhere along the way they got out and walked through dense bush and woods, and down into Feldbachtal. There, in a small ditch, Kroll raped the tiny body and watched his victim drown. Ilona's body was discovered in a park in Wuppertal, close to a playground, and once again the killer had removed steaks from the buttocks and shoulders.

On June 22, 1967, Kroll lured ten-year-old Gabrielle Putman into a cornfield and showed her some pornographic photographs. The young girl fainted, but as Kroll attempted to rape her, he heard the sirens from a nearby coalmine going off, indicating that the miners would be leaving work. Soon the area was swarming with miners on their way home, but Kroll managed to escape unnoticed, leaving Gabrielle frightened, but still alive.

Two years later on July 12, 1969, Kroll came across Maria Hettgen on a path near the Baldeneysee in Essen. She was not so lucky, he raped and strangled her, leaving his normal trademark.

Jutta Rahn was walking home from school on May 21, 1970, taking the short route between Hösel Railway Station and her house through a wood. She was approached by Kroll, raped and left for dead. Her boyfriend, Peter Schay, was suspected of her murder and spent 15 months in prison.

THE BLOCKED DRAIN

On July 3, 1976, four-year-old Marion Ketter was playing with friends in a playground in the Duisburg suburb of Laar. It was an extremely hot day and she was only wearing a pair of knickers. As she played, she was approached by a balding, kind-looking man who spoke to her and persuaded her to go for a walk with him. The young girl called him 'Uncle' and went off quite willingly, taking hold of his hand as they went. When her mother realized that her little girl had gone missing, she rushed down to the police station and reported that her daughter had been abducted. The police moved into the area in force, and started to make door-to-door enquiries.

During their investigations one of the residents told the police that his neighbour, a lavatory attendant named Joachim Kroll, had just told him not to use the lavatory on the top floor as it was blocked. When the man had enquired, 'With what?' Kroll had replied, 'Guts!' The man just presumed his neighbour was having a joke with him. A plumber was called out to investigate the problem, and it soon turned out that Kroll was not joking at all. The toilet was in fact blocked with the internal organs of a small child, including the lungs.

The police returned to Kroll's apartment and asked if they could have a look around. What they found made them sick to the stomach. Inside his deep freeze were plastic bags which contained parcels of human flesh, while bubbling on the stove they found a child's hand with some carrots and potatoes. Kroll was immediately arrested and the reign of the 'The Ruhr Hunter' came to an end.

ANYTHING BUT A MONSTER

Kroll, who was a brown-eyed, mild-mannered little man proved to be anything but a monster. It was obvious to the police from their questioning that Joachim Kroll was mentally subnormal, as his admission to his neighbour had indicated. He told the police that he was looking forward to being able to go home, and felt that after he had had an 'operation' to make him harmless to women, that he would be allowed to go free.

As the police interrogated the pathetic little man, it became obvious that he had committed many more cannibalistic murders than they had originally thought. Kroll was quite willing, and indeed talked quite freely about his obsession with sexual murders. He told them that he lived alone in the apartment, which turned out to be full of electrical gadgets and rubber sex dolls. He told them that he used to strangle his dolls with one hand whilst masturbating with the other. It became apparent that he was not capable of having sex with a conscious woman, as he was far too nervous and self-conscious, and he started to satisfy his sexual urges with rape. He told them that he had devoted most of his life to this 'occupation'. He told the police that he would wander around, sometimes for hours on end, waiting to find a girl who was walking on her own. Next he would follow her home, and possibly study her movements over the next few days, waiting for the chance to catch her on her own. He said he couldn't possibly remember just how many girls he had raped and killed.

Kroll also said that his cannibalism was in no way connected to his sexual urges, he just took the meat as he thought it was a good way of saving money on food. He told the police that he only took steaks from his victims if their flesh looked suitably tender. It was quite obvious that it was a combination of both stupidity and an animal cunning that allowed one of Germany's worst serial killers to operate for more than 20 years.

The trial against Joachim George Kroll started on October 4, 1979, in Saal 201 of the Duisburg Schwurgericht. He was charged with eight counts and 1 attempt of murder. The trial lasted for 151 days and on April 8, 1982, Kroll was sentenced to nine terms of life imprisonment. Kroll died on July 1, 1991, at Rheinbach prison, of a heart attack.

Stanley Dean Baker

*Stanley Dean Baker was no
ordinary cannibal – he was actually
proud of his eating habits*

BAKER, UNLIKE KROLL, was not a shy cannibal, and loved to boast about his fetish. He claimed to have developed a taste for human flesh while undergoing electroshock therapy for a nervous disorder.

It was Saturday, July 11, 1970, at around three o'clock in the afternoon. A man was relaxing on the banks of the Yellowstone River in Montana, pursuing his favourite pastime, fishing. All of a sudden he saw his float bob and presumed he had got a bite. He reeled in his line but instead of a struggling fish on the end, he had snagged a human body. He stood frozen to the spot for a short while, but on regaining his composure he drove to the nearest ranch to call the police. Deputy Bigelow was stationed at the entrance to the Yellowstone National Park, and he responded to the call.

The deputy waded into the turbulent river and, with the help of some local men, managed to drag the body out onto the bank. Accustomed to routine cases of drowning, Bigelow was shocked to find that the head was missing and immediately knew that he had a murder case on his hands. The Deputy phoned the Sheriff who subsequently bought the coroner to the scene. The victim was a male, clad only in shorts and, apart from the missing head, the arms had been severed at the shoulders and the legs chopped off at the knees. His abdomen and chest were covered with stab wounds, and there was a particularly large, gaping wound on his chest.

Even the Coroner had to admit that he was shocked by what he saw, and told his colleagues that he had never seen anything like it before. He said he felt the man was possibly in his early twenties and, apart from the fact that he had been stabbed around 25 times, his heart was missing. The chest had been cut open and the heart had been removed.

The Sheriff knew that it was going to be very difficult to identify the body, because all the usual means of identification had been removed. He felt that it was probably some form of cult murder, as there had been a number recently that had been connected with a secret group of devil-worshippers.

The torso was taken away so that a proper autopsy could be carried out, in the hope that it might throw some light on what had happened to the man. The Sheriff sent details of the victim to other neighbouring states in the hope that someone had been reported missing. Despite thorough searching of the banks and the river in and around Yellowstone Park, no traces of the missing limbs were found. Meanwhile, the police had to wait until someone was reported missing.

Monday morning threw some light on the case of the headless torso. A message came through to the Sheriff's office in Livingstone, concerning a missing person who resembled the description of the body in the morgue. His name was Michael James Schlosser, aged 22, and he had been reported missing from the town of Roundup, about a hundred miles away, that very same morning. Apparently he had set out on the Friday to Yellowstone Park in his Opel Kadett sports car, but had failed to turn up for work the following Monday. His office colleagues went round to see his landlady, but she told them that he had not returned home that weekend. The description of Schlosser – 6 ft tall and weighing around 200 lbs – fitted the considered age and size of the torso. The Sheriff immediately put out an alert for any sightings of the Opel car, which could possibly have been dumped in the area of Yellowstone Park.

Just one hour later a report came in of an accident involving a yellow Opel Kadett sports car that had been in a collision with a pick-up truck on a dirt road in Monterey County, California. The car had been reported travelling at speed on the wrong side of the road. The truck only suffered a dented bumper, but the car was a complete write-off. The driver of the truck, who was a businessman from Detroit on holiday, got out of the cab and approached the car. As he approached the Opel, two young men climbed out, both apparently unhurt, and both with the appearance of typical Californian hippies, with long hair and beards. One was blond and one was dark. The blond man was about 6 ft tall and very powerfully built, and the businessman was prepared for trouble. However, to his surprise, both the men were friendly, and he asked them if they could exchange driver's licences. When the hippies replied that neither of them had one, the businessman took the registration number of the vehicle and suggested that they accompany him to the nearest telephone so that they could notify the police of the accident. Both the hippies agreed to this and climbed into the front of his truck. When they arrived at a service station in the town of Lucia, instead of accompanying the businessman to the telephone, both the young men jumped out of the truck and ran off into some nearby woods.

The businessman phoned the police and told them what had happened and gave them the registration of the Opel car. It turned out to be the car that belonged to the missing Schlosser, and the California Highway Patrol were told to be on the lookout for two hippies who were possibly wanted in connection with a murder. A patrol-man, Randy Newton, on receiving the call on his radio, decided to turn off the highway onto a dirt side-track, figuring that the two men couldn't have got too far on foot. Just as he suspected, he came across the two hippies about two miles further on, trying to hitch a lift. Although they carried no identification, they openly admitted that they were the two men who had been driving the Opel Kadett that had been involved in an accident. Patrolman Newton arrested both men and radioed for assistance. When the other officers arrived, the two men were handcuffed and advised of their rights.

The blond man seemed very willing to talk, in fact almost too eager, and identified himself as 22-year-old Stanley Dean Baker. His companion was 20-year-old Harry Allen Stroup, and they were both from Sheridan, Wyoming. He told the police that they had been travelling companions since June 5, and got around by hitching rides. The two men were searched and in Baker's pockets the police found small lengths of bone. Patrolman Nelson was curious and studied the bones more carefully and then asked Baker what they were.

'They ain't chicken bones,' blurted out Baker. 'They're human fingers.' He paused for a moment, stared at the patrolman and then added, 'I have a problem. I'm a cannibal'.

The patrolman was taken aback, and ordered the two men to get into the back of his patrol car. On their way back to the police station in Monterey, Baker talked quite freely about his compulsion to eat human flesh. He told Nelson that he had developed the taste for it when he was 17, following electric shock treatment for a nervous disorder. He also referred to himself as 'Jesus'.

BAKER'S STATEMENT

Back at the police station the two men were questioned by Detective Dempsey Biley. Baker, still very eager to talk, almost bragged about how he had killed the owner of the Opel Kadett. He made it clear that his companion, Stroup, had not been with him at the time and that he had had nothing to do with the murder. Apparently the two men had split up at a place called Big Timber, because Baker had managed to hitch a ride with James Schlosser. When Schlosser told Baker that he was going to Yellowstone Park for the weekend, Baker asked if he could go along for the ride, and the two men eventually set up camp for the night close to the river.

Baker went on to say that in the middle of the night he had stealthily crept over to his sleeping companion and shot him twice in the head with a .22 pistol that he always carried with him. Next he proceeded to cut the body up into six parts, removing the head, arms and legs. When the Detective asked Baker what he had done with the man's heart, he replied, 'I ate it. Raw.'

He told Biley that he had removed the man's fingers so that he could have something to chew on later on. Then he dumped the remainder of the body in the river, together with the pistol, and then drove off in his victim's car.

Some time later he met up with Harry Stroup who was walking along the highway, and offered him a lift. He continued to insist that Stroup had had absolutely nothing to do with the murder of James Schlosser.

Both the men were thoroughly searched and among Baker's possessions was a recipe for LSD and a book called The Satanic Bible. It turned out to be a hand-book of devil-worship, which gave instructions on how to conduct a black mass.

Baker described to the police the location of the camp where the murder had taken place and, following a thorough search of the area, they found sufficient evidence to charge Baker. The earth was splattered with dried blood and a bloodstained hunting knife was found nearby. They also found human bone fragments, teeth, skin and a severed human ear.

Baker and Stroup were flown back to Montana and were brought before District Judge Jack Shamstron on July 27, 1970. They were both remanded in custody and Baker was sent to Warm Springs State Hospital for psychiatric evaluation. Harry Stroup, who had remained silent throughout the whole proceedings, was apparently guilty of nothing more than having become friends with a homicidal maniac. The pieces of bone that were found in Baker's pocket were sent to a pathologist, and they proved to be the bones from a human right index finger. There appeared to be no motive for the crime, other than the fact that Baker had a lust for human flesh.

Stanley Dean Baker was judged to be insane and confined to a mental institution.

Arthur Shawcross

An unrepentant cannibal who
munched on two girls during his
tour of duty in Vietnam

ARTHUR SHAWCROSS BOASTED that he was never happier than when he was serving his tour of duty in Vietnam. He claimed to have killed women and children indiscriminately while fighting for his country. Not only did he torture, mutilate, and dismember his victims, he also roasted their flesh for his dinner.

Arthur John Shawcross was born on June 6, 1945, two months premature, to Corporal Arthur Roy and Bessie Shawcross. Bessie took her newborn to her sister-in-law's in Watertown, New York, and remained there until her husband had completed his military service.

Many of the Shawcross family already lived in and around the Watertown district, but unfortunately Arthur found it hard to interact with other people. He tried various ways of attracting attention, and up until the age of six still talked in baby talk. He became a chronic bed wetter and his chiding by family members only seemed to make the matter worse. In an effort to get the attention of his mother, Arthur started to run away from home but would either return of his own accord or be brought back by the authorities.

Sadly, Arthur's school life was no better than his home, as the other children teased him constantly which meant he spent many hours on his own. His grades suffered and he always felt like he was a misfit. In an effort to gain recognition with the older children he started to bully the younger children, but apart from reducing his victims to tears, it had little of the desired effect. Around this time Arthur also developed a violent temper, and, if provoked, would fly into an uncontrollable rage. He also took to carrying an iron bar around with him.

As the months went by Arthur became more and more withdrawn and his grades suffered because he fell so far behind in his school work. At home he also became more introverted and to avoid further punishment due to his appalling school reports, Arthur would often escape to his grandmother's house.

OBSESSION WITH SEX

Arthur Shawcross had an obsession about sex from about the age of eight, and can never remember a time when his mind was not preoccupied with sexual thoughts. He spent many hours masturbating and then progressed into oral sex with friends of both sexes. He also claims that his sex was not just limited to humans, and he experimented with animals, such as cows, sheep, a horse and also killed a chicken whilst in the process of having intercourse with it.

Arthur had an 'Aunt' Tina, who he said introduced him to the delights of oral sex, and from this experience he always found it to be the most rewarding form of sexual gratification. Arthur claimed to have been regularly having oral sex with his sister Jeannie and his cousin Linda by the time he was 14.

Soon Arthur's desire for oral sex became insatiable and he would perform it whenever and wherever the opportunity presented itself. However, something happened one day on his way home from school, which was to change his view of sex forever. Arthur was walking down the road when a car stopped and offered him a lift. The man driving the car took them to a secluded spot and held a knife to the boy's throat as he performed fellatio on him. However, being so frightened, Arthur was unable to obtain an erection which made the man angry. He turned Arthur over and brutally sodomized him before dropping him back to his house. From this point on Arthur was unable to reach an orgasm unless there was some form of pain involved.

For the next four years Arthur became something of a waster and seemed unable to hold a job down for very long. He also took to stealing on a small scale for which he was occasionally caught.

In 1964 Arthur got married, but the relationship was

only to last for about four years, although the couple did produce one son.

THE TURNING POINT

It seems as though the turning point came in Arthur Shawcross's life when he was conscripted into the army and was posted to Vietnam. This became a significant period in his life because he was trained to kill, something which seemed to give him an unexpected thrill. Shortly before leaving for Vietnam, Arthur married for the second time to Linda Neary, following a very brief courtship.

Arthur was given the job of despatch clerk when he arrived at Vietnam, which made him responsible for flying out to the various war zones in a helicopter carrying ammunition. Initially he found he was horrified by the atrocities and savagery of war, but soon became very keen to join his fellow soldiers in the fighting. He seemed to enjoy the thrill of hunting down his enemy and playing the part of a predator.

Soon the horrors of the conflict brought out his bloodlust and he soon started to commit his own atrocities. On one occasion he found two Vietnamese women hiding in the bushes, and he told of how he shot one in the head and tied the other to a tree. Although the first woman was still breathing he cut off her head and put it on top of a pole for his enemy to find. Next, feeling the urge to eat human flesh, he took a slice from her thigh, cooked it and then sat down and ate it. He forced the second woman to perform oral sex on him, then he raped her and shot her in the head.

Vietnam became a real-life story of horror and blood-lust for Arthur, and he was later reported to have said that the war and its barbarity brought out the animal instinct in him. When he was eventually interrogated he said he felt he was justified in what he did because:

'The VC put razor blades up whores' vaginas. Shoved them inside a deep cut in where you'd never know until it was too late. When the GI's would fuck 'em they would slit their penises to shreds or cut them clean off . . . I was with some guys, ROK Koreans, who took a whore and put a firehose inside her and turned on the water. She died almost instantly. Her neck jumped about a foot from her body. Another time we took another whore and tied her to two small trees, legs to the trees, bent down. She had a razor blade inside her vagina. She was cut from her anus to her chin. Then the trees were let go. She slit in half. Left her there hanging between the trees. This may be why I did what I did to those girls.'

AFTER THE WAR

Following the Vietnam war and back at home with his wife, Arthur found it impossible to settle back into a normal routine. He constantly had visions of his blood-soaked orgies back in Vietnam and started to believe that he was possessed by the spirit of a 13th-century cannibal named 'Ariemes'. He felt that he was being driven to rape and murder and commit more acts of cannibalism. He started to beat Linda and was becoming more and more aggressive as the weeks went by.

His wife consulted a psychiatrist who made an assessment of Arthur, and the doctor told Linda that her husband needed to be committed for treatment and rest. However, Linda was a Christian Scientist and did not believe the doctor and subsequently refused to sign the papers for Arthur's committal. However, without the therapy that he desperately needed, Arthur's mental state started to decline and eventually he was driven to murder once again.

In 1972 Arthur Shawcross murdered ten-year-old Jack Blake and eight-year-old Karen Hill, in Watertown, New York. The children's bodies were discovered only a few days apart and Arthur was arrested for the murders. He was sentenced to 25 years and was released on parole in April 1987 after having served only 15 years.

A SECOND CHANCE

After his release Arthur eventually settled in Rochester, after residents in two other communities objected to his presence due to his sinister past.

Whilst in Rochester Arthur married Rose Whalley who was his third wife. However, around the same time he met a woman called Clara Neal, who became his mistress. Arthur lived in the centre of town and worked at night as a food processor. He didn't own a car and could often be seen riding a woman's bicycle along the banks of the Genesee River, a favourite spot for local fishermen. The people of Rochester weren't aware of his past and they described him as a friendly and mild-mannered man. Little did they know that around this time Arthur Shawcross saw the return of his old 'friend' Ariemes.

In the spring of 1988 women began to disappear from the streets of Rochester, the bodies later turning up in culverts or wooded areas surrounding the city. In March of 1988 the body of a 27-year-old prostitute was found floating in Salmon Creek. In September another body was discovered, and over a year later in October 1989, a third body was found. In early November a fourth, and later the same month a fifth body turned up. Police believed the murders to be the work of the same person, and realized that they had a serial killer loose on the streets of Rochester.

Arthur followed the news of the murders very carefully, and even took the precaution of warning his wife and Clara to be on the lookout. He hung around the local coffee bars and talked to the police about the case.

In late November another body was discovered by a man who was out walking his dog. Four days later another body was found, and by the end of the year three more bodies were added to the list of deaths. The Rochester police felt they needed help to solve this crime, and asked FBI agents who specialized in serial killing to assist in the case.

The FBI's first job was to make a profile of the killer

– white male, thirties, mobile, trusted by women who apparently got into his car without hesitation.

On January 3, 1990, the state police struck lucky when they were doing a helicopter search of a rural area near Rochester. As they circled over the area they saw a body in the icy waters of the Salmon Creek. On a bridge overlooking the creek, a man leaned out of his car and urinated into an empty bottle. The helicopter immediately alerted some patrol cars, who surrounded the area. On spotting the helicopter, Arthur climbed back into Clara Neal's car and drove off in the direction of the nursing home where she worked.

As soon as he pulled into the parking lot in front of the nursing home, a police car pulled in behind him and he was taken to the police station for questioning. Even though Arthur didn't really fit the profile constructed by the FBI, when they read up about his past convictions they immediately became suspicious. Through lack of evidence they were forced to let Arthur go, but were able to impound the car for further examination.

During an inspection of the inside of the car they discovered a pink earring that matched one found on one of the victims. Arthur was once again brought in for questioning and for hours he denied any involvement in the crimes. However, he eventually bent under questioning and admitted to killing 11 women since the spring of 1988. He gave them all the gory details and even led the police to two, as yet undiscovered, bodies.

Shocked investigators, and later psychiatrists, listened as Arthur told of how he had cannibalized the vaginas of several of his victims, often returning to the decomposing remains several days later. By the time his case came to trial, in October, Arthur Shawcross refused to testify, and tried to get an insanity claim.

Whilst under hypnosis Arthur spoke as an 11-year-old 'Arttie' and even as a reincarnated medieval English cannibal. He was found guilty after an ineffective insanity plea, and was sentenced to ten consecutive terms of 25 years at the Sullivan Correctional Facility. He is still being held at Sullivan and there is no possibility of him ever receiving parole.

WEDDING NUMBER FOUR

On July 10, 1997, Art married his long-time mistress, Clara Neal in a very simple ceremony held in the prison's visiting room. Arthur's previous wife, Rose, had died in the spring of that year, which left him free to marry his true sweetheart. Under the state Department of Correctional Services policy Clara and Arthur will be entitled to conjugal visits. Clara says she loves her cannibal husband and will stand by him 'no matter what'.

Arthur Shawcross was punished with two years in solitary confinement on September 19, 1999, for allowing agents to sell his paintings on the Internet auction site, *eBay.*

Armin Meiwes

At his trial Armin Meiwes confessed to a lifelong obsession that eventually led him to eating a fellow human being

GERMANY WAS GRIPPED by a horror story recently, when a man was arrested for killing and then eating a man he met on the Internet.

Armin Meiwes grew up in a large house in a German town near Kassel with a very domineering mother. His father left when Armin was only eight, and former school friends recall him being publicly ridiculed by his mother. She constantly intruded on his private life, even going as far as accompanying him on dates and to troop outings in the early 1980s when he was in the German army.

As a young boy Armin seemed to have no real friends and spent a relatively secluded life being loyal to his mother. He was constantly lonely and would create stories and even invented a make-believe brother called 'Franky' with whom he said he could have proper conversations because he was the only person who listened to him.

At the age of 19 he joined the army but still continued to live at home. He had a real problem interacting with the other recruits, and even when he did want to bring friends back to his house, his mother always made it a problem. He was always unsure of his sexuality, and constantly questioned himself about what his preferences were.

In 1991 he met a group of sailors and was invited to go sailing. This turned out to be his greatest joy – he absolutely loved sailing. In the late '80s his mother became bedridden and totally dependent on her son, so when she died in 1999 Armin was thrown completely off balance and didn't know hope to cope without his powerful mother figure.

After his mother's death, Armin left the army and went to work as an engineer, and was well respected in the village where he lived. He led an outwardly quiet life and was described by one woman as a 'friendly and sensitive' person. He started to frequent a local brothel, and started to fabricate stories about his girlfriends when he was drinking at the bar.

The house he lived in was a very old-fashioned, rather dilapidated farmhouse, and he decided that if he wanted to attract friends back to his house, he would need to do some renovation. He had started to use the Internet at home and was getting interested in a lot of the cannibal chat sites where he found people that said they would like to be eaten. This had always been a fantasy of his since childhood, he knew he wanted to eat human flesh so that that person could become a part

Above: A policeman searches Ed Gein's rubbish-filled kitchen for vital clues. By the end of the investigation, human skulls and other body parts had been found.

Right: Ed Gein being escorted to court to face trial. He is seen as one of the most bizarre, cannibalistic serial killers of the twentieth century.

The mystical and isolated Easter Island was once home to a cannibalistic society. By 1600 the population of this island was about 15,000 and the pressures on resources led to cannibalism being more of a necessity than a ritual.

Jeffrey Dahmer at his court hearing. Dahmer murdered, dismembered and devoured at least 15 people. Amongst other human remains, detectives found hands in a kettle, skulls in the cupboard and a torso in in the freezer. He believed that if he ate the flesh of his victims they would come alive again within his own body.

Left: Jim Jones, leader of the People's Temple cult in Jonestown, Guyana, was responsible for the deaths of over 900 of his followers. He ordered them to take a lethal poison as it was time to depart to a 'better place'.

Below: The bodies of some of Jim Jones's followers who took the lethal poison. Officials also found victims who had been killed by gun shot wounds to the head.

The smiling, yet chilling face of Charles Manson at one of his many parole hearings – which have been refused each time. After his trial Charles Manson was placed in a strangely favourable light by the media, and his story has been re-told on stage and film. His bewitching charisma is what made many young girls follow him and his beliefs.

Above: Marshall Herff Applewhite, one of the two founders of the Heaven's Gate cult. He believed that a UFO was following the Hale Bopp comet and co-founder Bonnie Nettles would be on board to take him and his flock to the next level.

Below: One of the 39 Heaven's Gate members who committed suicide, wearing their Nike™ trainers and covered in a purple shroud.

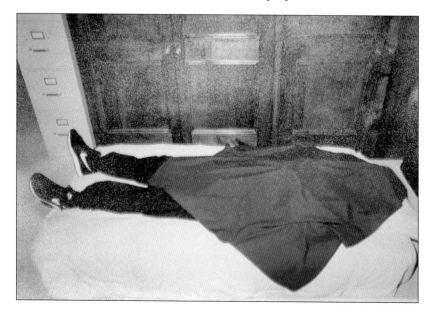

Left: Branch Davidian leader, David Koresh inspecting one of his many weapons prior to the fire that was to end his life and the lives of 76 of his followers.

Above: The inferno at the Mount Carmel complex, Waco, where the Branch Davidians perished.

The unmistakable uniform of the Ku Klux Klan. When this photograph was taken in the 1920s, the KKK was a greatly influential group, with four million members at its highest point. Thankfully today numbers have decreased immensely although there are still people who fight wholeheartedly for the cause.

of him, just like 'Franky'. As he read and talked to more and more people with like minds on various websites, Armin decided to post an advertisement on the internet under the alias of Franky and it read:

i search a young boy between 18 and 25 y/o.
Have you a normal body, i butchering you and eat
your horny flesh.

Franky

On the outside the house looked perfectly normal and Armin had made it very presentable on the inside as well, putting in bathrooms upstairs so that he could invite friends to stay. But what no one knew about was the 'slaughter room' he had constructed which contained a large cage.

His advertisements and photos on the internet had started to attract attention and it wasn't long before like-minded psychos wanted to see his slaughter room. His fantasies about killing and devouring someone grew stronger and stronger. He would take his new found 'friends' to his room, haul them up on a pulley and then mark their bodies with a marker pen, showing the most choice parts to eat. However, so far his guests had been unwilling to go further, that is until he was contacted by Bernd Juergen Brandes, a 43-year-old microchip engineer from Berlin.

Brandes used the name 'Cator' on the internet and over the next few months the two of them exchanged numerous explicit e-mails. Eventually they arranged to meet and Brandes made arrangements to come to Armin's house. Before leaving Berlin, Brandes sold his possessions and wiped clean the hard drive on his computer so that he could not be traced. When he eventually met up with Meiwes at the train station, he said, 'I am your Cator. I am your flesh'.

That evening, March 9, 2001, the two men sat naked drinking coffee. After a while they climbed the stairs of the rambling old house and went into Meiwes' bedroom. So as not to experience too much pain, Brandes first swallowed 20 sleeping tablets and drank half a bottle of schnapps. Then, using a kitchen knife Meiwes cut off Brandes' penis, with his full agreement, and then fried it for them both to eat for their supper.

By this stage Brandes was bleeding heavily and Meiwes talked him into having a bath whilst he read a Star Trek novel. In the early hours of the morning, Meiwes finished off his victim by stabbing him in the neck, but not before kissing him first. Next he chopped up his victim into pieces and put several pieces of him into his freezer – right next to a takeaway pizza. Finally he buried his skull in his back garden.

Over the next few weeks he defrosted pieces of his friend and cooked the flesh in olive oil and garlic. He managed to consume around 20 kg of Brandes' flesh before the police eventually knocked on his door.

The police were tipped off by several people who had seen his advertisements on the internet. When they started to search Meiwes' home they found neatly packaged body parts in a freezer in the kitchen. Each package was labelled with the specific body part. In the back garden police found other body parts buried because they were presumed inedible. Meiwes openly admitted to the police that the parts had belonged to Bernd Juergen Brandes who he met on the internet, but said that it wasn't murder because Brandes had agreed 'to be slaughtered'.

He told police that the two men had enjoyed a final meal together. Brandes had agreed to be castrated and the two sautéed his penis and testicles, which they washed down with a German white wine. Meiwes also gave the police a video tape he had recorded of the whole procedure. It showed that after the meal Brandes willingly allowed himself to be hanged from a butchers hook and slaughtered just as you would a calf.

During his trial Meiwes testified in his own defence saying that when he ate the body he felt that a part of Brandes was inside him. Investigators on the case discovered that Meiwes had been in internet contact with more than 200 people who shared his fantasies, while the cannibal himself claimed there were thousands more like him.

Armin Meiwes was convicted of manslaughter and sentenced to eight years and six months in prison. Meiwes has said he plans to write his memoirs in order to persuade other people with similar fantasies to seek help before it is too late.

Sascha Spesiwtsew

*With the help of his mother, Sascha killed and
ate his hapless victims*

SASCHA SPESIWTSEW WAS born in Nowokusnezk a
town in Siberia. He spent his entire childhood living in
fear of his abusive father, who not only tortured Sascha,
but his entire family.

When he reached adulthood Sascha shared a flat with
his mother and his beloved dobermann dog. Unfortunately Sascha had inherited the traits of his father, and
his mother had to put up with his permanent abuse.
His sister was extremely successful in her career, and
worked as a secretary at the court for a famous judge.

The depth of Sascha's brutality and atrocities was not
disclosed until 1996, when it was uncovered by chance.
No-one would have believed just how far his tendency
to torturing would go.

A broken water-pipe had forced the neighbours to
call a plumber. The plumber needed access to Sascha's
flat to stem the leak, but when no one answered the
door, he had to break in by force. However he could not
have been prepared for what he saw.

When he entered the flat the first thing the plumber noticed was blood covering the majority of the walls. In the kitchen there were bowls everywhere that contained pieces of human body. In the bath they found the mutilated body of a girl with the head missing, and another girl was found lying seriously wounded on the sofa. The plumber called an ambulance who took her to the hospital where she was able to tell the public prosecutor exactly what she had had to go through. Unfortunately, she died from the severity of her injuries 17 hours later.

Apparently Spesiwtsew's mother had lured the girl, along with two other girls, into the flat where Sascha raped and continually hit them. He killed one of the girls and then forced the other two girls to cut her into pieces in the bathtub. Then Spesiwtsew's mother cooked the girl's body parts for dinner. The second girl was killed by Sascha's dobermann who bit through her throat.

During a thorough search of the flat, the police found a notebook which contained details of the murders of 17 other girls.

Although Sascha had managed to escape over the balcony when he heard someone forcing the door, he was later caught as he attempted to rape a young girl.

Sascha Spesiwtsew was tried, along with his mother, and he was declared guilty in all 19 cases and sentenced to death. His mother, who denied complicity through-out, was sent to prison for life.

EVIL CULT KILLERS

Evil Cult Killers

IT IS ESTIMATED that in the US alone around five to seven million citizens have been involved in a 'cult' at some point in their lives and approximately 180,000 new members are recruited every year. Numbers are much lower in the UK. Cultic statistics are rather ambiguous as firstly it is extremely difficult to define what a cult actually is and secondly many groups are underground associations that do not make their membership numbers available or do not even record them. Nevertheless every country has groups and movements that worry the non-involved inhabitants, but the question is, is there a need for concern?

DEFINING THE WORD 'CULT'

The word cult and the usage of such a word can be highly controversial as it is always people on the outside of the specific group or movement who deem it a 'cult'.

The word has many meanings, and a dictionary definition shows just how intricate it really is. The Oxford Modern English Dictionary defines the word as:

cult /kʌlt/ *n.* **1** a system of religious worship, esp. as expressed ritual. **2 a** devotion or homage to a person or thing *(the cult of aestheticism)*. **b** a popular fashion, esp. followed by a specific section of society. **3** (*attrib.*) denoting a person or thing popularized in this way (*cult film or cult figure*).

A definition more specific to religious movements, that can be found on the *Victims of Violence* website, states that a cult is:

> *a religious movement which makes a fundamental break with the religious traditions of the culture and which is composed of individuals who had or seek mystical experience.*

Throughout modern times the word cult has meant anything from a fad of a certain era, such as the mods and rockers of the '60s or the Acid House movement of the late '80s and early '90s, to certain eating habits such as the Atkins Diet or vegetarianism. The word is often given to things that become popular very quickly and then just as rapidly, fade out.

Certain alternative, non mainstream film and music genres have what is deemed 'a cult following', but it is always the lack of understanding by people who are not involved that label such things so and the word always becomes associated with difference.

The majority of non mainstream religious groups are also negatively deemed cults as they are offering ideas and practices that are so alien to the majority that it is hard to understand what draws people to their teachings. Whenever the word cult is used within a religious sense it always denotes negative feeling. But for the purpose of categorization, sometimes the word cult is the only word that will do.

CULTS AND RELIGION

No one believes that the religious movement or hobby that they are interested in is a cult as they see their beliefs or interests as completely normal. Even within each specific group of people there are many individuals with opposing views and feelings to one another.

The problem is that the word has the tendency to cluster many extremely different ideas and movements under one banner and connotations of 'weird behaviour' and 'brain washing' become rife. In her book *Cults*, Shirley Harrison reiterates this point:

No one ever considers their own religion a cult. Christian Scientists are offended to find themselves linked with the Unification Church, Jehovah's Witnesses will not preach to the likes of Scientologists. If you are a Muslim you regard the Baha'i Faith with disdain. If you practise Transcendental Meditation you are not following a specific religion at all. The Church of Christ believes that mainstream Christianity has departed from the teachings of Jesus. The truth is that neither the word cult, nor the softer alternative 'New Religious Movement', can be applied to all these groups. Each is different. Very few are all bad.

The word causes ongoing debates and questions, such as: why should The Branch Davidians be called a cult but Christians or Jehovah's Witnesses not, when both groups can be defined as a 'system of religious worship'?

Maybe it becomes easier to call a religious group or movement a cult after an event that has rocked them and brought their ideas negatively into the mainstream as it is these events that have given other peace loving harmless groups a bad name.

Although the word cult has been used in conjunction with modern culture, the idea of cults and sects is by no way a new notion. Cults, in some form or another, have been around since the beginning of religion. There have always been offshoots and movements that have not been accepted by the majority due to their fanaticism and instead have been negatively described as unorthodox or spurious.

Back in the time of the Crusades, around 1118, a knight of the First Crusade, Hugh de Payens, founded 'The Templars'. The Templars consisted of ten knights who stayed in the holy land after the crusade and provided escort for pilgrims travelling from Jaffa to Jerusalem. Over the years this small group of 'do-good' knights grew in numbers, in fame and in power. By the Second Crusade they had gained the right to wear a red cross, the symbol of God, on their white mantles. But with fame and fortune also came stories that The Templars were rash and aggressive, with the best spy network in the Middle East. They soon spread as far as Europe and owned huge amounts of land that they used to earn revenue that could be sent back to their Templar brothers in the East.

The knights soon became a worry for monarchies and governments around the world, and whether or not they were doing anything bad did not seem to matter, they were seen as a threat, especially to those in power. By 1307, the King of France, Philip the Fair had the majority of Templars arrested on charges that ranged from sodomy to witchcraft and with the help of propaganda it wasn't long before the public had turned completely against them.

This can be related to many modern day groups, it just takes a few pieces of bad press for a whole movement and ideology to be seen as a threat to society, just because the ideas they are teaching or the way in which the group are living are not 'the norm'.

CULTS THAT BECOME DESTRUCTIVE

On the flip side, there are groups which are tarred with the description of cult as they are a danger to people and society as a whole.

Thuggee was an Indian cult in the 16th century that was made up of Muslim and Hindu members who worshiped Kali, the Goddess of Destruction. They were responsible for the assassination of travellers for monetary gain and each murder was completed in an extremely ritualistic fashion. The Thugs believed it was their religious duty to commit such atrocities, and a holy and honourable profession.

It was because of their fanatical belief and worship to Kali that the Thugs had become such dangerous people, who really believed that there was nothing wrong with what they were doing. In this respect the Thugs could be seen as a dangerous cult that needed to be stopped.

In recent times there has been an uprise in alternative religions and beliefs. This has had a lot to do with travel becoming easier, the movement and amalgamation of cultures have seen people exposed to many foreign theories and practices that are subsequently moulded into something new. Even something such as Yoga has made people in the West spiritually aware of a very Eastern practice which 60 or 70 years ago would not have been so accessible.

The practice of a non-mainstream religion or of a new belief that is not common is not the problem, as humans should be free to choose what they believe in, if anything. The problems with 'cult activity' come when people are sucked into a group that has a detrimental effect on their health and also on their brain and thought process which ends in them either killing themselves of others. These groups could be termed 'destructive cults'. Groups, such as the Branch Davidians, Aum Shinrikyo and The Order of The Solar Temple were perfectly respectable groups, with the best intentions that for whatever reason ran out of control. Even after events such as mass suicide, many survivors of these destructive cults still praise their leaders, but is that because they were so severely brainwashed that they will never again think for themselves?

It is a myth that destructive cults prey on emotionally low people of low intelligence in need of guidance. Through various studies and personality breakdowns of former cult members we can see that an alcoholic divorcee has just as much potential of becoming involved in a life changing movement as a university professor. Although there is not one single personality type for people who join cults, in the West common traits are: middle class, white, non-religious and around 18 to 30 years of age, who are in a transitional phase in their lives.

It could even be argued that cults that embark on mass suicide should be left to it as they are all adults who can think for themselves. But it is never as easy as that as many times children are either brought into a group by their parents or are born into such a movement. It is the children who need rescuing as they know no different and are not able to make their own choices.

The problem with destructive cults is that people can be recruited dishonestly and new members are manipulated into conforming to certain rules and regulations that take away their freedom and interaction with family and friends on the outside. It can be extremely hard to distinguish between a destructive cult and a cult that is in fact just a radical new movement as leaders can come across as very saint-like and angelic who convince their members that they are going to feed the hungry and clothe the poor.

As soon as a group takes away your opinion to exercise your God-given privilege of free-will, it is a cult that definitely has the potential to be destructive and evil.

SECTION ONE
CULT SUICIDES

The Heaven's Gate UFO Cult

Mass suicide in San Diego

THE HEAVEN'S GATE were known by various names during their 22 years of existence. At the beginning they did not even have a name, therefore it was people outside the cult who first christened them. A sociologist who studied them in the early years referred to them as the 'Bo and Peep UFO Cult' and media articles often referred to them as 'HIM' – Human Individual Metamorphosis. Yet it wasn't until a couple of years prior to the end of their existence in 1997 that the group settled on Heaven's Gate as a name, the name they had been using for their website.

Marshall Heff Applewhite was born in Spur, Texas in 1931 and had studied at various institutes before finally dropping out to follow a career in music. At the beginning this career path looked rather promising when he became music director at the First Presbyterian Church in Gastonia before obtaining the post Professor of Music at St. Thomas University in Houston. Things took a turn for the worse in 1972 when he was dismissed from his post due to a scandal involving a male student. This incident ruined both his career and his relationship with his family. Applewhite subsequently suffered a mental breakdown and signed himself into a psychiatric ward in order to 'be cured of his homosexuality'. It was at this vulnerable time in Applewhite's life that he met nurse Bonnie Lu Nettles. Applewhite felt that his sexuality was secure with Nettles and their relationship, although intense, was strictly platonic.

Bonnie Nettles was born in 1927, little is known about her background apart from her interest in metaphysical studies. She was a member of the Theosophical Society and had an avid interest in channelling. In contrast, Applewhite came from a traditional Christian family upbringing with a father who had been a Presbyterian minister – he had always been interested in religion but it wasn't until he started hearing voices in his head that he became hungry for more. Nettles used Applewhite's vulnerability to benefit her thoughts and beliefs by magnifying his delusions and although they had many differences in nurture, they soon discovered a mutual interest in UFOs, the paranormal and science fiction.

BO AND PEEP

A year after their chance encounter the couple began wandering around the American West living a rather nomadic lifestyle. They cut themselves off virtually from all other human existence and submerged themselves in a private world of visions and metaphysics. Having plenty of time for contemplation and reflection it was at this point that they decided they were the two witnesses written about in the *Book of Revelations.* Their belief drew on an ideology that they were two prophets whose destiny it was to die and be reborn. They had many childlike nicknames for their duo such as 'Bo and Peep' 'Guinea and Pig' and 'Ti and Do' and to this day cult and theological analysts are still trying to work out what the reasons behind the names are.

'The Two', as they also referred to themselves, embarked on creating a hybrid religion that was a mixture of Christianity, Theosophical teachings and the paranormal. They often reportedly had contacts with beings from other planets whom would tell them to 'abandon their worldly pursuits'. The *Book of Revelations* went on to state that after 1,260 days of showing their witnesses the truth, their enemies would attack and kill them. This event would be followed by their rise to heaven by cloud. The cloud would take the form, Applewhite believed, of a UFO.

TWO BECOME HIM

It didn't take long for 'The Two' to start attracting media attention, many people who had the same thoughts and beliefs as them but who maybe needed a little guidance to act upon it started to join them on their walkabout.

Applewhite educated his followers into believing that himself and Nettles were representatives from the 'higher level' of existence who had taken on a human form at this lower level in order to guide aspirants through the journey to the higher level of existence.

At one point, with around 200 recruits in tow, Bo and Peep spilt the members into small groups with vague instructions regarding preparation for the resurrection. Bo and Peep disappeared into the wilderness, and for about six months small groups of their followers were roaming the country awaiting news from their leaders.

After half a year of nomadic wandering, news came that Bo and Peep could be reached at a post office box in Mississippi. Within a few months, around one hundred followers had reassembled behind a much more mature leadership.

By the beginning of the '80s 'The Two' had become 'HIM' with around 50 or 60 solid members. The group wandered around the Mid West before making camp near Laramie, Wyoming. They were an extremely peaceful and contemplative group of people who were dedicated to their cause – more likened to monks than a cult. Over time, more and more rules were being thought up by Bo and Peep, and members – their sheep – were strictly regulated by what was termed the 'Process'. They yearned to eliminate sex and all human emotion from themselves and their followers. It was almost as though because Applewhite had such a problem dealing with his own emotion and desire that he felt such feelings should be deleted from existence.

Followers came and went but 'HIM' maintained a hardcore following, and through members inheritances the group managed to set up two residencies, one in Texas and the other in the Rockies.

LIFE AFTER TI

In 1985 Nettles, (who had actually been rechristened 'Ti' to Applewhite's 'Do' at this point) at the age of 57, died of liver cancer. In Applewhite's eyes Nettles had always been his superior and from the day of her death he started to refer to her as his 'heavenly father'. He told his followers that Nettles was definitely an advanced member of the higher level and reported right up until his own death in 1997 that he was in constant communication with her.

Applewhite continued to sail his ship onwards and upwards so to speak. He lectured followers that if they wished to board the spaceship to heaven they would have to embark on even more disciplined training. His disciples had to give up practically everything, including family, friends, alcohol, tobacco and sex. Applewhite was surgically castrated and five of his male followers followed suit.

The group adopted a whole range of space related jargon in order to describe their ideas. Applewhite was the Captain and his followers were the crew. Food turned into 'fuel' and their bodies were the 'physical vehicles' that would help take them to the heavenly space ship.

Members wore identical uniforms which consisted of collarless monotone tunics, Nike™ trainers and, male and female alike, all had cropped hair cuts. Their tunics were disturbingly similar to something that could easily be associated with a sci-fi television programme such as *Star Trek,* and it is believed that many of the group's members were in fact avid sci-fi fans.

According to Applewhite, the Bible provided an array of proof regarding what their ideologies entailed. Passages from the four gospels and the *Book of Revelations* could apparently be interpreted to show references to UFO visitation.

As the years went by each of the members individuality lessened. They had been given new names by Applewhite which helped crumble their sense of past, they were no longer the people they had once been, they had been completely brainwashed for the cause of the higher level. This mind-control was supported by members being assigned a partner. If one half of the pair was falling out of the much needed mind-set the other crew member was there to put them back on track. The individual thought process had been predominantly wiped out, except maybe the individual thoughts of Applewhite himself.

NEW RECRUITS

In the early '90s the group came out of seclusion and began a campaign to get their message across to as many people as possible. They recorded video messages, held open meetings and lectures, took out advertisements in national newspapers and set up their own website called *Heaven's Gate.* The website allowed access to the group's sacred text: *How and When Heaven's Gate May Be Entered* and also contained essays by both Applewhite and his students explaining their theories and where they were going. An 'Earth Exit Statement' posted on the site by a student named Glnody discusses the dominant and corrupt governments of the world and how due to technology there is no longer such a thing as freedom on earth. It was around the time that their website went live that they started loosely calling their movement Heaven's Gate . . .

In 1993 news broke of an incident at Waco, Texas where 81 members of the Branch Davidian sect including leader David Koresh had died in a fire after a 51-day siege with ATF and FBI agencies. This caused Applewhite to panic about his own cause, Heaven's Gate already felt disassociated from governments and forces, so guns were purchased and stored in preparation for an attack. By 1995 they had built a cement strong hold but a message from Nettles advised Applewhite to abandon such attempts at war. Applewhite believed that their cause was far greater than anything that had gone before it.

HALE-BOPP

Another event happened in 1995 that caused Applewhite to sit up and take note. Two astronomers, who were hundreds of kilometres apart at the time, were looking at the globular cluster M70 when they noticed a fuzzy object come into view. It soon became apparent that they had both fallen upon a previously undiscovered comet within seconds of each other. It was given the name of Hale-Bopp due to the surnames of the two discoverers and was to become the most photographed comet of all time. Hale-Bopp was such an amazing discovery as it was visible to the naked eye for over a month. The comet was estimated to be between 40 and 100 kilometres wide, and was described as a dirty snow ball with an extremely long gassy tail. From the day of its discovery Hale-Bopp became rather a mystical comet and reports started to circulate that there was more to it than science as we know it.

In November 1996, amateur photographer Chuck Shramek took a photo of Hale-Bopp using a 10 inch SC telescope and a CCD camera. In the photo there appeared to be another object following behind the comet's tail. Shramek described it as a 'Saturn like object' due to the ring-like form that seemed to embrace its strangely shaped body. This was all it took for Applewhite to believe that closure of the lower life was imminent. He went on to preach to his crew that the saturn like object travelling behind Hale-Bopp was the spacecraft coming to take the Heaven's Gate members to the higher level. Applewhite believed that Nettles had contacted him to inform him that Hale-Bopp was the sign that the apocalypse was getting close.

HIGHER LEVEL CALLS

At the same time the Heaven's Gate crew had managed to acquire enough internet skills to set up a company called *Higher Source* that designed websites for other customers. The money from this enterprise allowed the group to rent a $7,000 a month Spanish style villa just outside of San Diego. The villa was to become the home of 40 members. they would wake up at 3 a.m. to begin prayer, eat two bland meals a day and make themselves as genderless as possible so as not to arouse any form of sexual attraction from other members.

Members began recording video diaries where they happily stated that they were looking forward to leaving the Earth behind to join Ti (Nettles) on the higher level. Applewhite constantly stated that his crew members were allowed to leave at any time, and many of them did, but so powerful and controlling was his mind that it was the weaker crew members who stayed – maybe people who would have had suicidal tendencies even without being in such a cult? One member even wrote a passage on the website stating that even if they were wrong and there wasn't a higher level, there wasn't anything to live for on Earth anyway so it was worth a try. People who feel that low about themselves, maybe depressed about how their lives have gone so far, of course will embrace the idea that life on Earth is in fact meaningless and there is something better to come from the 'next stage'. If an idea is expressed in an interesting enough way it will cause people to think, even if they do not necessarily agree with the statement in question, it will get their mind working – is that all it takes to get inside the mind of another human and completely change their destiny?

Applewhite had made his crew members believe that the only way for them to progress to the next level was through an Older Member, so without Applewhite, they did not stand a chance; they needed him. Therefore the logical process would be to leave this world when Applewhite left.

THE YEAR OF SUICIDE

The Heaven's Gate crew members enjoyed their final year on Earth. They went to a UFO conference and purchased insurance against alien abduction. At the beginning of March all 39 members went on a four day coach trip that took them to Golden Beach, the place where Ti and Do had held one of their first meetings in 1975. They went on day trips to the local zoo and some members went to San Diego Sea World. They ate out every night; pizzas, burgers and steaks were consumed. On March 21, the entire crew went for a final lunch at a Marie Callendar restaurant in Carlsbad where they ordered 39 identical meals of chicken pot pie, cheesecake, and iced tea. That was the last time they were to be out of their villa.

On March 26, 1997, the San Diego Sheriff's department received an anonymous phone call stating that there had been a mass suicide at the Rancho Santa Fe.

The bodies of 39 people were found in the villa just north of San Diego. At first it was believed that they were all men ranging between 18–24 years old. But after a closer look it became clear that there were 18 men and 21 women whose ages ranged from 26–72. The confusion had arisen because all the bodies looked identical and sexless.

The bodies were found in various rooms of the villa, each person was lying on their back with their hands by their sides as if asleep, and all except two had a purple shroud covering their heads. All members were in their regimentary tunics and wearing their Nike™ trainers.

It became apparent that the 39 people had committed suicide in three separate sittings over the course of a few days. Fifteen on the first day, 15 on the following day and the final nine on the third day. The careful way in which each shift had died concluded that it was definitely planned. There were no signs of distress and one of the first officers on the scene even described what he encountered as being rather serene and tranquil.

The suicide was very ritualistic and each person died in the same way they had lived within Heaven's Gate, in a very ordered fashion.

Some members assisted others with their death, cleaned up, and then went off to take their own lethal cocktail. In each top pocket of the 39 bodies was a five dollar note a few coins and a recipe for death. The recipe said:

Take the little package of pudding or apple sauce, and eat a couple of teaspoons to make room to put the medicine in and stir it. Eat it quickly, drink this vodka mixture and then lay back and rest quietly.

After autopsies it turned out that the 'medicine' the recipe referred to was phenobarbital which is an anti-seizure drug that in a high enough dose and mixed with alcohol can cause death. The drug would also make its user extremely drowsy, so plastic bags had been used as part of the ritual to make sure death came either from poisoning or suffocation. The last two bodies to die still had the plastic bags over their heads. All other members had died with plastic bags on their heads, but these had been subsequently removed and replaced with purple shrouds by the remaining members. The last two members alive must have removed the bags from the the other seven in their group and then killed themselves.

FAREWELL

In the house, along with around ten computers, investigators found video tapes that had been made in the weeks prior to the suicide. There was a statement from each of the 39 members. each stating their joy and excitement at leaving their earthly vehicles in order to board the heavenly ship that would take them to the higher level. One such video statement from a crew member known as Stmody stated that:

We watch a lot of Star Trek, a lot of Star Wars, it's just like going on a holodeck...we've been on a holodeck, we've been in an astronaut training program . . . we figured out a day equals one thousand years . . . played it out mathematically . . . it's roughly 30 minutes . . . we've been training on a holodeck for 30 minutes, now it's time to stop and put into practice what we've learned . . . so we take off the virtual reality helmet, we take off the vehicle that we've used for this task. We just set it aside, go back out of the holodeck to reality to be with the other members in the craft, in the heavens.

Each member seemed totally at ease with what they were about to do, in their minds – however the thought had got there – they were about to take part in a perfectly normal and reasonable act. An act that was much more than suicide, it was departure. Departure on a new journey to a more fulfiling and enlightening place.

Whether the Heaven's Gate ever reached their destination remains to be seen, but maybe the important thing is that in their minds they were about to succeed and that was contentment enough? On the other hand, had they never met Bo and Peep the 38 crew members would have become wolves instead of sheep and hunted and fought for a decent life on Earth as it was the only one they were going to get.

David Koresh
Sent to Earth by God?

What really happened at Waco?

VERNON WAYNE HOWELL was born on August 17, 1959, in Houston, Texas. The son of an unmarried teenage mother, Vernon never knew his father and was brought up by his grandparents. His childhood was quite a lonely one and often got teased by other children who called him 'Vernie'.

Whilst at high school he was diagnosed as having dyslexia, but by the ninth grade he had dropped out. Although he had no interest in school Vernon was a keen guitarist, with a great love for women. He was also very interested in Biblical scriptures and although he had no formal religious training apart from what he had learnt at his mother's Seventh-day Adventist Church, he had the remarkable talent of being able to recite and explain long passages of Biblical scriptures.

In 1979, after getting expelled from the church for being a bad influence on other young members, Vernon moved to Hollywood with the idea of making it as a rock guitarist. By this point in his life he had gained a lot of confidence as well as a theatrical and assertive nature that would be expected of a try hard rock star. But two years later, after realising just how difficult it was to make it in the music industry, he returned to the state of Texas and moved to Waco.

Howell joined the Mount Carmel religious Center and it wasn't long before other members were taken in by his extraordinary way of being able to teach and explain complex scriptures to them.

It was here that Howell met Lois Roden. Roden was the amiable 67-year-old leader of the Branch Davidian Seventh-day Adventist group – which descended from a schism in the Seventh-day Adventist Church.

Lois Roden had become leader of the Branch Davidians when her husband, Benjamin Roden had died in 1978. The year before in 1977 Lois Roden claimed to have had a vision in which she saw the Holy Spirit. Roden claims that she had learnt from this vision that the Holy Spirit was a female.

Howell and Roden soon embarked on an intense sexual relationship and eventually moved in together. Howell got deeper and deeper into the thoughts and beliefs of the Branch Davidians and the couple even travelled to Israel on a pilgrimage for their beliefs. It was on this trip, in Jerusalem, that Vernon claimed that he was given a direct revelation about the Seven Seals together with the knowledge and ability to teach it to the world. Vernon was rapidly working himself into a position of influence and had Lois completely on side.

VIRGIN BRIDES

In 1984, at the age of 24, Vernon Howell married a 14-year-old named Rachel Jones and it soon became apparent that he was a womanizing sexual deviant with the need to satisfy physical lust. He may not have stayed faithful to his relationship with Lois Roden but he did stay faithful to her Davidian cause.

When Louis Roden died in 1986, a battle for power began between Vernon and Roden's son George as to who was to become the new leader of the Davidians. The majority of the Branch Davidians' members sided with George Roden and at gun point Vernon Howell and his meagre following were forced off the Mount Carmel sight.

By this time Howell had acquired two more wives. In March 1986 13-year-old Karen Doyle became his second wife and then five months later he wed 12-year-old Michelle Jones in secret.

Howell relocated his group in Palestine, Texas as an offshoot of the Davidians with the intent of being a peaceful and religious commune; or so it was thought. That was until 1987 when Vernon and seven of his trusted followers returned to Mount Carmel in full camouflage gear. They had nine guns and 400 rounds of ammunition and by the end of the siege George Roden was left with gunshot wounds to his chest.

Vernon and his group were arrested for attempted murder but at the trial neither he nor his compatriots were convicted.

INSIDE THE MIND OF DAVID KORESH

By 1990, Vernon Howell had become leader of the Branch Davidians and it was in this year that he legally changed his name to David Koresh. On the legal document the reason for his name change was stated as being 'for publicity and business purposes'. But his main reason was from his belief that he was now the head of the biblical House of David. Koresh came from the Hebrew translation of Cyrus, the name of the Persian king who allowed the Jews held captive in Babylon to return to Israel. David Koresh believed he was the new Messiah sent by God to spread the word.

Once in control of the Branch Davidian Seventh-day Adventist group, Koresh embarked on annulling the marriages of members stating that only he, as leader, could be married. Several members left following this announcement but many followed his orders. Koresh then declared that due to his status he was owed at least 140 wives and was entitled at any time to claim any of the females in the compound young or old. Girls as young as 12 were soon to fall pregnant and forever be in his grasp.

Elizabeth and March Breault broke out of the group at this point as they were not happy with his teaching. They wrote many letters to their friends alerting them that the teachings of the man that called himself David Koresh were false and inaccurate. Their campaign did some good and by the summer of 1990 the majority of all Australian and New Zealand members had broken away from Koresh.

Koresh was seen as a man of many sides, a 'Jekyll and Hyde' character, full of contradictions. He could be funny but also extremely serious, he was loved but at the same time feared. His students would see him at times as a loner, deep in communication with God, and then on the flip side part of the crowd taking part in group activities.

PREPARATION FOR THE END?

Control of his students got more and more intense, Koresh even dictated what and when they could eat. He would enforce strict rules, and then moments later break them. He could basically do what he liked as he was a prophet sent by God.

By the the winter of 1990 Koresh had become more and more volatile and aggressive, he started to instruct his followers to watch violent war videos on a regular basis and had begun purchasing firearms. They were accumulating weaponry stock as part of a seemingly legal selling trade, solely for the purpose of making money.

They were also building up an impressive larder of food that could have seen them through a whole year if the need was to arise.

Even though it is believed by many people (apart from the FBI and government) that the weapons were only there as a means of making money, it does seem on the other hand that the Branch Davidians were beginning to obtain a militaristic mentality. According to some ex-members, Koresh wanted to know how far his followers would go in standing up for the faith that they believed in.

Koresh is reported to have said around this time that the Apocalypse would begin when the American army attacked their Mount Carmel compound. They even buried a school bus which was to be used as a bunker if the situation arose.

By 1991 there had been multiple reports made to the local authorities by ex-members of the Branch Davidians who were unhappy with the way life seemed to be going at the compound. Investigations started to take place due to allegations that Koresh was mentally and physically abusing the children in the congregation.

INVESTIGATIONS

In the spring of 1992 two parallel investigations of the Mount Carmel compound began. The first was the *Waco Tribune Herald* which, with the help of some former Davidian members, began in-depth research into the Davidians with the notion of publishing a seven part article at the beginning of 1993. At the same time The Bureau of Alcohol, Tobacco and Firearms (ATF) launched an investigation into Koresh and his followers.

On February, 1993, the *Waco Tribune Herald* published the first installment of its piece on Koresh and the Davidians. This was the beginning of the mess that was to come over the next 51 days. The newspaper article, built mostly on accusations from the disaffected members, portrayed Koresh as being a potentially aggressive, sexual deviant and his followers as brainwashed and deluded people who had forgotten how to be rational human beings.

It is also declared that three of the people who were interviewed by the paper were also working closely with the ATF, and the paper had also discussed the article with the bureau before going to press.

As the article went out and was read by locals the ATF planned a raid for the following day in order to arrest Koresh on charges of possessing unlicensed firearms and illegal explosives in order to protect the local community from impending danger.

Bizarrely enough, at the end of 1992 Koresh had invited the ATF agents to the Mount Carmel compound in order to examine his weaponry stash and its corresponding paperwork but the ATF had declined this offer.

The bureau were intent on going ahead with their February 28 raid but due to lack of planning and over eagerness, by the time they arrived all 131 Branch Davidians and a couple of local television news crews were already there to greet them. Without thinking through the situation, and without foreseeing what could happen, the ATF stormed straight in, carelessly and unnecessarily.

The major problem was that it was more than just a case of a siege against David Koresh. There were children within the compound, innocent people whose lives should have been made priority over the search warrant on Koresh – but they weren't.

As the ATF stormed Mount Carmel there was a retaliation, gun shots were heard and soon it became apparent that six Branch Davidians and four ATF officers had been shot dead. Many others on both sides of the battle were injured.

The FBI came in at this point and they were clearly not aware and failed to understand why David Koresh and his followers were refusing to back down and walk out. It appears that as soon as the ATF arrived on the fateful February day, Koresh believed that this was the beginning of the end – as he had foreseen time and time again. Koresh believed that the attack was in some way related to the Fifth Seal of the Revelation – the last major event before the end of the world. The confusing thing to Koresh was that he had not expected the Fifth Seal to arrive until 1995.

The FBI and the ATF did not understand anything to do with the Branch Davidians or the Bible extracts that Koresh was reciting therefore they were totally lacking in the knowledge and understanding needed to diffuse the situation peacefully, without endangering the people within the compound.

Whether or not Koresh was a deluded, mentally unstable person will never be known for sure, but throughout the 51-day siege he believed that he was dealing with acts of God together with overthrowing the godless people of the world in the form of the US government and law enforcement agencies and this belief was to overshadow the initial reason for attacking the compound. There could have been many more than ten deaths on that day if the Davidians had been intent on attack rather than self-defence.

Between March 1 and April 18, around 14 adults and 21 children left the compound by their own choice, but that meant over 100 people stayed with David Koresh, in order to see the situation until the end.

PSYCHOLOGICAL METHODS

When the FBI took over the raid after the shoot out, they were toying with the idea of using what was dubbed as 'psychological torture', that they believed would eventually break the Davidians into giving themselves up.

Igor Smirnov from the Moscow Institute of Psychocorrection was the chief advisor in this campaign and he had spent ten years developing a device that could allegedly implant thoughts into a subject's mind. In this instance the FBI wanted this tool to be used to implant the voice of God into David Koresh's mind, telling him to surrender. And the voice they were going to use as God's – none other than that of the actor Charlton Heston.

This method was eventually rejected, but the thought had been there nonetheless. Did the fact that the FBI even considered using such a new and unknown field show the disregard and thoughtlessness they had for the Davidians', their beliefs and their culture, however brainwashed they may or may not have been?

THE SIEGE CONTINUES

Over the weeks, trained FBI negotiators were brought to the scene with the intention of peacefully ending the stand-off whilst at the same time federal commanders worked opposite tactics. On March 7 a memo went out to the FBI agents listing certain 'tactical activities that might be used to increase the stress and anxiety inside the compound' such as flooding the Mount Carmel building in lights throughout the night, cutting off all the Davidians' communications with the media, and hindering the supply of milk to the children inside.

Surely such acts were never going to get a group of people who thought that the end was upon them any closer to coming round to a new way of thinking?

David Koresh asked to speak to somebody who would understand what he had to say, someone with a learned knowledge of the Bible – this request was denied on a number of occasions even though the FBI had many religious and theological contacts that they had been using for translation purposes whenever they entered biblical conversations with Koresh.

Doctor Michael Haynes, who had a PhD in theology and psychology, even suggested that he be allowed to negotiate directly with Koresh. Dr. Haynes thought he may be able to talk Koresh out of the compound by promising to help him spread the message of God. Again this request was denied.

Negotiations were discussed throughout March and people who had voluntarily left the compound were allowed to return in order to tell the remaining Davidians's that they were being treated well and they should not fear coming out.

By March 19, Koresh was speaking to negotiators, promising that he was not going to commit suicide and neither were any of the other members within the building. He requested that the FBI did not destroy any more Davidian property and that in time they would come out. But accounts of the siege state that released children who were interviewed by a psychiatrist from the University of Baylor suspected that they had heard talk about suicide from the adults.

Each time negotiations broke down the FBI bulldozed an area of wall or removed property from the grounds, but again this did not help matters as the Davidians were going 'beyond this world'.

It then became apparent that another reasoning behind the stand-off was the fear of prosecution. Once the members realised that Kathy Schroeder was being charged with murder it made them all believe even more that there was no reason to leave their safe haven, maybe that the final judgement in this crazed situation would come from God?

The final Davidian to exit the compound came out on March 23, 1993. Three days later on March 26, a negotiator told Steven Schneider, a high ranking Davidian, that ten more people must be released by midday. Schneider reportedly got angry at this and said that the remaining Davidians did not care as they only feared God.

GAS, GUNFIRE & INFERNO

A meeting was held on April 7 for all the agencies involved in the Branch Davidian siege. The FBI reported to the Attorney General that they had concluded from the meeting the possibility of using tear gas as a resolution. By April 12 managing attorneys in the Criminal Division received a briefing from the FBI that CS gas would be released into the compound if the Davidians did not come out by the end of passover. This action had been ordered by the Attorney General herself, Janet Reno. It was believed by the agencies that they were at a stale mate with the Branch Davidians and there was no other alternative. Also, if the children inside the complex were getting physically and mentally abused they needed to be removed as soon as possible. But surely gassing these people out was always going to do more harm than good?

As armoured vehicles cleared cars from the front of the property on April 18, Davidian members were reportedly seen holding children up at windows in a tower with a sign saying: 'Flames await'.

At around 6.00 a.m. on April 19, 1993 the gassing began. A negotiator telephoned the compound and told Schneider what was about to happen. He was informed that the gas was not deadly and they should come out peacefully. Schneider responded by ripping the phone out of the wall. The message was announced again over loud speaker but as the gassing vehicles approached Mount Carmel, gun-shots were fired towards them.

The gassing continued for several hours, and at the same time the armoured vehicles began smashing holes in the building to weaken it for entrance and exit purposes. Three hours into the demolition and the main entrance had been broken down.

At noon, several fires started around the compound and shortly after the Davidians fled the building. They were the lucky ones, as rapidly the wooden structure of the building became engulfed in flames and even though openings had been made in the building no one else survived the fire. David Koresh and 76 of his avid followers, including 20 children, died on that grim afternoon.

MYSTERY

To this day so many things related to the Waco disaster remain questionable. It will never be known for certain who fired the first shot on February 28. ATF agents who were part of the raid testified in court that the Branch Davidians had fired first. Immediately after the raid (and off the record) however, one of the ATF agents told an investigator that a fellow agent may have fired the first shot when he killed a dog that was roaming around just outside the compound. The agent later withdrew his statement. Surviving Davidians still maintain that they did not shoot their guns until they were fired at.

It can also be questioned whether negotiations should have continued for longer before resorting to a gas attack. Were Koresh and his followers given the freedom of speech and belief that is meant to be part of the American Dream? Many lives may have been saved if people with more theological and biblical knowledge had been allowed to talk directly to the Davidians as opposed to going through an agency that are more renowned for shooting first and asking questions later. Was it right to use the FBI as a peace-making tool?

It seems more factual and fair-minded to spread the blame between the government agencies and the Branch Davidians, as, with a bit more rationality, maybe events would have turned out differently.

As to who started the fire that was to end the siege, and many lives, again remains to be seen. Independent arson experts concluded that the fire was deliberately set from within the compound and a Texas jury ruled that the US Government were not to blame for the deaths of the 80 Branch Davidians. Jurors heard audio tapes made inside the compound which contained conversations between unidentified Davidians asking incriminating evidence such as 'Start the fire?' and 'Should we light the fire?'.

Even if the Branch Davidians can be seen as responsible for the act of starting the fire maybe the government should be held responsible for not dealing with such a complex situation in a more discerning manner.

The Branch Davidians may not have become aggressive if they had not had a provoking aggressor such as the FBI or the ATF on hand to persecute them but then again it may have become worse if the situation had been left any longer. Only the people who were inside with Koresh really know what went on and if abuse to children really happened.

Maybe if religious groups such as the Branch Davidians were not so taboo and demonized within everyday life then it would have been easier to understand how things had got to this stage and the situation could have been diffused silently and carefully.

David Koresh may have known exactly what he was doing form the beginning, he may not have believed anything that he was saying and if this is the case he was an evil criminal with innocent hostages. On the flip side if he believed he was the Messiah then he was a religious fanatic with fanatical followers. Either way innocent people, however they had got themselves in the situation, could have been saved.

Just how much the Branch Davidians brought their end on themselves is hard to say, and will never really be known but it was definitely a situation that could have been handled in a more humane manner by the authorities. David Koresh went out of the compound most days so therefore could have been picked up at anytime by the ATF in a peaceful manner.

All we can definitely say is that this was a mass tragedy and although a certain amount of brain-washing may have taken place, the lives of these men, women and children could have been saved.

One question that nobody seems to have thought of though is, maybe he really was the Messiah? . . .

The Order of the Solar Temple

Jo Di Mambro & Luc Jouret

WHEN THE FIRE service was called out to a blazing property in the well-known ski resort of Morin Heights in Quebec, they treated the call as they would any other emergency. Unfortunately though, on reaching the scene, it appeared that they had arrived too late to save the former occupants, and two charred bodies were recovered from the burned-out wreck of the building. The property was owned by Jo Di Mambro, so it was assumed that one of the bodies must be his. The other, they thought, would be that of his friend, Luc Jouret. But an autopsy revealed this not to be the case.

Di Mambro had leased the property out to the Dutoit family – a couple and their young son – and as the autopsy proved that one of the bodies was female, this seemed to provide the answers to the identity of the corpses. It did not explain however, where their three-month old child was at the time of the blaze.

With the fire out and the site deemed safe for further

inspection, a team of forensics went into the property. A more thorough search discovered another three bodies crammed in a cupboard – that of a man, a woman, and a small baby. This was the family to whom Di Mambro had rented his property. They, however, had not died in the fire. The bodies were punctured with multiple stab wounds and covered in blood. Experts estimated they had all been dead for a couple of days before their bodies burned in the fire.

This gruesome discovery solved the mystery of the boy's absence, but it opened a completely new enquiry as to why this family had been killed, and whose were the two bodies originally discovered?

It turned out that the family had once belonged to 'The Order of the Solar Temple', a sect run by Jo Di Mambro which was believed to have in the region of 600 members. News spread to the police that Di Mambro had believed the young boy to be the anti-Christ and had therefore sent his henchmen to the property to murder him. A warrant for Di Mambro's arrest was immediately issued.

CHEIRY, SWITZERLAND

The following day in Switzerland, the Cheiry fire department was called to an equally gruesome scene at a farmhouse owned by the elderly Albert Giacobino. Having extinguished the fire, they entered the building and discovered a man's body lying on a bed. He had been shot in the head and a plastic bag had been tied over his face. They also found a collection of explosives around the farmhouse.

A police team was called, and they made a search of what they thought was Giacobino's garage. It appeared to be more like a meeting hall, and inside were the belongings of several different people but no evidence of any further bodies.

There were no internal doors in the garage, but the space inside the hall did not fit the perceived size of the building from the outside so inspectors began to test the walls. One wall appeared to be hollow, and so the team opened it up.

A very strange sight met their eyes. Around a triangular altar, with their feet at the centre and their heads outward, lay 18 bodies. They were all dressed in identical robes, and bottles of champagne littered the floor around them. Similarly to Albert Giacobino, most had plastic bags tied around their heads, where they had been shot. Some had been suffocated, and some also beaten. Another three bodies were found in a second secret room. Bags of petrol were discovered in a chapel situated next to this building. From the explosives in the house, and these rigged devices, it seemed that an attempt to set fire to the whole place had failed.

GRANGES-SUR-SALVAN, SWITZERLAND

The same night, again in Switzerland, another fire was reported. Three ski chalets in the resort of Granges-sur-Salvan were alight. The fact that all three houses were burning suggested that it was no accident. Indeed, it wasn't. Numerous petrol bombs had been suspended and exploded, and in total 25 bodies were recovered. Again, most had been shot in the head.

A link began to emerge between the two Swiss fires. After the difficult process of identification, it transpired that all the victims had belonged to the Order of the Solar Temple. The buildings were in fact the property of the sect. Autopsies proved that overall, 15 of the deaths had been suicide. The rest were murder.

Meanwhile in Canada, the two bodies found in the rented home of the Dutoit family were identified as Gerry and Collette Genoud, a Swiss couple who also belonged to Di Mambro's Order of the Solar Temple. The incidents were clearly related.

JO DI MAMBRO

Born in France in 1924, Jo Di Mambro originally trained as a horologist, but his real interest was in religion and spirituality. He was a member of the 'Rosicrucian Order' (Ancient and Mystic Order of the Rosy Cross) for 13 years, but during this time he developed his own religious ideas and beliefs and decided to move east, close to the Swiss border, to set up his own school, the 'Centre for the Preparation of the New Age'. Charges of fraud and swindling may have precipitated this departure. Followers whom he had met and influenced while in the Rosicrucians went with him.

Di Mambro had radical ideas. He claimed to be reincarnated, but the identity of his former self changed frequently – sometimes religious, sometimes political. He also named the members of his group as reincarnations of famous people. He organised marriages between his followers and dictated who amongst them was permitted to produce children. His own children, he claimed were exceptional. His son would shape the world, and his daughter was one of only nine 'cosmic children', a Messiah who would bring about his much-prophesised New Age. He took money and personal possessions from his followers in order to care for the needs of the community. With donations from some of the more wealthy families, Di Mambro purchased a mansion in Geneva. He was even attracting devotees from outside the community who had heard of his teachings and generously donated cash sums to his cause.

LUC JOURET

'The Foundation of the Golden Way', which Di Mambro founded in 1978, became the Order of the Solar Temple (officially known as the International Chivalric Organization of the Solar Tradition) in 1984 after Di Mambro had recruited the charismatic Luc Jouret. Jouret was a Belgian doctor and obstetrician, and his entry into the group was a turning point for Di Mambro. He was a charming and compelling man and worked ceaselessly for Di Mambro in recruiting new members and acting as guide and prophet. A medical doctor by training, he had also embraced spiritual healing and homeopathic medicine while travelling in India, and many people came to the Order of the Solar Temple, attracted by him.

Jouret believed himself to be both the third reincarnation of Christ, and also a former member of the Knight's Templar, a secret, 14th century Christian order founded by French crusaders in Jerusalem. It was therefore rumoured that he was in possession of a deeper spiritual knowledge and guarded deep religious secrets. He preached that when death came and the spiritual body departed from the physical body, only the members of the Order of the Solar Temple would ascend and meet again on the star Sirius where a better life would continue for them. He warned though that they may have to make this transition before their physical body had died naturally. The earth was slowly being destroyed by war, pollution and human neglect, and the end was nigh. He told the members that they would have to leave before the world self-destructed, and the only way to make the journey to Sirius was through fire. Fire, although destructive, had the ability to transform and it was therefore the only medium through which to pass.

This obsession with fire may have come from Jouret's belief in his own reincarnation from a member of the Knight's Templar. Members of this group were known to have been burned to death at the stake by the ruling monarchy who feared the power and secrecy of the order. The spirits of these persecuted and holy men lived on, he proclaimed, in the elders of the Order of the Solar Temple.

By the end of the 1980s, membership was international and spread mainly across France, Switzerland and French Canada where Jouret had led lecture tours. There were also a few followers in the US, Spain and French Caribbean. The sect had amassed a fortune of 93 million dollars through donations and sales of property offered to it by its members.

CONCERN AND SUSPICION

But Jouret's radical prophecies of an ecological apocalypse caused concern and suspicion amongst the group and membership began to dwindle. Rumours also crept in that the Order was a hoax and that the members had been swindled out of their savings and possessions.

Perhaps under pressure from these accusations and the creeping group discontent, Di Mambro was fast losing patience with his partner too. He was aware of the commune's displeasure at the controlling way in which Jouret conducted his lessons and preachings. Despite his magnetism and inspirational style, Jouret had previously been voted out of another group, 'The Renewed Order of the Temple', as Grand Master by his followers. This displayed a severe lack of confidence, and Di Mambro feared that the same could happen within the Solar Temple.

The disillusion spread amongst the group, when a

couple of members left and began to denounce the group in Quebec. They claimed that the Order was dangerous, demanded their money back and encouraged others to do the same. They did, and Di Mambro was faced with numerous lawsuits and financial demands.

Di Mambro was also coming under scrutiny from the banks and financial institutions who were beginning investigations, suspicious of money-laundering, into the vast sums of cash which he'd been investing in his accounts. His health was also suffering. He was diagnosed with diabetes and kidney failure, and believed that he had also developed cancer.

Neither were his family supportive. His daughter, whom he had heralded as one of the 'cosmic children', no longer wanted to be involved in her father's premonition of the New Age and instead wanted to be with the other children of her own age, doing the things they were doing. His son condemned him as a fraud, which led to many more of the Order's followers demanding their money back.

The police also became involved when, through Jouret's association with illegal arms dealers, two members of the Quebec group were arrested for the possession of handguns with silencers. Jouret was also charged. The suicides at Waco and Jonestown did not help Di Mambro's cause either as unorthodox groups were now regarded as dangerous and viewed in a very negative light.

With the world seemingly bearing down on Di

Mambro, the only explanation he could offer his confused followers was that the end of the world was nearing and that this negativity was intended to encourage them to seek out a better life, and to push them towards their salvation. They had to depart together. Consequently Di Mambro and Jouret began to expedite their plans to take their followers to Sirius.

VITAL EVIDENCE

In the aftermath and investigation into the Swiss and Canadian suicide fires, letters were offered to the police from relatives of those who had died, written in advance of the events, and as a means of explanation for what was to come. They told of how some 'traitors' would have to be executed, but that mostly they were going to carry out the killings as a way of helping the members of the group who were not strong enough to make the journey themselves. Those who were prepared to kill themselves were the more spiritually developed and superior. They believed that they would transcend to a higher spiritual level by taking their own lives and those of others, and would reach a state which they could not achieve on earth. Earth, they claimed, was heading for destruction anyway and soon no one would live there at all.

These notes however, albeit written before the events, were mailed afterwards. Therefore some of the members of the Order of the Solar Temple were still alive.

It was originally believed that Di Mambro and Jouret had planned these murders with no intention of taking their own lives, but instead lying low and then emerging when the dust had settled to spend the money their followers had donated to their cause. It was therefore surprising when their bodies were discovered amongst the dead in Switzerland. They died separately, Jouret first at Chiery, and Di Mambro afterwards at Granges-sur-Salvan. It appears that they had genuinely believed their own prophecies and predictions.

DUTOIT MURDERS

The reasons for the first murder, that of the Dutoit couple and their son in Quebec, soon became known. Tony Dutoit used to help Di Mambro with one of his greatest 'tricks' – creating the illusion of conjuring up the elders of the Order to materialise before the assembled followers in their communal enlightenment rituals. This was all achieved with the use of lasers, and it was not long before Dutoit became disillusioned with this fraudulent practice and the false claims which Di Mambro was making. He disclosed the secret of this 'phenomenon' to other members of the group and then tried to claim back some of the money which he'd donated to the Order. Nicki Dutoit, Tony's wife, also displeased Di Mambro by becoming pregnant. Di Mambro had forbidden this as he did not want any children to threaten his daughter's prophesised place as the new messiah. They therefore left for Quebec, where they had their son. Di Mambro heard of the birth of their baby, and declared him to be the anti-Christ. The child, and their parents who were clearly trying to stand in the way of spiritual progression with their disobedience, had to be disposed of.

With the damage Dutoit did in exposing Di Mambro and having the audacity to defect, it was clear to see why he became Di Mambro's first victim.

GRENOBLE, FRANCE

One year passed without incident before another mass suicide was committed. This time, 16 people were found dead near Grenoble in France. Not all of them had departed willingly it seemed, as one woman had suffered a broken jaw, indicating a struggle. Fourteen of the bodies, lay together in the same circular arrangement as the bodies in Switzerland, but two bodies lay separately. These, it is believed, were the bodies of two people whose responsibility it had been to shoot the weak and to start the fire. All the deceased had been members of the Solar Temple, and the incident was therefore immediately linked to the preceding three mass suicides.

But the families of the victims of Grenoble were not satisfied that the perpetrators had all died. They believed that some of the group were still at large.

Police monitored the behaviour of the remaining members of the group carefully the following year, especially during the solstice and equinox seasons, but nothing aroused their suspicion, and there were no reported fires or suicides. They believed that the practice of the Solar Temple had finally come to an end.

It hadn't. One last journey to Sirius was made on March 22, 1997, from St. Casimir, Quebec. It was almost a failed attempt as the fire-starting devices did not go off. Having been given this reprieve though, the children in the group begged for their lives and were allowed to leave. They were released on the condition that they took sleeping pills and went to stay in a neighbouring workshop. They knew that their parents would be dead when they awoke. A second attempt was made, and this time it was successful. This took the total number of followers who had taken their lives to 74.

MICHAEL TABACHNIK

With continued pressure from the families of the Grenoble victims, the police led a search for the remaining members of the Order of the Solar Temple and uncovered several of the leaders. One of whom was the Swiss musician, Michael Tabachnik. He went to trial for his involvement in what was now being termed a criminal organization and for his alleged knowledge of the murders before they occurred. Apparently lined up to be Di Mambro's successor, Tabachnik had written quite a lot of the group's literature and had declared the final mission of the group just before the first deaths happened. This, the prosecutors claimed, meant that he was conditioning people to die. Tabachnik's own wife had died in the Cheiry suicide.

Tabachnik, it was asserted, had travelled with Di

Mambro to Egypt and it was there that they had taken the decision together to found the Golden Way. The principles of this sect were the same – members would achieve peace only in death. When they recruited Luc Jouret, the Golden Way became the Order of the Solar Temple.

Tabachnik pleaded not guilty to all charges. He said that he had not been a member of the Order for over five years, and claimed to have had no knowledge of the intended mass suicides. A lack of hard evidence to prove otherwise meant that Tabachnik was found not guilty.

With no high-profile arrests the commotion surrounding the sect died down, and it is now believed to be more or less dissolved. If there are any members still practising the beliefs of Jo Di Mambro, they are certainly not considered a threat, and are of no concern to the authorities. The ritual of mass suicide and murder perpetrated by the Order of the Solar Temple is believed to be defunct.

Movement for the Restoration of the Ten Commandments

A mass suicide in the Ugandan jungle

IN THE LATE 1980s Credonia Mwerinde was in a cave just outside the Ugandan town of Kanungu when another vision of the Virgin Mary seemingly came to her.

Mwerinde, who was born on July 30, 1952, was a daughter of a Roman Catholic catechist. She was a school drop out who had had a number of unsuccessful and unhappy marriages and ended up as a prostitute in the Kanungu trading centre.

It was while being involved in this age-old profession that she met a local man who wished to take her on as his seventh wife. Again, her marriage turned sour, this time due to her inability to conceive, even though she had three children from previous relationships. It was during this time that Mwerinde started to get blinding visions from the Virgin Mary. Her current barrenness the Virgin said, was caused by a decision of Mary herself to 'withhold' the unborn child.

VIRGIN MARY

The Virgin Mary started to appear regularly to Mwerinde, in her bedroom, on the sides of rocks and in the caves – which she returned to time and time again.

Credonia tried to convince the Vatican of these miracles that had so unselfishly appeared to her, but there was not enough evidence or credibility for the Vatican to take it any further. Luckily for Ms Mwerinde a failed politician by the name of Joseph Kibwetere was on hand to listen and believe every word that she said.

LOVING FATHER?

Joseph Kibwetere had lived peacefully within the luscious green countryside of southern Uganda. He was a loving father and husband who rarely argued with his family and was known by many Ugandans for 'his piety, his prayer and his good works'. He was active in Ugandan politics and was a devout Roman Catholic from which he founded a Catholic school and became a supervisor for other schools in the region.

It is reported that from as early as 1984, Kibwetere was having visions and frequently hearing conversations, between Jesus and the Virgin Mary. In these conversations, the Virgin Mary complained about the world's lack of regard for the Ten Commandments and prophesied that the world would end on December 31, 1999.

MEETING OF MINDS

Kibwetere joined his ideas and prophecies together with similar-thinking excommunicated Roman Catholic priests Joseph Kasapurari, John Kamagara, Dominic Kataribabo and two excommunicated nuns. There are conflicting stories as to when exactly their group was founded but in 1994 they registered as a non-governmental organisation.

When Joseph Kibwetere met the self-styled visionary Credonia Mwerinde he believed wholeheartedly about her revelations and asked her to come and live with him and his wife. Mwerinde continued to have visions of the Virgin Mary and word started to spread about these amazing apparitions. Many people, mostly those suffering from infertility started to arrive at Kibwetere's house with the hope of reaching the Virgin Mary through the human form of Mwerinde. Over the months, more and more people seeking retribution and answers, started to stay at the Kibweteres' home and the group began to call themselves 'The Movement for the Restoration of the Ten Commandments of God'. The group kept growing and at one time had increased to several thousand members with followers even in the neighbouring country of Rwanda. This caused Kibwetere's relationship with his own wife and children to become strained and although his family had initially joined the movement they soon fell out with other members who called them 'sinners' and burned their clothes. Things at the commune got so bad that Kibwetere's own family, including five of his own sons and daughters ran away. The last time the family were to see Kibwetere was in 1995 when he came to the funeral of one of his children who died of natural causes.

The Movement for the Restoration of the Ten Commandments of God placed themselves within a remote farming community in the unstable south-west corner of Uganda and led a relatively uneventful existence as far as the media and the police were concerned until the horrid events that were to unfold in the year 2000.

LIFE WITHIN THE CULT

As with many African countries Uganda has a whole range of religious movements and groups, spreading a variety of messages and ideologies. The Ten Commandments of God had been fairly inconspicuous and was a registered charity that portrayed itself as being intent on spreading the word of Jesus with the aim to make as many people as possible adhere to the Ten Commandments. The link with the Roman Catholic religion was apparent, with small statues of Jesus and a crucifix decorating their modest headquarters. The headquarters interestingly enough, had one time been the family home of Mwerinde. She became the sole owner of the property after her three brothers mysteriously died one by one.

In 1992 the group moved from Kibwetere's home, in the countryside, and by 1998 the group had become a flourishing natural community who lived together on land bought by combining the money gained from individual sales of their properties. They built churches in amongst the plantations and had their own primary school. The followers all lived together in dormitory style accommodation and local villagers described the members as being completely disciplined and very polite but with some strange habits, such as on certain days speaking entirely through hand signals. The reason for this was so as not to break the ninth commandment (eighth commandment for Roman Catholics and some Lutherans):

'Thou shalt not bear false witness against thy neighbour.' (Exodus 20:16; KJV).

It was in this year that the group had some problems. The local authorities took away its charity licence because the school was breaking public health requirements and there were rumours that children were being poorly treated.

During this time Joseph Kibwetere merged his leadership with Credonia Mwerinde who had increasingly become a dominant force within the group. She was often referred to by other members as the 'programmer' as all of the Virgin Mary's 'orders' were channelled through Mwerinde's body and voice.

Some people say that Mwerinde ultimately took over and shadowed all of the other leaders. Kibwetere was just a figure-head for her to use as a pawn in her quest for fame and money. She was seen by many as a violent, vindictive, unstable woman who was a pyromaniac and had killed before. Her ex-husband was quoted as saying:

'She was only happy when she was making money.'

With these views circulating does it bring us any closer to the events that were soon to take place?

WELCOME

Kibwetere and Mwerinde kept their followers isolated. Any contact with people from outside the group was strictly monitored and mostly forbidden. People outside the group were deemed 'sinners' but new members were warmly welcomed and always had the nicest food and warmest beds, until they became so reliant on the group that there was no chance of them leaving. When that time came they were treated just like all other members, they were encouraged to be celibate, unable to speak unless in prayer, worked long hours in the fields and lived on a nutrition lacking dish of beans. In order to become a fully fledged member of the movement newcomers were required to read a book entitled A Timely Message from Heaven: The End of the Present Time even though the Bible was the group's sacred text much of the governance came from this book. It was was written by Kibwetere and foretold the destructions that would come to Earth and wipe out the majority of the human race, due to their evil, disrespectful ways.

STRUCTURE OF THE MOVEMENT

The Movement consisted of separate groups. The first group was made up of new members who had read *A*

Timely Message From Heaven. These were the novices and they were required to wear black. The next group were the people who had sworn to follow the commandments, they wore green. The fully fledged members were those who were 'willing to die in the arc' and they wore white and green. Although this vow was referring to burial requirements of members, it may have had an ulterior motive for occurrences to come.

The whole community was based around the 'second generation' apostles. It was second generation as the movement believed that at the second coming, both the Virgin Mary and Jesus would return. For this reason six men and six women made up the leaders.

Members grew increasingly tired and hungry and due to the lack of contact with the outside world started to rely on the group for all of the emotions that as humans we rely on to survive.

Even though the majority of the group's members were Roman Catholics, they were taught that the Catholic Church was an enemy, badly in need of reform. Their own rules as well as those from the handbook, came direct from the Virgin Mary so they must be the right rules to follow – surely?

Doomsday predictions were endlessly lectured by Mwerinde and the other leaders to their flock. When the predicted day passed without any world-ending events the date would be pushed forward. By the time the world had entered the year 2000 it is said that some cult members may have started to suspect something, but Mwerinde calmed these feelings in a constitution.

She stated that the world would end 'before the completion of the year 2000'. There would be no 2001. For many of her members she remained true to her word as on March 17, 2000, a terrifying fire was to take place that would mean the end of the world for hundreds of innocent people.

INVITATION TO CELEBRATE

On March 15, 2000, Joseph Kibwetere issued a letter to government officials describing the world changing events that were about to take place. It spoke of the end of the current generation of people and of the world. The messenger dropped off the letter and bid farewell. The members also started to take part in activities that can be seen as preparation for the end or in preparation of a celebration, or both. They slaughtered cattle and bought a large supply of soft drinks such as cola. At the same time members started to travel across the country inviting both current and old members back to the compound in time for March 17. Members were reported as saying that on this day the Virgin Mary was to appear. Many members of the commune started to sell products to the nearby villagers for little or no profit and many debts within the community were settled. A local shop keeper alleges to have sold one of the apostles – Father Dominic Kataribabo – 40 litres of sulphuric acid which he claimed was needed to replenish power batteries.

BLAZING INFERNO

On the night of March 15, 2000, the members consumed the beef and drinks and had a celebration in honour of their new church, which they had recently constructed. On March 16, the members spent most of the night praying and then met early on March 17, in the new church. It is reported that around 10 a.m. they were all seen leaving the new church to enter the old church, which was now being used as a dining hall.

Did the hundreds of devout worshippers know that this would be the last time they saw the fresh air or did they think they were going to carry on with the celebration feast in the dining hall? When the members finally realised what was going on were they too exhausted and confused to resist?

Approximately 600 people went into the old church on this day and stayed where they were as the windows and doors were boarded up and nailed shut around them. At around 10.30 a.m. nearby villagers heard a massive explosion and when they arrived at the scene a gargantuan inferno had rapidly taken hundreds of lives.

The victims of the blaze included people from all generations; men, women and children perished. The death toll even today is still not accurately known but reports state that between 300 and 600 people died on that 'apocalyptic' morning. It is not even known if the leaders of the movement perished with their followers.

Joseph Kibwetere's family believe that he is dead

although his body has not yet been positively identified. A ring believed to have belonged to Kibwetere was found on the finger of a charred body amongst the rubble of the burned church. But is this enough to prove that the 12 apostles burnt together with their followers?

There are mixed views as to what happened to Credonia Mwerinde. A few days after the fire police claimed to have found her body, but some people believe that she is still alive. One local business man claims to have discussed selling cult land, vehicles and property just days before the fire. There have also been sightings of her in surrounding countries including the Democratic of the Congo where due to the lack of laws in the country there would be no way of her being faced with any kind of justice or arrest.

SUICIDE OR MURDER?

Straight after the inferno news spread of the mass suicide by the Movement for the Restoration of the Ten Commandments, but soon discoveries were made that brought a new question into the equation – was this in fact mass murder?

Four days after the fire, five bodies were found buried under fresh cement in the compound's latrines. When the people died and who killed them remains a mystery.

On March 25, 2000, 153 further bodies were found under the house of Dominic Kataribabao. The bodies were killed in a variation of ways; hacked, strangled and poisoned. How these murders were carried out without raising any awareness from surrounding neighbours is alarming. Local villagers heard no shouts or screams for help. The only sounds were of the diggers hard at work. When asked what they were doing by local villagers they answered that they were digging new latrines. What it seems like in hind-sight is that the members were digging their own graves.

The mass graves still remain a mystery. Everything is just speculation. The graves are believed to date back to a year or more prior to the blaze. One conclusion for why the graves were there, could be due to the strict categories that the members belonged to. It is possible the lower groups, who did not have fully-fledged members that were 'willing to die in the arc', lost their lives here anyway.

GOVERNMENT COVER-UP/PUZZLE

As well as the theory that Mwerinde and/or Kibwetere had in fact set up and murdered their followers, there is also another belief circulating that the whole thing could have been a government cover-up, with the Movement for the Restoration of the Ten Commandments being the scape-goat.

There are so many conflicting news stories reported and written on this case that mass suicide, murders and government/police cover up are all equally plausible theories.

Newspapers showed pictures of the mass graves that were found in the weeks after the fire. The images showed dead bodies piled up on top of each other. Whereas the police said that these had been added one by one, another source said that the way the bodies were piled looked more as though they were buried all at once, and had been thrown off a dump truck all together.

Another queer event was that a police spokesman had declared that a number of policemen had died in the fire. If this is the case, what were they doing there?

The Ugandan government were also happy to use the tragedy to enforce the restriction of non-mainstream religious groups.

Professor of Religious Studies, Irving Hexham, goes as far as to believe that after the initial number of deaths – which tallied with the number of registered group members – was used as a cover up and stated: 'Some enterprising police and army officers may have decided to use the tragedy as a cover to dispose of the bodies of murdered political prisoners.'

It could have been easy for this to have happened. It wouldn't have taken much for the media to start spreading 'evil-cult' stories, which would immediately draw the audience in to believe that it was a weird bunch of people brain-washed by the belief of a heavenly after life. People then would get so carried away with that thought process that the government could then start to back it and confirm that this was the truth and no one would even start to think that there could have been conflicting evidence. The media were eager for another story like the Jonestown incident that had happened in Guyana, South America, in 1978.

BLURRED HISTORY

The problem is that there is not enough known on the people involved in the group or the years running up to the tragedy. So many actions and events went unnoticed for so long that a factual account and the truth will probably get further and further away the more years that pass.

It has already become something of an urban legend for the new millennium. People make up their own account of what actually happened depending on their political and religious standpoint. Easy answers come from stating that the leaders were evil beings possessed with greed for money, or that they were a sect brainwashed with twisted religious ideas. Either may be the case but there is definitely a lot more to it. Due to the location of the Movement for the Restoration of the Ten Commandments of God and the lack of inside information it is difficult to paint a completely true and factual picture of what went on within this group. Reporters and local citizens of the area are so culturally different that any facts will be interpreted a thousand ways, and anti-cult groups have also forced their own beliefs about the tragedy into print, that it is hard to filter out what is the truth from what is just hearsay and whisper.

All this text can do is lay everything out for individual interpretations to be made but there are definitely no answers as to how or why such a massive tragedy took place whether it be murder or suicide.

Reverend Jim Jones

The People's Temple

AT FIRST IT was believed that the deaths of 913 people in the Guyanese Jungle were a mass suicide. As the gruesome details of the last few days in what had become known as 'Jonestown' came to light however, the horrendous truth emerged that the deaths may not all have been voluntary, and that one man may have been responsible instead for mass murder. The deceased all belonged to a group known as 'The People's Temple', led by the Reverend Jim Jones.

Jim Jones was born in Lyn, Indiana, on May 13, 1931. Lyn was a farming town, and Jones did not have many friends as a child. Home life was difficult for the family as, due to a severe lung disease, his father was unable to work and therefore relied upon only a minimal pension to maintain his family. In order to bring in some extra money for the family, Jim Jones's mother worked in a factory. Embittered by this hardship, Jones's father, a veteran of the First World War, began to sympathise with the racist activities of the Ku Klux Klan. This leaning always seemed strange to the young boy though, as Jones's mother was of

Cherokee Indian descent. He did not understand how his racist father could support such a relationship, and therefore saw flaws in his father's beliefs and values. He did not want to be a follower of this hypocritical ideology.

Perhaps because he had not been shown a clear religious path by either of his parents, Jim Jones took an exceptional interest in Bible Studies at school. In all other classes he was an average student. Inspired by what he learnt and the more he came to believe in the Christian faith, the more active he became in it. When the other children would leave school together and play, Jim Jones returned home, took up his position on his parents' front porch, and preached to the people who passed by the house.

At the age of 18, Jim decided to enrol on a religious studies course at Indiana University, and took a job as a porter at a Richmond hospital to fund this education. One year later, Jim became a pastor and also married Marceline Badwin, a nurse at the hospital. Now directly involved in the running of the church, Jim decided to introduce black worshippers into the congregation. One of his main pursuits was the running of the racially integrated church youth centre.

RESISTANCE AND DISAPPROVAL

In a segregated society such as that of Indianapolis, this was a move which met with much resistance and disapproval, not only from the bigoted members of the community, but also from the conservative affiliates of the church. Jones was not deterred however, and became even more determined to put a stop to this racism. His determination encouraged some of those who had initially wavered in their support to back him more fervently. As this support grew stronger, Jim Jones came to be seen as a leading figure in the fight for black people's rights. His following soon became large enough to enable him to break away from his former church and set up his own, which he named 'The People's Temple'. It was a church for all races, and nobody was turned away. Jones prided himself on his bi-racial background and his Cherokee heritage. As a result, the area became a magnet for black people and the ethnic minorities of Indianapolis.

With the large majority of his congregation being black, Jim Jones turned to well-known, influential black preachers to guide him, and modelled his manner and performance on them. One of his mentors was Father Divine, a black preacher and faith-healer from Philadelphia. He asserted such influence over his flock, that they responded by bestowing gifts and luxuries on him. He led a very comfortable life based purely on donations and contributions from his followers. This opened Jim Jones's eyes to what he himself may be able to achieve. He decided to put his own following to the test.

Over the course of a couple of weeks, Jones reported to the people of his church how the violence generated against him by the racists of the community and in particular, the Ku Klux Klan, was on the increase. He told them he had been attacked, his property had been vandalised, and his family were receiving threats. The stories appeared in the local press, leaked to them by Jones himself. Consequently, Jones was offered a job, fully paid, on the Human Rights Commission of Indianapolis and he received full support and backing by his followers in this role. Encouraged by the strength of this allegiance, not only of his own congregation but also of the mayor in offering him this role, Jones's confidence grew. He soon seized what he thought would be an opportunity to test this commitment to the extreme.

JONES DISCOVERS GUYANA

America was in the throes of preparing herself for the threat of nuclear war, and millions of families were building themselves fall-out shelters. In a spoof article, a magazine responded to this nationwide panic by listing the top ten safest places in the world to be to maximise chances of survival in a nuclear war. Jones read the article in all seriousness, and his eyes fell upon Belo Horizonte in Brazil. He spoke to his congregation, telling them that he predicted wholesale nuclear destruction, but that he could lead them to a place where they would be safe. He went out ahead to explore the area, funding the trip entirely from the finances of the church. He did not like what he found though, and deemed the area unsuitable as a place to begin a new life and base his community. However, on the return journey he did stop over in Guyana for a couple of days.

To Jim Jones, Guyana was a much more viable option. A newly independent socialist democracy, it was the perfect place to live out his harmonious and socially equal ideal.

In view of this new and exciting discovery, Jim Jones returned home to an eagerly-awaiting congregation and told them that in fact, the threat of nuclear war had lessened and that consequently there was no immediate rush to move out to Brazil as he had originally planned.

Jim Jones continued his activities in The People's Temple, embarking upon faith-healing to attract more followers to his church. News of his healing powers spread, and worshippers at the church witnessed those who claimed to have previously been sick and crippled, leap up in the middle of his sermons professing themselves to be cured of their illness or disability. No doubt these 'miracles' had been fixed in advance by Jim Jones, but they had the desired effect and more people came.

A CLAIM TOO FAR

But things got out of hand. Perhaps encouraged by Jones, the followers at The People's Temple began to make claims that not only was their reverend curing the sick, but that he had actually brought no less than 40 of the faithful back from the dead. This attracted the unwanted attentions of the State Board of Psychology. Sensing the urgency and possible danger of this situation, Jim Jones gathered his followers together and fled for the Redwood Valley near Ukiah, California. It was a wise decision. As it was the mid-'60s and a haven for hippies and drop-outs, Jim Jones and The People's Temple slipped in unnoticed and were left entirely to their own affairs.

CHARITY WORK

Wisened by the brush he had with the authorities and the negative reports he had been subjected to in the media however, Jim Jones decided to safeguard himself against the possibility of such damaging press occurring again. He ingratiated himself with the local community by telling his congregation to take unpaid charity work, and to offer their homes up to foster children. Jones himself turned his attention to influential politicians and before long had been proclaimed foreman of the County Grand Jury. His only aim in acquiring this political power, he declared, was to use it to enforce greater social equality. In order to help him, citizens were asked to make donations to The People's Temple, which consequently became a state-registered, tax-exempt religious body.

As Jones's finances grew, he was able to establish a new church in San Francisco for his now 7,500-strong congregation. He never failed to impress as officials and the press watched on to see him distributing food and care for the poor and disadvantaged on a daily basis.

As more and more people handed over their income and life savings to The People's Temple, not only did

Jones's finances grow, but his name spread far and wide too. His attentions now turned to South America, and to the starving children he believed he could 'help' out there. In particular, he wanted to spread his aid to Guyana. He was supported in this endeavour not only by his own followers, but now by the politicians and civic leaders who looked to this exemplary missionary and praised his ceaseless fight for the poor and underprivileged of the world.

THE ROAD TO 'JONESTOWN'

Perhaps carried away by his own phenomenal success however, Jim Jones began to get more and more extreme and puritanical in his views and preachings. He gave lengthy sermons about the evils of sex, and was beginning to encourage some of the married couples in the church to divorce so that he could choose more suitable partners for them from the Temple. As leader, he claimed he had the right to have sex with any of the female members he chose and forced them into many sexual acts against their will. He abused them sexually, and enjoyed watching them suffer physical abuse too. He would arrange fights, partnering children against adults to see the young ones knocked out. Some kids were tortured with cattle prods.

Yet he was still the golden boy in the eyes of the press. He kept the journalists away from some of the more sinister goings-on in the Temple by diverting their attention with the Temple Awards, huge financial rewards for reporters who had made 'outstanding journalistic contributions to peace and public enlightenment'. The police department was also on his side, as grateful as they were for the charitable contributions he was making to the families of police officers who had lost their husbands, sons and fathers in the line of duty.

The bubble was about to burst though. News of Jim Jones's remarkable, altruistic mission was spreading far and wide and it came to the attention of the White House that perhaps a little more unbiased investigation should be done into the activities of The People's Temple. Knowing what probing any deeper than the superficial exterior of his mission would uncover, Jim Jones knew the time had come. The money he had been so generously sending to Guyana had in fact been used to procure a plot of land in the Guyanese Jungle, soon to be known as 'Jonestown'. Accommodation had also been built, with space enough for Jim Jones to bring 1,000 followers. Here they would set up and live out Jim Jones's utopia.

In November 1977, Jim Jones and 1,000 of his faithful followers left for Guyana, and behind them San Francisco breathed a sigh of relief that the problem of The People's Temple was no longer its own. All of San Francisco that was, except for one man – Leo Ryan.

LEO RYAN

Ryan was a local politician, and rather than waving Jones off, pleased to see the back of him, his concerns grew for the 1,000 citizens he had taken with him. He had already heard disturbing reports from the relatives of suicide victims who had belonged to, and attempted to leave, The People's Temple while in San Francisco. Already, news was reaching him from the friends and family of those who had left for Guyana, that they were being held against their will, and that they were prisoners in Jonestown.

Ryan decided that he had to get out there, to see for himself the conditions in which these people were being held, and if indeed, they were being held against their will at all. He arranged the trip with the agreement of State Department officials, and also sent a telegram to Jim Jones to announce his forthcoming visit. Jones imposed some conditions on the visit, banning media coverage and insisting that the Temple's legal counsel be present in all discussions.

When the time for the trip eventually came, Leo Ryan landed in Guyana to find that Jim Jones had retracted his permission to allow him to visit, and he was barred from even getting out of the plane. Lengthy negotiations ensued, and eventually Ryan was allowed access to Jonestown. What he found there confirmed his fears, and disturbed him greatly. The members, although professing complete devotion to their saviour Jim Jones, were indeed trapped – Jones had taken their passports from them. What's more, they were in a poor physical state, weak and undernourished. Ryan addressed the group, telling them that any one of them was at complete liberty to leave with him, and that he guaranteed them total protection should they decide to do so. Out of the silent and slightly shocked group, one person stepped forward.

Ryan stayed on in Jonestown to talk further with the members of The People's Temple. The journalists he had travelled out with, left to stay the night in a neighbouring town. When they were safely out of Jonestown, one of the journalists read a note which had been secretly passed to him by one of Jones's followers. 'Please, please get us out of here,' it said, 'before Jones kills us.' Four people had signed the piece of paper. The second journalist claimed that one of the group had whispered the same thing, barely audibly to him.

On their return to Jonestown the next day, the journalists found Leo Ryan sitting with 15 people who had dared to say they wanted to leave. The plane in which Ryan and the journalists had made the trip to Guyana was only small, and it would have been impossible to carry the additional passengers back with them. So it was decided that they would have to call for a second plane to come and get them. The group was divided into two. Ryan was going to stay at the settlement and see if he could persuade any others to defect, but as the journalists and the defectors were about to leave, one of the Temple's elders lunged at Ryan with a knife. He missed him, and Ryan was hauled onto the departing vehicle by his travelling companions. They travelled immediately to the airfield but the second plane had not yet arrived and they had to wait 40 minutes. As they reached the runway, a vehicle drove out at them, firing at them as it gave chase. Leo Ryan, one reporter, a cameraman and a photographer were killed straightaway. Then one of the followers, undoubtedly planted amongst the infidels by Jones, opened fire and murdered the pilot.

THE END OF THE IDEAL

Clearly already aware of the fate of Leo Ryan and his accompanying party, Jim Jones could forestall the inevitable no longer and knew that before long his 'utopia' would be destroyed. He gathered his community in front of him, and told them that it was time for them to depart to a better place, and that they were too good for the world they currently inhabited. He was talking about the complete destruction of everything he had created, and as he spoke, a concoction of cyanide and sedative-laced soft drinks was brought out to his people. Babies were brought forward first, and the deadly liquid injected into their mouths. Remaining children were the next to die. Finally it was the turn of the adults. One by one they queued up to take this poison, but some showed their fear. Their belief failed them and they didn't want to die. Those who refused the poison had their throats cut by Temple elders, or were shot in the head. Jim Jones was taking his entire congregation with him.

CARNAGE

The scene which greeted the Guyanese soldiers who

arrived the next day was complete and total carnage. Only one or two terrified survivors were found, having crawled into tiny spaces underneath buildings and hidden to save themselves. Others were missing, presumably having escaped into the jungle. Of a total of 1,100 people believed to be in the compound, 913 were found dead. The body of Jim Jones was found with a single bullet wound in the right temple, believed to be self-inflicted.

Investigations into the massacre at Jonestown, and into The People's Temple revealed that in fact, Jim Jones had been preparing his people for this mass suicide for many years. He was paranoid that the American government was planning to destroy him, his people and his work and had instilled the idea in the minds of his followers that he was their salvation, that as long as they obeyed and trusted only him he would look after them. Therefore, when the order came from their leader, their 'father', that the enemy was finally upon them and about to slaughter them all, they were trained to follow his instructions and believed that in so doing, they were taking a noble and dignified path to a better place.

The bodies, many unidentifiable, were brought home to the United States, where many cemeteries refused to bury them. Eventually, the Evergreen Cemetery in Oakland agreed to take the bodies – 409 in total. A memorial service is held there annually to remember those who died. The remainder were buried in family graveyards, or cremated.

Sadly, the 913 deaths recorded in Jonestown were not

the end of the story. Members of the Temple who had survived the mass suicide in Guyana, took their own lives, and the lives of their children, within months of returning home anyway. Ex-members of the Temple, who presumably felt safe speaking out against Jim Jones and his followers following the disaster, were found shot dead.

Jonestown, having already been looted by locals, was destroyed by fire in the early 1980s.

Siberian Satanist Cult

Incited murder, or suicide?

IN 1996, IN the Russian city of Tyumen in Siberia, 1,400 miles east of Moscow, five young people were found hanged between the months of April and October. Police who investigated the individual deaths at first recorded them simply as suicides – tragic, but arousing no suspicion or cause for any further enquiries. However, when a link began to emerge between the five youths, the cases were re-opened, and a much larger investigation began to take shape.

Scribblings relating to secret and mystical beliefs were found amongst some of the possessions of the suicide victims. Decipherable, these related to an initiation ceremony, the final stage of which was ritual asphyxiation. Although the five youths had not died together, it was firmly believed that the deaths were somehow connected and that they had been involved in a very sinister organisation.

It emerged that this group of five had in fact been friends. Their ages varied, ranging from 17 to 22, but they all assembled together regularly in a basement. The basement, police discovered, contained a satanic altar, and the walls were adorned with signs of the devil, and secret messages which could not be understood.

The fourth of the quintet to die, Sergei Sidorov, had confided in his mother prior to his death that he was involved in something from which he could not escape. He told her that he was a satanist, but that even though he knew it was wrong he could not break out. When the father of Stas Buslov, a friend of Sergei who had died just before him, was informed of the details which were coming to light, he did some research of his own. He discovered that, in the previous year in the Tyumen region, 36 deaths by hanging had been recorded. All were aged between 12 and 22.

Despite having amassed no evidence to confirm that these were the actions of cult members, police believed that the deaths must have been the work of some kind of satanic cult. In March 1997, they launched a search for its leaders. It is rumoured that the head of the cult was a man in his early forties. With the help of two, younger assistants, he is believed to play on the naivety of the innocent, local children, persuading them to join him and his followers. Whether the deaths of the children of Tyumen were acts of murder, or whether their suicides were encouraged, or even demanded, is unlikely ever to be revealed. The police enquiries have so far been unsuccessful and it looks increasingly improbable that the truth will ever be revealed.

SECTION TWO

CULT KILLINGS

Adolfo de Jesus Constanzo

Murder in Matamoros, Mexico

IN 1989, ONLY three months since New Year's Day, 60 people had been reported missing in the region of Matamoros, Mexico. Whether or not this was common knowledge, it would not have deterred the spring-break students of that year who had been planning their holiday, as generations of college-leavers had done for over 50 years before them, in the vice-ridden border town. Matamoros was the obvious choice for the fresh-faced students who had just completed their exams and wanted to party in a town where prostitution, sex-shows, drugs and alcohol were freely available. Matamoros was easily accessible across the Rio Grande from Brownsville in Texas, and so the students, an estimated 250,000 per year, came in their droves. In March 1989, Mark Kilroy was one of the college students to make the same time-honoured journey. Yet, unlike the others, he was never to return.

Mark Kilroy, however, did not simply become the 61st person to go missing. When his disappearance was reported his family demanded action, and his was a family with connections in high places. Immediately, a $15,000 reward was offered for either returning Mark safely to his family, or for information on who was responsible for his disappearance. The US Customs Service, who feared the involvement of Mexico's evil drug traffickers, and the Texas authorities, kept up the pressure on the case in the USA, while in Mexico, the police in Matamoros began to question 127 of the area's known criminals. In spite of trying to extract the required information by way of beating and torturing, the Mexican police were given no leads. It seemed to them that Mark Kilroy had simply 'disappeared'.

OCCULT ACTIVITY

As the search for Mark continued in Mexico, the police were beginning another of their routine drug crackdowns. Knowing that they were not able to permeate the inner circles of the Mexican drug barons directly, the police used roadblocks at border towns to catch those who did the dirty work of passing the drugs from country to country for them. At one such road-block just outside Matamoros, known drug-runner Serafin Hernandez Garcia failed to stop at the police checkpoint and ignored the police who followed him in hot pursuit signalling continuously for him to pull over. The police tailed Garcia until he eventually stopped at a nearby derelict ranch. Inside the property, the police found not only evidence of drugs but also of occult activity.

Garcia and another man, David Serna Valdez, were arrested on drug-related charges, yet their behaviour in custody disturbed the police. Their situation appeared to be of little concern to them, and they claimed that their fate was in the hands of a much higher power which they knew would protect them. Unnerved by the pair's comments, the police returned to the ranch where they spoke to a caretaker who confirmed that the property was used frequently by members of a drug ring run by Garcia's uncle, Elio Hernandez Rivera. On the police's presentation of a photograph, the caretaker also confirmed to them Mark Kilroy had visited the ranch, but just one time.

On receipt of this information, the police returned with no delay to interrogate Garcia in custody. To their surprise, Garcia disclosed further details willingly. He told police that Mark Kilroy had indeed been kidnapped and killed, and that he himself had been involved in his murder. Yet, he didn't describe it as murder but rather as human sacrifice, one of many he claimed, which were performed in order to ensure occult protection over the drug syndicate. He called it their religion, their 'voodoo'. The leader of this group, according to Garcia, was Adolfo de Jesus Constanzo. He was a master of magic and ordered the murders of the victims, first raping them and then making a 'magic stew' from their internal organs and dismembered bodies.

Police needed to amass the evidence, and so took Garcia back to the ranch. He accompanied them willingly and led them straight to the makeshift graveyard where he showed them where to begin digging to uncover the remains of the first of 12 bodies. One of the bodies was that of Mark Kilroy, his skull was split in two, and his brain had been removed. Garcia led police to where they could find the missing brain – floating in a mixture of blood, animal remains and insects in a cauldron located in a nearby shed.

With all the evidence they had collected at the ranch, and Garcia's willingness to assist them with their enquiries, the police were now evaded by only one last detail – the whereabouts of Adolfo de Jesus Constanzo.

ADOLFO DE JESUS CONSTANZO

Adolfo de Jesus Constanzo was born to a Cuban immigrant in Miami in 1962. He had two siblings, and all three children had different fathers. The priest who blessed the infant Adolfo at the age of six months declared to his mother that the child was the chosen one, and destined for great things. The priest was of the Palo Mayombe religion, and blessed the young boy accordingly. Palo mayombe is an African religion, and believes that everything on earth is controlled by the spirits. Accordingly, its followers practise communicating with the spirits in order to control their own fate. It is considered an amoral religion as it allows each worshipper to create his own destiny using either black or white magic and drawing no distinction between the two.

When Adolfo's mother moved her family to Puerto Rico, she kept their Palo Mayombe faith a secret and allowed the San Juan society to believe that her son had been baptized a Catholic. In private however, she was devoted to her faith and began Adolfo's education in witchcraft and magic with fellow followers in both San Juan and Haiti. When they moved back to Miami in 1972, Adolfo began his formal training with a priest in Little Havana.

In school, Adolfo was a poor student. He was far more interested in the secrets of Palo Mayombe and chose to spend his time with his teacher. They went together to dig up graves in order to steal the contents for the sacrificial cauldron known to the religion as a 'Nganga', around which the main worship and practice of palo mayombe is carried out. Adolfo also began to get involved in petty crime, and within a couple of years had been arrested twice for shoplifting. He believed his 'powers' to be increasing though, and his mother and teacher proclaimed him to be developing strong psychic abilities.

Adolfo's faith took a sinister turn in 1983 when he chose Kadiempembe, Palo Mayombe's equivalent of Satan, as his own patron saint and henceforth devoted his life to the worship of evil for profit. Encouraged by his mentor, he carved symbols into his own flesh and declared his soul to be dead. This signified the end of his training.

MAGICAL POWERS

Later the same year, Adolfo took a modelling job in Mexico City and when he wasn't working he went down to the red light district to tell fortunes with tarot cards. He became increasingly popular and developed a reputation as being a clairvoyant and having magic abilities. He attracted supporters and admirers, and took two male lovers from the group who followed him. He did return to Miami when the modelling was over, but he came back to Mexico City the following year. He moved in with his two lovers, and began a profitable career as a fortune teller and cleanser of enemy curses. His services were expensive, and it is recorded that some of his clients paid as much as $4,500 for just one treatment. Adolfo added magical potions to his list of services offered, and used the heads of goats, zebras, snakes and other animals in his costly concoctions.

Ordinary citizens provided Adolfo with a steady and satisfactory income but the real money, he was soon to discover, was to be made from Mexico's drug dealers. They came to him to predict the outcome of larger deals and to forewarn them of police raids. They even paid him for magic which they believed would make them invisible to the police. For the money they were paying him, Adolfo realised that he would have to put on more of a performance than he had been and so his magical ceremonies became all the more elaborate. It was at this time that he began robbing graves of bones to add to his own cauldron.

Adolfo's clientele became more and more high-profile. He even attracted members of the Federal Judicial Police, amongst them the commander in charge of narcotics investigations, and the head of the Mexican branch of Interpol. They were not just convinced by Adolfo's fortune-telling and magic tricks, but revered him as a kind of god – he was their direct link to the spirits. Through his connections in the corrupt Mexican police force, Adolfo became acquainted with more of Mexico's major drugs dealers and his profits began to soar.

HUMAN SACRIFICES

It is not known at what point Adolfo stopped using the remains of those who were already dead, and instead began to make his own human sacrifices. It was, however, a massive drawing card for the drug barons he sought to impress, and his readiness to mutilate and murder both strangers and friends secured him what he believed to be firm connections within the upper echelons of the drug-dealing cartels. He had perhaps got a little carried away. He approached the Caldaza family, whose business and interests he had been closely protecting and nurturing over an entire year, and declared that he and his powers were the sole reason for their success and mere existence. He claimed that he should be granted full partnership in the association accordingly. The Caldaza family was one of the largest and most notorious drug cartels in Mexico, and they refused his presumptuous request.

Adolfo did not take this rejection well. Days later, the head of the family and six of the household disappeared. One week later, police found seven bodies, which had been dumped in the Zumpango River. They had been tortured, mutilated and some parts of the bodies had been removed. In Adolfo's cauldron, these missing fingers, toes, hearts and genitals were bubbling away satisfactorily.

SARA MARIA ALDRETE VILLAREAL

Across the border in Brownsville, Texas, Sara Maria Aldrete Villareal was a conscientious and successful student at the Porter High School. A model pupil according to her teachers, she was encouraged to pursue a college education but she became distracted by the attentions of Miguel Zacharias. They married, but it was not to last and after only five months they had separated.

With her failed marriage behind her, the Mexican-born Sara returned home to her parents' house in Matamoros, but also resumed her academic career and enrolled at Texas Southmost College to study physical education. Once again, she excelled in her chosen field and quickly became one of the college's most out-standing students. She devoted a lot of time to her studies and even commenced part-time work as both an aerobics instructor and a secretary in the college's athletic department. She was so busy that she only went home for weekends and holidays. When she did go home, she spent time with her boyfriend, the drug-dealer Gilberto Sosa, who had close links with the notorious Hernandez family.

The relationship with Sosa brought Sara swiftly to the attention of Adolfo de Jesus Constanzo who had been carefully monitoring Sosa's movements in order to assess his position on the Mexican drug scene, and to evaluate his possible connections. When he spied the tall, athletic and very beautiful Sara, he engineered a meeting.

Adolfo swung his Mercedes into Sara's car as she drove through Matamoros one afternoon in July 1987, choreographing the accident to ensure that he just missed her. He got out of the car, and apologised profusely to Sara. Instantly she was attracted by his good looks and charming manner, and there was clearly a very obvious attraction between them. They became friends, and slowly Adolfo set about destroying her relationship with Sosa. He achieved this by planting doubt in Sosa's mind about Sara's fidelity. Finally, he made an anonymous phone-call to Sosa and informed him that Sara was cheating on him. Despite her protestations of innocence, the jealous Sosa finished with Sara and she turned to Adolfo for comfort.

The pair did embark on a sexual relationship, but Adolfo's homosexuality could not be suppressed, and the physical side of their relationship soon petered out. By the time this happened though, it mattered little to Sara who had, in quite a short time, become completely brainwashed by Adolfo's beliefs and practices. She became fascinated by the occult and discarded her passion for her physical education at college to pursue a deeper interest in magic and witchcraft. To Adolfo she became 'La Madrina', the godmother.

THE HERNANDEZ FAMILY

Sara had retained her links, originally established via Sosa, with the Hernandez family, and Adolfo was keen to exploit them. He predicted that the family would consult Sara over a problem, and that when they did, she was to introduce them to him. It all came to pass.

Adolfo's plan couldn't have been orchestrated at a better time. There was much discontent in the Hernandez family and their position on the drug scene was threatened by heavy competition. Adolfo walked in with the answers to all their problems – magic. For the nominal fee of 50 per cent of their wealth, and their complete compliance with his instructions, Adolfo promised to rid them of their enemies. He would not only dispose of the rival drug dealers, but would do so by sacrificing them to the spirits. This way the spirits would offer safety and protection to the family. He also claimed that by trusting him implicitly, he could make the family members and their employees invisible to the police and resistant to their bullets.

And so the killing began, becoming more blood-thirsty and sadistic with every sacrifice. According to Adolfo, excruciating suffering was fundamental to the beliefs of Palo Mayombe and the more agonising the death, the more pleased the spirits were. When two members of the Hernandez family were abducted by a rival drug gang, and subsequently released unharmed, Adolfo claimed that they had been saved purely by a ghastly torture and sacrifice that he had conducted, and by the family's faith in him and in Palo Mayombe.

Adolfo increased the slaughter, and drug dealers were sacrificed indiscriminately. Adolfo even murdered a 14-year-old member of the Hernandez family, realising too late who the young boy was. There were however, no consequences. Adolfo stole contraband from all the dealers he murdered, and by early 1989 had accumulated 800 kilos of marijuana. He decided to smuggle it into the US, but realising that it was such a big job, knew that he would need a very special sacrifice to ensure a safe journey. Having struggled with a previous sacrifice whom he ended up simply having to shoot, he instructed his followers to go out and bring back someone who would not fight, but who would really scream. They returned with Mark Kilroy.

AFTERMATH OF THE KILROY KILLING

Adolfo did not expect the reaction which the Kilroy murder triggered.

Perhaps society had turned a blind eye to the dark and sinister dealings of the drugs world, and allowed the dealers and henchmen to operate within their own rules. Maybe they felt that those who had suffered such gruesome deaths deserved their fate. But when an innocent college student met with such a violent end, there was silence no longer.

Kilroy's family, with the support of the US and their political connections behind them, demanded that Mark's killer be found. The Mexican police were forced to take action, recognising that by killing an American – and a wealthy, white one at that – Adolfo had this time gone too far. They were going to have to bring him to justice to avoid a disastrously damaging international outcry.

In spite of the fervour building up around him, Adolfo still had to complete his deal on the 800kg of marijuana. He decided that Gilberto Sosa, Sara's former boyfriend, would make the necessary sacrifice. The deed done, he successfully smuggled the drugs across the border.

ADOLFO ON THE RUN

But the net was closing in on Adolfo. Serafin Hernandez Garcia had been arrested by police and had led them to his ranch, where evidence of his sinister and sadistic rituals, and the mutilated corpses of the victims themselves, had been discovered. Showing less faith in the protection of the spirits than his disciple Garcia, Adolfo fled, taking Sara, two male lovers, and a hit man from the Hernandez family with him.

His first thought was to run to Miami, but the authorities knew that this was where his mother lived, and were already looking for him there. So he remained in Mexico City, relying on his followers to hide him for short periods each.

Media attention was on the increase and shocking television shows were aired which detailed the events in Matamoros. These were broadcast internationally. Nationwide sightings of Adolfo and Sara were repeatedly reported but none of them confirmed. The police presence at border controls swelled and everyone was on the look-out for the fugitives, but they were nowhere to be found.

PARANOIA

Adolfo turned to his tarot cards, and in them read betrayal. He became more and more paranoid that his close friends were going to turn him in. He hardly slept, threatened everyone with the power of the spirits, and kept a submachine gun with him at all times. When he saw on the television news of April 22, 1989, that arsonists had burnt his ranch to ashes, and witnessed priests exorcising the remains with holy water, Adolfo flew into a blind fury and destroyed the apartment in which he was hiding.

Two days later, another of Adolfo's disciples was arrested. He, like Garcia, held nothing back when questioned by police and confirmed all the statements they had already received detailing the occult practices at the ranch, and naming Adolfo de Jesus Constanza as the leader, El Padrino.

On April 27, Adolfo moved himself and his elite entourage one last time. Still unable to leave Mexico City, they moved to an apartment on Rio Sena.

Witnessing the daily change in Adolfo and his increasing paranoia, and consequently fearing for her own safety, Sara secretly wrote a note which she threw from the window on to the street below. It read:

Please call the judicial police and tell them that in this building are those that they are seeking. Give them the address, fourth floor. Tell them that a woman is being held hostage. I beg for this, because what I want most is to talk – or they're going to kill the girl.

The note was discovered, but discarded. Its finder believed it to be a joke in very poor taste and thought nothing more of it.

In spite of her failed attempt, Sara did not have much longer to wait. On May 6, police were conducting a routine door-to-door enquiry, looking for information on a missing child, completely unconnected with Adolfo's crimes. They arrived at the building on Rio Sena. Within an hour, Adolfo de Jesus Constanzo lay dead.

SHOOT-OUT

Adolfo had spied the police from his window and lost his nerve, assuming they had come for him. He opened fire, raining bullets down on them. The unsuspecting police very quickly called for help and were instantly joined by their backup. In total, 180 policemen surrounded the building. The shoot-out continued for 45 minutes, until Adolfo realised that he was never going to escape. He gave his gun to the former Hernandez hitman and ordered him to kill him and one of his male lovers. At first, the order was refused, but Adolfo became angry and threatened him with eternal damnation. The gun was fired, and Adolfo slumped to the ground. Police charged into the building, found the two dead bodies, and arrested the three survivors.

SENTENCES FOR THE SURVIVORS

With El Padrino dead, the Mexican authorities turned their attention to the surviving members of Adolfo's cult – the three they had pulled out of the apartment on Rio Sena, and the many who had already been arrested and had happily confessed to participating in the slaughters.

All but Sara Aldrete admitted to their own involvement. She however, claimed that she had been a victim. Her lengthy protestations gave her away though, and instead of clearing her of guilt, they exposed the knowledge she had had of the secret and brutal rituals of the cult. She received a sentence of 62 years from the Mexican courts, and should she ever be released from prison there, then the US authorities are ready to try her for the murder of Mark Kilroy. Over 20 other members of Adolfo's cult were brought to justice – the longest sentence passed was 67 years.

Yet Mexico is still not breathing easy. Many suspicious crimes cannot be explained, and some ritual murders remain unsolved. Former members of Adolfo's cult, including Sara Aldrete, claim that their religion has not reached its conclusion and that Adolfo's practices continue. Mexican authorities believe that Adolfo de Jesus Constanzo was responsible for the majority of the crimes, even some for which they cannot posthumously convict him. They fear though that he didn't commit them all, but that somebody else, who has yet to be identified, did.

The Kirtland Killings

Jeffrey Lundgren and his
Mormon splinter group

JEFFREY DON LUNDGREN was born on May 3, 1950 in the city of Independence, Missouri. The Lundgrens seemed like an average American family in many ways, Jeffrey's father Don went to work whilst his mother, Lois, stayed at home to look after him and his younger brother and keep the house looking presentable.

The family were avid church goers, and like many Independence residents, were part of the local Reorganized Church of Latter Day Saints (RLDS) congregation, which is an off-shoot in between Christianity and Mormonism. The vision statement of the RLDS reads as follows:

We believe that the future belongs to God and that the promise of God's kingdom shall be fulfiled. We have a vision of that kingdom where the name of Jesus Christ is truly honoured, where God's will is done on earth, where the hungry are fed, poverty is alleviated, sinners are repentant, and sin is forgiven. We believe that love is the proper foundation of our relationship with others, that opportunity to grow in the likeness of Christ should be fostered, and that the resources of the world can be managed to respect and preserve their creation and purpose. We have a vision of a time when all evil is overcome and peace prevails. Impelled by this vision, we will be an international community of prophetic vision, faithful to the risen Christ, empowered by hope, spending ourselves courageously in the pursuit of peace and justice.

Although there was nothing extremely unusual about the Lundgrens, and they did try their best to raise a respectable family, it was noted on many occasions that Don Lundgren was an overly authoritative father with many strict rules. He would often severely punish both Jeffrey and his brother for childish pranks that they did not deserve such reprimand for. In comparison Lois Lundgren was quite a distant mother who did not give her sons much maternal love, she was a stand-offish, unapproachable woman whose main priority in her role as the housewife was definitely the home rather than the children.

Jeffrey Lundgren went to a local school and was seen by the majority of his peers as a loner with a pretentious streak. Throughout school nothing much really kept his attention, but through his father he found one hobby that kept his interest – shooting guns. Don had had this pastime for years and when Jeffrey got to his teens Don thought he should share his hobby with his son. They would spend hours together practising target shooting as well as gun maintenance and also hunting and wilderness survival, these were all skills that Don Lundgren thought any respectable American male should have.

Jeffrey managed to graduate from high school, and was accepted on an electrical engineering course at the Central Missouri State University. In his first year at University he met some students that he was able to befriend at the RLDS student house; one person in particular would prove to have a life changing effect on him. This person was Alice Keeler.

A SUITABLE PARTNER

Alice was born on January 21, 1951 in a small town about 20 miles outside of Independence, called Macks Creek. She possessed many similarities to Jeffrey whilst growing up, preferring her local church group to her school and peers. She was the eldest of four siblings and had a relatively happy childhood up until the age of 12 when her father found out he had multiple sclerosis. As her father got weaker so did the family. He was no longer able to provide for them so Alice's mother had to get a job as a secretary at a local firm. This meant that as the oldest child, Alice instinctively took on her mother's role as carer for her three siblings and her infirm father. This misfortune caused her to become even more introverted at school but she managed to stay on top of things with the help of the church youth group which continued to take precedence over school activities. When everything else had crumbled around her, her faith had kept her going.

Despite her problems at home and school, Alice graduated from high school and gained a place at the Central Missouri State University where again she became an active member of the student church youth group. It was here that Jeffrey and Alice first met and it was not long before they became an item.

Alice fell pregnant to Jeffrey in 1969, and to the disappointment of both sets of parents, they dropped out of their university courses. Jeffrey's parents were so enraged by their son's behaviour that they refused to go to the wedding when the couple married the following spring.

Jeffrey needed to start providing for his new family so he signed up to the Navy and was enlisted to serve as an electrical technician. He served four years in this position and by the time he came out on honourable discharge his second son had been born.

The family of four settled in San Diego, California and rekindled their interest in the RLDS. Before long they were strong members of the congregation who spent a lot of their spare time organising and participating in the churches events and making a conscious effort to enlist new members, trying especially hard to convert any friends, old and new, who were of different beliefs.

Things started to take a turn for the worse in the late '70s. Ever since he had left the US Navy, Jeffrey had found it extremely difficult to find a job that would bring in a big enough income to support his ever growing family. He decided to relocate his family back to Independence hoping that finding a job would be easier there, but the job market did not seem to be the problem as whenever Jeffrey did manage to get a job he could not hold it down due to his dream-like, irresponsible personality.

VIOLENT STREAK

When the Lundgrens' third child, Kirsten, was born in 1979 Jeffrey seemed to switch from being annoyingly irresponsible to downright aggressive, and started to abuse his wife and children. It is reported that Alice even needed surgery once after Jeffrey pushed her down a flight of stairs.

In the September of 1980, Alice gave birth to the Lundgrens' fourth child – family and friends have speculated that she became pregnant in order to try and save her rapidly crumbling marriage; to stop the abuse and curb Jeffrey's roaming eye.

TOO LIBERAL

Around this time, in the early '80s, the RLDS was having a spring clean and started to change some of their archaic rules. When, in 1985, they announced that they were going to start allowing women to become ordained as priests, Jeffrey knew it was time to move onto something new. Jeffrey felt disenchanted with these liberal ideologies, and the lay minister desired to return to the fundamentals of the Mormon faith, which among other things, taught women to be submissive to men.

Jeffrey believed that the truth lay somewhere in the Scriptures and even though the RLDS was not going to help him, he would still find the answers. It was not long before a Mormon splinter group had formed, with Jeffrey Lundgren in command and other disillusioned RLDS members as his followers.

Bible teachings and study groups were held regularly at the Lundgren house and soon many of his friends and family moved away from the RLDS and into his arms.

Even though as a boy, Jeffrey had been quite a loner, over the years he had learnt how to come across as confident and this side of his personality was what shone at this time of his life. He had a real way with people and it did not take long for his followers to become convinced that he had uncovered the true meaning of the Scriptures. The strange effect that he had started to have on people even caused some followers to donate money for the upkeep of his family – did this start Jeffrey Lundgren's brain ticking with ideas, or did he think it was God's way of saying thank you?

The sums of money that Lundgren was receiving were helpful but modest, and it wouldn't be long before greed would start to take over.

Lundgren soon declared that God had spoken to him

and told his followers that they needed to move to Kirtland, Ohio to start a revolution. He told his congregation that they were going to do good deeds such as feed the hungry and help the poor, much in the way that Christ had done over 1,500 years previously, and very true to the ideologies of the RLDS. Such positive statements enthralled his followers and they wanted to find out more.

So, in mid August, 1984, the Lundgren family and a handful of followers arrived at the Chapin Forest Country Park, a few miles from the Kirtland Temple.

The Kirtland Temple was built by Joseph Smith Junior, the 1830 founder of the Latter Day Saints in Western New York. The temple started to be built in 1833 after Smith apparently received a revelation from God telling him that a place of worship was to be constructed in Kirtland and it has become a source of history and divinity ever since.

It was in Chapin Forest that Lundgren declared his revelations to his flock, funnily enough they were much like Joseph Smith Junior's revelations, and described how they would have to use the original RLDS temple for a while. Both Alice and Jeffrey managed to get jobs as temple guides, due to their extensive knowledge of the faith. The job gave them a small salary and also free lodgings and meals. This was a perfect set up for the vision that was starting to grow within Lundgren's head as he knew he would be able to use his position to subconsciously pass his views onto the temple visitors, and maybe even sway some more recruits.

THE MAKING OF A LEADER

Slowly, the greed that was growing inside Lundgren started to take over, and he began pilfering from the donations that the church received and from the earnings of the visitor centre, that both he and Alice had easy access to. Nobody suspected that such a religiously moral man would do such a thing, that he got away with daylight robbery. In fact, people were starting to see Lundgren as the opposite to a petty criminal and more like a saint.

Jeffrey restarted his home seminars and bible groups in Kirtland and his group of followers grew quickly. He mesmerised people with his endless knowledge of the Scriptures and his promises of kindness yet to come. In 1984 one of Jeffrey's old navy friends, Kevin Currie, was visiting Kirtland Temple and was surprised to find Lundgren there working as a guide. Currie was be-witched by Lundgren's wisdom and aura that he immediately relocated to Kirtland and moved in with Lundgren's ever increasing flock, Currie even surren-dered his monthly earnings to the Lundgrens cause. More and more people would re-think their lives after going on one of Jeffrey's temple tours, many saw him as a prophet and believed that to get close to God they would have to be close to Lundgren.

Dennis and Tonya Patrick had known Alice and Jeffrey from their days at University and had moved to Kirtland, from Independence with their daughter Molly. Like all the others before them they were so taken aback by Lundgren's teachings that they thought that there was no alternative, even though they did not like the way in which he treated his children – the abuse was continuing – they looked past it, and selfishly thought of themselves.

Throughout the year Lundgren's teachings became more and more extreme and rigid, violence started coming into play, but like many extreme religious groups, balanced thinking gets replaced with abiding by the prophet's rules. Lundgren was by this point seen as the next step from Joseph Smith Junior, and in Mormon terms, you couldn't get much higher on Earth therefore his instructions even surpassed the importance of the Scriptures.

By the end of 1986 Lundgren started claiming to his flock that he had received prophecies from God regarding the end of the world. The prophecy, Lundgren claimed, stated that Jesus would return to Earth and destroy everything except those righteous few who were within the Kirtland Temple. He gave his followers two dates on which this would happen, but each time the date came and went with no avail. So Jeffrey quickly changed his prediction. He stated that his group should take hold of the Kirtland Temple on May 3, 1988, conveniently enough this date was also Lundgren's birthday.

It was around this time that member Kevin Currie decided enough was enough and left the group as he could no longer handle the teachings of Lundgren. The rest of the congregation started to prepare for the day of the siege. Lundgren ordered his flock to wear military style uniforms, they had to march everywhere and were trained, just as Jeffrey had been by his own father, to load, unload and fire guns proficiently. They regularly practised combat tactics and watched violent Vietnam style war films in order to psyche themselves up for the main event. Lundgren had them believe that they were the good people of the world fighting a true and just cause of worldly evil.

In 1987 a family that Lundgren had known from his religious seminars in Independence, the Averys, moved to Kirtland in order to join the Lundgren cause. Jeffrey had never liked the family but upon their arrival in Kirtland he could not do enough for them, he knew too well that they had collateral from the sale of their house and once he had convinced them that he would care for them like he would his own family, they donated $10,000 of their savings to him. They were convinced that it would make them better off in the future as surely giving up such a huge amount of money to such a saintly person would make them slightly more god-like themselves?

Lundgren had become so obsessed with his personal plight that it was not surprising when officials from the RLDS started to question his practices and went as far as to annul all the religious titles that he held. This angered Lundgren and he immediately cancelled his membership of the church, left his job, and moved into a large farmhouse property that would soon house both his family and many of his followers. They settled on their 15-acre farm and prepared for the day that they would meet God, which in turn would be their final day on planet Earth.

At the beginning of September, Kevin Currie the member who had left, decided he had made the wrong decision and reinstated himself as a member of Lundgren's clan. Currie had felt extreme guilt after leaving the first time and decided to return and this time not listen to the part of his consciousness that was questioning Lundgren's authenticity.

Throughout the latter part of 1987, Lundgren managed to stock pile a vast amount of ammunition and weaponry which his eldest son, Damon, was in charge of. Jeffrey Lundgren's children had been part of their father's ever growing strangeness since birth, they did not know a different life, to them their father spoke the truth and it was the only one they knew.

At the beginning of 1988 Kevin Currie once again left the group, this time for good, as he could not get certain quirks of Lundgren's out of his head. All Currie had wanted was to be a godly righteous man, but as Lundgren's teachings went on he became more and more disillusioned by them and his mind had stayed strong enough to break out while he still could. Currie wanted to make a clean break, but Lundgren's strange ways kept playing on his mind, so much so that he filed a report to the Federal Bureau of Investigation. The FBI just presumed that it was a hoax, and if not a hoax a minor problem that could be sorted by the local authorities so they passed the information onto Kirtland police department. The police chief immediately started investigating Lundgren and his group as he had a feeling that it was much more than a hoax.

Lundgren had no idea that an investigation had started on him, but he was extremely angry that Currie had walked out for a second time, this anger was to build when a lady by the name of Shar Lea Olsen also decided to leave. Shar had joined the group in 1987 after she had spent the weekend in Kirtland visiting a couple of friends who were already solid group members. She had been extremely impressed by Lundgren and had wanted to learn more. But by the time Shar left she had a rather different view of Lundgren and his enlightenments. She had wanted to leave for many months before she finally did so but had become so scared for her life that it took her time to build up the courage to make the final break.

THE SHOW GOES ON

Jeffrey Lundgren may have lost two of his followers but he still had many more who were willing to do anything for him and follow his every instruction. By the autumn of 1988 Lundgren was holding lengthy scripture lectures that would last well into the night, he got into the habit of wearing military combat gear during his lectures and kept a loaded gun at his side. His scripture lectures became more and more violent and he translated the meanings for his own purpose. Anything he didn't like about his flock he would bring to their attention in the following lecture and say that the Scripture stated that it was a sin.

The main promise that kept his flock so obeying was that Lundgren had sworn that they would get to see God. Over the months Lundgren started to analyse this promise and decided that God would be so angry with the sins of man when he returned to Earth that the Kirtland group would be at his mercy. This did not bode well, so to rectify this Lundgren amended his divine forecast. He told his followers that he had had another vision which told him that he needed to sacrifice the Avery family in order to save the rest of them. Lundgren demonstrated this by claiming that Dennis Avery was dismissive and did not listen to his teachings, Cheryl Avery was too obstinate to be virtuous and their children were uncontrollable. All these signs, Lundgren told his flock, showed that they were sinners who should be sacrificed for the good of the rest of them. Lundgren's flock did not question his statements, in fact now Lundgren had mentioned it, they too could see what sinners the Averys were – sinners who deserved to be punished. In Lundgren's warped mind, killing the Averys in the name of God was the only sensible thing to do.

SACRIFICE

By the beginning of April 1989, a plan for the demise of the Averys started to come together. Lundgren instructed that a pit should be dug in one of the farm's outbuildings which would conceal the bodies. Lundgren told his flock that it was imperative that the murders happen and once they had they would all abandon the farmhouse and reform at a new venue. At the same time he informed the Averys to pack up their belongings and told them that they were all going on a pilgrimage.

A motel room was booked for the Averys and all their belongings were brought from their rented accommodation to the farm house. They suspected nothing, Lundgren had so many rules and regulations that anything was possible.

On April 17, 1989 the group prepared for what would be their final meal together. After dinner the Averys' fate became real. Once Dennis Avery seemed to be deep in concentration in whatever he was doing, Lundgren gathered five of his right hand men in his bedroom. He produced a pistol from his belt and asked for a show of hands to confirm that the men were all in allegiance with him, and they were. So the plan, that unbeknown to the Averys had been discussed over the previous few weeks started to be put into action. They had decided that the best way to do it would be to lead the family one by one into the barn and kill them separately, and this is what they did.

First to meet their fate was Dennis Avery. Ron Luff, who was seen by Lundgren as one of his most righteous brothers, someone who never questioned his teachings, walked out of the barn and back into the house. He went over to Dennis and asked for his assistance in the barn to help with packing the equipment for the subsequent pilgrimage that they were about to embark on. Dennis, of course agreed, and why wouldn't he? He followed Ron into the barn where they were met by Richard Brand, Danny Kraft, Greg Winship, Jeffrey's son Damon and of course Jeffrey himself. As soon as Dennis got close to his comrades his was shot at by a stun gun. The desired effect of this was to silence him but the stun wasn't strong enough and instead he cried out in pain and then in mercy as it was now obvious to him that the end of his life was close.

The five men grabbed Dennis, bound his arms and gagged his mouth with duct tape, and threw him into the ready made grave. Greg, who was now outside, was given the signal to start the chain saw in order to muffle the sound of things to come, whilst Jeffrey took aim. Two shots were fired straight into Dennis's back and the chain saw stopped. The men stood in silence and one by one filed into the area of the barn where Dennis's body now lay in a blood stained crumpled heap, and took stock of the gruesome murder they had all been involved in. A few contemplative moments later Ron left the barn and made his way back up to the barn to collect the second victim.

Cheryl Avery, Dennis's wife, was pottering around when Ron reached her, completely oblivious to the fact that Dennis was lying dead in a shallow grave a few metres from where she was standing.

Ron told Cheryl that Dennis needed her help in the barn packing their bags, again it was an extremely normal request, so she immediately accompanied Ron back to the barn. As they entered, Cheryl was met with the stun gun which for the second time did not have desired effect, she was in pain but still totally conscious and aware. Unlike her husband, Cheryl did not scream or beg for her life, she just slid down onto her knees whilst she was bound with the tape. Ron and Richard dragged her over to the pit where her husband lay and threw her in, at the same time Greg started the chain saw. Ron and Richard then stepped out of the room and Jeffrey prepared to take a second life. He fired three shots, two hit Cheryl on the right side of her chest and the other hit her in the stomach. Like her husband she was dead in an instant.

After this murder, there was no time to stand around looking at the aftermath, as Jeffrey was worried that the shots may have been heard, so he ordered the men to check the area. Everything was done in the style of a commando operation; quickly and quietly. Once the men were sure that they had not been heard, Jeffrey instructed Ron to go back to the house for a third time to get the first of the Avery children.

The three daughters had been sitting in the living room playing computer games and discussing the next day's trip, a couple of the females who were part of the plan were with them in order to make sure they didn't stray. Ron entered the living room and asked Tina Avery to accompany him. The 15-year-old followed Ron into the barn and stood completely still, in complete shock and confusion as the men bound her. A few minutes later and she was lying in a pit with her dead mother and father. Jeffrey Don Lundgren, still completely calm and in control pulled the trigger for a sixth time and the bullet shaved past the top of Tina's skull. She attempted a muffled scream of pain but moments later she was shot again, this time the bullet went directly into her skull. Tina Avery had met the same fate as her parents, callously murdered in cold blood.

The men were now possessed, no human remorse was apparent on that day, whether or not guilt was being felt inside may never be known. Lundgren and his flock continued with their task. Next on the hit list was 13-year-old Rebecca Avery. Ron re-entered the living room and asked Rebecca and her younger sister Karen if they wanted to see the horses. Ron said that they could only go one at a time so as not to scare them. Karen waited with the women as her older sister was escorted by Ron back to the barn.

Once in the barn the men pretended they were playing a game and picked her up and bound her. They lowered her into the blood-spattered pit and she was placed on top of her dead mother. For the fourth time that evening Greg powered up the chain-saw, the routine was well rehearsed now, it was automatic. Jeffrey fired the gun and the bullet pierced her thigh. A second shot was fired which hit Rebecca in the chest. She was left spluttering for her life. Jeffrey never fired a compassionate shot to put her out of the pain she was in so Rebecca Avery was left to die a slow, painful and lonely death.

So with four out of five sacrifices complete, Ron went back to the house for the last surviving member of the

Avery family. Six-year-old Karen Avery was so excited about seeing the horses that she jumped up onto Ron's back and was given a piggy back ride to her fate. The same routine took place and after Jeffrey Lundgren had fired two shots their mission was complete. All five members of the Avery family were now lying in a heap in the make-shift grave. Lundgren ordered a couple of the men to smother the bodies with a lime solution and then cover them with dirt. Afterwards, bin bags were placed on top of them and the job was complete. The men made their way back to the farm house.

Whilst the murders had taken place, Alice Lundgren had left the compound with the younger children. After confirming that the job had been done she returned. Soon after, Alice went with son Damon and husband Jeffrey to the motel where some of the Avery belongings had been stashed, and removed them. Upon their return Jeffrey called the rest of the group into the classroom for a late night prayer meeting. There was silence throughout the class and it is reported that Richard Brand was the only one brave enough to speak. He believed that no one deserved to die in the way that the Averys just had. Lundgren was quick to give an explanation for the events stating that it was God's will that it had happened.

After what must have been quite a disturbed night's sleep, the group prepared for their departure from the farmhouse. Lundgren ordered them to split up into smaller groups, leave at intervals, and meet up in Pennsylvania for further instructions.

The group did this, they were extremely fearful of their leader now, but also of their fellow members, no one knew who could be trusted, therefore any angst was not relayed to the others. Lundgren finally found a well-hidden campsite in West Virginia that they were ordered to make base for the next few weeks, he loved the new power he now had over his flock and adored being feared. He often boasted to members of the group who had not witnessed the massacre, about the events of that horrid night; Lundgren was indestructible.

Back in Kirtland, the police officer who had been contacted by the FBI after Kevin Currie had left Lundgren's group for a second time, was doing a routine patrol past the farmhouse the day after the murders when a ghostly shiver travelled up and down his spine. Deputy Ron Andolsek noticed that the farmhouse was deserted and he thought to himself that it was odd that the group had just suddenly disappeared. But there was not much he could do as they had not, he thought, done anything wrong. Little did he know that a family of five were laying murdered in a shallow grave within one of the barns on the farmhouse's land.

With the soldierly base camp now up and running in West Virginia, Lundgren embarked on a tough regime. There was round the clock guard duty and Lundgren instructed the men of the group to shoot down anybody or anything that came towards them, they even had an anti-aircraft sub-machine gun for use if helicopters were to attack. Jeffrey Don Lundgren was at his most paranoid and at his most vicious, and by August 1989 his teachings had become as extreme as his personality, he even ordered that the men surrendered their wives to him so that they could be cleansed and purified by his godly seed.

On October 13, 1989, Lundgren decided that it was time for his flock to move on. He knew that a friend of one of his women had an empty barn just outside of Chilhowee, Missouri that they had been given permission to use temporarily. The group stayed there for around ten days before Lundgren decided that they should all split up for the winter, get jobs, save their salaries, meet back up in the spring and pass their earnings over to him.

Was Lundgren now scared that he was going to get found out for what he had done? Was he worried that his flock were about to turn on him? Did he really think that after the winter break his flock would still be willing to return to their master?

The winter parting was the moment a few of Lundgren's trustee members had been waiting for. It was their chance to escape from Jeffrey's throws without any worries. Richard Brand and Greg Winship, both of whom had been heavily involved in the April massacre, had started to see the past few months from a new perspective, they could no longer live with the past or live with a future at the hands of Lundgren and his teachings. The two men left camp at the end of October and were followed closely after by Ron Luff and two of the women, Sharon Bluntschly and Kathy Johnson, who were both carrying Lundgren's children.

By December, Jeffrey was starting to panic, realization hit him that many of his members were probably glad to be out of his clutches and may even feel the need to confess to either friends or the police about their lives under the rule of him. The Lundgren family and a few others decided to move on to California, where they would lay low and see if any investigation arose. Lundgren stored all his weapons and ammunition in a safety deposit box and waited.

On December 31, 1989 Keith Johnson was crushed, the guilt that had been building up inside him since April had finally exploded and he decided that he needed to inform the police about Jeffrey Lundgren and the murders that had taken place. He told the Kansas police everything about life under Lundgren's regime and gave detailed accounts of each of the five murders, ending his confession by drawing a map of where the bodies were buried. The map was immediately faxed over to the FBI department in Cleveland. The FBI agent who received the fax, did not for a minute believe what he was reading and thought it would be a waste of the bureau's time if they were to investigate the report. Instead, the FBI passed the telephone number of Kirtland police department onto Kansas police department. Thankfully the Chief of Police in Kirtland, Dennis Yarborough took the matter as serious, he knew that his Deputy, Ron Andolsek, had been commenting on the oddities of Lundgren and his flock for months now and appointed him the task of tracking down the Avery family – why they did not go straight to the barn as drawn on the map, is another matter altogether.

After a few days of speaking to friends and family members of the Averys, it became apparent that there had been no sight or sound of them for months. Cheryl Avery's mother, Donna Bailey, had always received letters from her daughter but they had recently stopped. Deputy Adolsek took this as a sign that a search of the farm needed to take place. He gained permission from the farmhouse owner and on January 3, 1990, both Adolsek and Yarborough made their way to the farmhouse that had been the Lundgrens home for over a year. With the map in hand that Johnson had sketched, the police officers made their way to the barn and could never have been ready for what they were about to encounter.

The first thing that hit the Chief and his Deputy was the putrid smell of decay, there is nothing quite like the smell of rotting flesh. When they reached the area marked on the map it did not take long for the policemen to work out what they had uncovered. They were standing next to the grave of the Avery family. The two men immediately called for back up and also requested the service of the fire brigade to help with the excavation.

Although they had been briefed on the situation, the firemen were not quite ready for the smell that rapidly got worse as they started to dig. The smell got so bad that many officers had to leave the barn and were violently sick. The ones that carried on were met with murky brown water with what looked like flesh floating on the top. After a few minutes they unearthed the first body which was less than a metre under the ground and there was now no getting away from what they had found. The FBI were called and this time they had to take the call seriously. They began an intensive search of the barn and the rest of the buildings.

It wasn't long before the horrific news was broadcasted over TV stations across the world and slowly members of Lundgren's flock came forward and gave themselves up, maybe hoping that it would help them get a lesser sentence.

Steven Tourette, a county prosecutor, was given the Avery murder case, and the more information that came in regarding the murders the more disgusted he became. There was no way he was going to let anybody involved in the crime get an easy ride. He immediately obtained arrest warrants for the 13 adults within the Lundgren clan and within hours Ron Luff, Susan Luff, Dennis Patrick, Tonya Patrick and Deborah Olivarez were at Jackson County Jail for questioning. It didn't take long for Sharon Bluntschly, Richard Brand and Greg Winship to give themselves up, but there were still five members at large; Kathy Johnson, Danny Kraft and the Lundgrens – Alice, Damon and Jeffrey.

MEXICO AND FREE?

Jeffrey was smart, if he made it to the Mexican border he would be free, whether it was the guilt that was making him run or if this was still part of God's master plan is anybody's guess, but he was determined not to get caught.

But Jeffrey was too trusting, he called his mother-in-law on January 5, 1990 and told her to go to California in order to collect her grandchildren. He gave her a phone number of where he could be contacted. Alice's mother agreed implicitly to his request but as soon as she was off the phone she contacted the police. The FBI traced the phone number to a Californian motel just six miles from the Mexican border. Jeffrey Don Lundgren was six miles from heaven.

The Ohio FBI agent in charge of the case flew south immediately as he wanted to be there when the arrest was made. Local Californian agents surrounded the motel and as soon as they spotted him they pounced – Jeffrey Don Lundgren was arrested on five accounts of murder. It was a much smoother arrest than it could have been as when they searched his motel room and safety deposit box they found a small arsenal, which they did not doubt that Lundgren would have used if he had been given the chance.

They also found Alice Lundgren, Damon Lundgren and the younger children all sitting in the motel room watching television awaiting their master's return. As soon as Damon saw the FBI he immediately told them that he hadn't done the shooting.

Compassion has to be felt for somebody like Damon, from a baby he had lived and learned from his father, but was also scared of his father due to years of abuse. How was he ever to know the real right and wrong, it is up to parents or guardians to nurture children into loving human beings and to teach them the ways of the world. All Damon had done was to obey his father but in the eyes of the law Damon Lundgren was as much at fault as every other group member over the age of 18. As an adult, law believes that Damon should have been able to work out the real right and wrong for himself.

With the three Lundgrens now under arrest there were just two more suspects at large. Danny Kraft and Kathy Johnson were found five days later on a San Diego motorway travelling south in Danny's pick-up truck. There was no chase, no fight, they knew it was now over.

IN THE COURT ROOM

The following months saw trial after trial as one by one the 13 religiously devout men and women stood up and took their oath to tell the truth, the whole truth and nothing but the truth so help them God.

By January 1991 they had all been sentenced. Sentences ranged from 18 months probation for obstruction of justice for Tonya and Dennis Patrick to five death sentences for Jeffrey Lundgren. Damon Lundgren was found guilty of four out of the five murders but his life was saved from death row after the jury heard statements from his friends and family, instead he was given 20 years to life for each of the four murders.

Alice Lundgren was sentenced to ten to 20 years for five accounts of kidnapping and 20 years for complicity to commit murder on five counts, with all sentences having to be served consecutively.

So, how could it have come to this, 12 people all with compassionate hearts ended up being part of killing five innocent people, including three little girls. How could 12 people who would have at one time never let such a thing happen, be twisted into believing that it was a call of God – an event that had to take place? Jeffrey Lundgren had scared them or brainwashed them into a new way of thinking and by the time the murders took place there was no free-thinking left, anything view or thought that came into those 12 people's heads had passed through Jeffrey Lundgren's mind first where it had taken on a different form.

And what about Jeffrey Don Lundgren? In a five-hour long statement, which he issued during his penalty phase, Lundgren declared that he: 'considered [himself] a prophet and through interpretation of the scriptures, God had told him that the Avery family were to be killed'. To this day whilst on death row Jeffrey Don Lundgren is still writing letters to anybody willing to read them stating his reasoning behind the murders and giving biblical proof for his actions.

TRYING TO UNDERSTAND

Ten years after the murders, in April 1999, some of Lundgren's flock opened up to the Cleveland Plain Dealer – Ohio's largest newspaper – and reported that they actually felt freer in prison than the whole time they had spent under Lundgren's grasp. One woman in paticular feels this a lot, and that is Susan Luff. She believes that she was deceived by both Lundgren and her husband Ron, who was the leader's right-hand man. Susan Luff insists to this day that she did not understand what was going on due to being so mentally brainwashed by her life in the cult. Now, in prison, she is once a again a free-thinker with no worries of death threats or abuse. She can also contact her friends and family whenever she likes, can study new subjects and can pray when she wants to, not when dictated to. In the Plain Dealer article on April 11, 1999, she was quoted as saying:

You see, there are no guns here, no death threats, and no one can even be verbally abusive here . . . I do not want to just be a survivor, I'm doing everything I can here to give back to society.

So how can these 'survivors' keep their faith after such a traumatic experience at the hands of religion? Why did God not strike Lundgren down when he saw what sins were taking place?

Ron Luff believes that he has to start his religion from the beginning again and re-learn everything he thought he already knew:

God had become so ugly I couldn't go any further, I just kind of had to take everything that I ever thought I knew about Scripture and put it completely out of my mind and start over.

It seems that the need for a spiritual presence in some people's lives is so strong that they stick with it even when it comes crashing down. Maybe their strong requirement for religion is the reason that they get so easily get caught up with in such destructive groups in the first place? People are made to feel special when they join such a group, recruits think they are about to be part of something remarkable, something worthy of a new sacred text.

If someone convinces you that they are the living prophet, spoken about in the religious text that you abide by, it is very difficult to shun that person away. It is a catch-22 situation, you can either follow the prophet's every word, even if it means murdering innocent people, or you can detach yourself from the cause but face the risk of being deemed a sinner on judgement day.

And what about the Averys? They were just as much in agreement with Jeffrey Lundgren as the rest of the flock. They were willing to watch his children be abused, they gave Lundgren a vast share of their life savings, they bought guns and ammunition to use against anyone who tried to stop them. If Lundgren had chosen another family to sacrifice who is to say that they would not have participated in the slayings? Of course, this will never be known, but they were just as much part of a brain washed flock as the rest of them.

Although another theory is that the Averys were about to leave the cult as they had become disenchanted with Lundgren's teachings. In doing so they would have become a real threat to Lundgren as other members could have been provoked into following suit.

Nobody will ever know if Lundgren was just a con-man who indoctrinated his followers, or a dilluded man who really believed what he was preaching.

Either way, Jeffrey Don Lundgren managed to get on side 12 intelligent, stable people who all played their part in committing five murders. Of course they are all victims, even Lundgren, if he is in fact mentally deranged, but three completely innocent children were killed that night, children who were not yet at an age to make any decisions for themselves. Their parents had taken them – unintentionally – into an unsafe environment in which they never got to live a true life. Is fanatical religion really worth that?

Aum Shinrikyo

The Aum Supreme Truth
Terrorist Organisation

CHIZUO MATSUMOTO HAD one ambition in life and that was to be rich. As the fourth son of a poor weaver, he had very little as a child. Times were hard for the family and they scraped together enough to be able merely to exist. Therefore, from a young age, growing up in southern Japan in the 1950s, Chizuo dreamt of being wealthy and having money to spend.

The young Chizuo also suffered from infantile glaucoma, a condition he had had since birth, rendering him blind in his left eye and only partially sighted in his right. To add to the misery of poverty, Chizuo was teased mercilessly for his disability and eventually his parents moved him to a government-funded school for the blind.

ROLE REVERSAL

The tables quickly turned and where Chizuo had suffered at the hands of the bullies in his former school, he now found himself, the only student with partial sight in a blind school, in a position of power which he exploited to the full. He dominated the other children and bullied them into doing whatever he told them to. His limited vision began to work in his favour financially too, and he would assist the other students in various tasks, but only if the price was right. The quest for money dominated his school life, and his reputation steadily worsened. So scared were the other children though, that nobody stood up to Chizuo and his behaviour was allowed to continue. By the time Chizuo graduated, a successful student with good grades and a black belt in judo, he had extorted a sum in the region of $30,000 from his fellow classmates.

With a good academic record behind him and a confidence gained by the standing he had achieved at his school (albeit a reign of fear rather than respect), Chizuo's attention turned to his career. He again aimed high and declared his intention to become Prime Minister of Japan. To achieve this he planned to study at the prestigious Tokyo University, but he was dealt a crushing blow when his application was rejected. This affected him very badly, and he returned to his home town embittered and angry.

He did not stay down long though, and within a couple of months he made his way back to Tokyo. Here he settled down quite quickly. He met and married Tomoko, an intelligent college student and they began to have children together. She steadied the impulsive

Chizuo, and together they began to plan a joint business – an acupuncture clinic to be run primarily by Chizuo. To help the young, newlywed couple achieve their goals, Tomoko's family invested money in the venture.

THE CLINIC

An instant success, the clinic began to make money immediately. An average three-month course of herbal remedies and yoga techniques would set one of Chizuo's clients back by around $7,000. And the reason the money rolled in so quickly? Chizuo was spending next to nothing on his 'miracle cures'. Far from the expensive herbal remedies he claimed to be selling, his medicines were knocked up in minutes. One was proved to be nothing more than alcohol-soaked tangerine peel. The scam came to light eventually and a fine of $1,000 was imposed upon the clinic. Chizuo hardly noticed, having made almost $200,000 already.

So it seemed that Chizuo was on course to realize the dreams of wealth and prosperity that he was only able to imagine as a child. Yet, he was not entirely satisfied. He told Tomoko that his life needed meaning, and he began to study religion, fortune telling and meditation. After long periods of meditation, an enlightened Chizuo claimed that he had the gift to 'see' people's auras and that he could identify evil. He decided that this new-found spirituality was the new course his life was going to take.

In this pursuit, he began to research both established faiths and unorthodox sects and cults. He encountered hundreds, but decided that an essentially Buddhist sect called Agonshu was most suited to his calling. In order to gain admission into the Agonshu, Chizuo enthusiastically began the 1,000-day training period of daily, lengthy meditation. However, it was a somewhat different and cynical Chizuo who completed this period of training, and he consequently turned away from Agonshu claiming that it had destroyed his peace of mind.

AUM ASSOCIATION OF MOUNTAIN WIZARDS & SHOKO ASAHARA

After such disappointment, in spite of his extensive research into the many religions and sects of Japan, Chizuo decided that he would have to establish his own sect and subsequently founded the Aum Association of Mountain Wizards, officially Aum Incorporated. To finance this sect, Chizuo returned to making and selling his dubious herbal remedies.

A trickle of recruits initially registered for Aum yoga classes, but following a carefully placed advert in the *Twilight Zone* magazine which showed Chizuo levitating through meditation, members began to enrol in their hundreds. Soon Aum was receiving enough money to open schools nationwide, and Chizuo's reputation as a caring and gentle spiritual leader was spreading.

Whilst on one of the spiritual retreats, which Chizuo found himself more and more at liberty to enjoy now that he could afford to leave the running of his schools in the capable hands of his deputies, he met a companion who informed him that Armageddon was imminent and that only a race pure in spirit could survive. As his friend spoke, Chizuo realized that this was the calling he had been waiting for. He was the chosen one, and he would lead this race to salvation. He returned back to his following, and declared that it was up to them to save the world. He also changed his name, to Shoko Asahara, as Chizuo Matsumoto was too plain a name for the saviour of their civilisation.

Shoko Asahara embraced this vocation with enormous energy and enthusiasm, travelling far and wide to spread his word and to meet other spiritual groups with whom he could ally. His followers were whole-heartedly supportive, and new recruits joined his school daily. An opportune photo with the Dalai Lama on a trip to India furthered his cause as he claimed that he had been selected by the Dalai Lama to reveal the true teachings of Buddha to the people of Japan. He was chosen in this mission, he said, as he had been given the mind of a Buddha.

Asahara came back and made personal appearances, wrote a book, and held classes in how to improve spiritual powers. Those who saw him came away convinced of the amazing results and talked wildly of how he had helped them to reveal their untapped potential. Realizing his own potential, Shoko Asahara soon declared that in fact he was closing down the Aum Association of Mountain Wizards, and opening instead the Aum Supreme Truth. What had begun as a simple yoga school which cultivated psychic ability was to become a global religion.

AUM SUPREME TRUTH

The most fundamental conviction of the Aum Supreme Truth, was its belief in the forthcoming Armageddon and the absolute certainty that only those who achieved spiritual enlightenment through the teachings of Shoko Asahara could survive the ever-nearing disaster. The payments flooded in from Japanese citizens who wanted to hear and learn from the teachings of Shoko Asahara and in so doing, safeguard their place when the day of reckoning came.

As Asahara's power and influence spread even further, so his already-slipping grasp on reality began to fade into oblivion. He was no longer just taking money from those who came to hear him preach but, for extortionate sums, offering them the chance to partake in ceremonies such as drinking his blood, which had magical powers, and selling them vials of his used bath water, or clippings of his body hair.

The membership figures for Aum Supreme Truth in Japan had reached 1,500 by the end of 1987, and a new office was opening in America, entitled Aum USA.

Joining fees, annual 'course costs', and all the additional donations offered by the faithful ensured that Shoko Asahara's mission could keep on expanding. In 1988, in a location at the foot of Mount Fuji, the live-in head-quarters of the Aum Supreme Truth was constructed. Here, for a fee of $2,000 per week, followers came to listen to Shoko Asahara, receive one meal a day, sleep on the floor, be encouraged to join Aum, and sever any contact with any non-members, be they friends or family. The 'truly faithful' even moved in permanently, offering up their savings, their estates, and all their material possessions to the greater good of Aum and Shoko Asahara.

REJECTION

The only disadvantage of Aum's ever-increasing wealth was the taxation levied upon it, so Shoko Asahara tried to register Aum with official religious status which would mean that he would be awarded substantial tax relief. At first the application was rejected. The status was only granted to religious groups which were run according to certain guidelines and word had spread about Aum separating parents from their children and punishing rule-breaking with food and sleep deprivation. Under the Japanese Religious Corporation Law therefore, Aum was not worthy of the concessions. The rejection infuriated Shoko Asahara and he consequently set his followers the task of hounding government officials, making threatening phone calls and writing threatening letters. When Asahara involved lawyers, who claimed that the officials were in violation of the religious freedom laws, the application was finally accepted and the heavy taxes alleviated.

UNWANTED PRESS ATTENTION

Although a success for Aum, the debacle had drawn unwelcome attention from the press, and several newspapers began to write about the twisted religion of the Aum Supreme Truth. When the editor of one such newspaper, faced with a furious Shoko Asahara and a group of his followers, refused to withdraw his article, a hate campaign was launched against him, his family and his place of work. When the poor editor suffered a fatal stroke, Shoko Asahara was pleased and believed that heaven had had its vengeance for the defamatory articles.

More and more people began to object to the practices of the Aum Supreme Truth, yet the authorities felt helpless to intervene. So sensitive was the new-found religious freedom on which Japan now prided itself that they simply could not be seen to be suppressing any kind of religious group, even though accusations of cult activities had been made against the organisation.

It was not only the weak-willed and easily led individuals of society who found guidance in Aum. Brilliant scientists, physicists and engineers also succumbed to the enchantment of Aum and the charisma of its leader. This empowered Shoko Asahara, and made Aum Supreme Truth all the more dangerous.

It was not only the outside world who were becoming uneasy about the activities of this ever-expanding cult. Inside the compound, disillusion was creeping in and a few members who felt that they had not achieved the spiritual enlightenment which they had been promised, began to voice their concerns. These 'dissenters' were summoned to the master and told that their irrational apprehension was caused by mental instability, all the more reason to stay with Aum and become stronger. Those who did not return to the fold, and declared their wish to leave Aum completely, were never seen again.

When the families of these victims tried to contact their loved ones and were told time and time again that they were in 'training', they turned to the police. Yet, although the police were being forced by the ever-mounting complaints about the cult to investigate further, they were still not taking the appropriate action, and therefore the friends and families sought legal support.

TSUTSIMI SAKAMOTO

One man, a lawyer who specialized in human rights and who, having taken on a similar case with the Moonies, had previous experience with cults, took on the case of one family who were trying to get their daughter back. Word soon spread though and before long, Tsutsimi Sakamoto was representing 23 families who wanted Shoko Asahara to release their children.

The further Sakamoto delved into the activities of the Aum Supreme Truth, the more resistance he met, and the more lies he heard. A committed family man himself, this only made him more determined. He made a claim for the families' rights to have proper access to their children, a request which met with the offer of letting one of his clients see their daughter. This was not good enough for Sakamoto and he fought for the same response for all of his clients. He went further, representing a former member of Aum, who had paid $7,000 to drink the magical, power-giving blood of Shoko Asahara, and having noticed no difference as a result wanted his money back. It could not be proved, he claimed, that the blood had magical properties, and he demanded to see the medical report which stated otherwise.

When the media heard of Sakamoto's involvement and interviewed him, wherein he announced that Aum had imprisoned its members against their will and under false pretences, all negotiations between him and Aum ceased. Shoko Asahara tried to damage Sakamoto's reputation, sending out flyers which made false allegations against him and threatening him and his family. Sakamoto refused to be intimidated and fought back even harder.

Realizing the potential problem he was now facing in terms of negative press attention and the possible revocation of his tax exemption, Shoko Asahara decided that ultimately and simply, he had to be rid of this man. A lethal poison was created, and injected by Asahara's henchmen, who had broken into the family home in the middle of the night, into the veins of Sakamoto, his wife, and his baby son. The bodies were brought back to the Aum site, where Shoko Asahara inspected them with pleasure, and they were then driven away and dumped in different locations miles from the Aum Supreme Truth.

It did not take long for colleagues and family members to notice Sakamoto's absence. They went to the lawyer's home and a search of the interior revealed a badge showing the insignia of the Aum Supreme Truth. The police were contacted immediately but on hearing of the possible involvement of Aum, they refused to pursue the matter, claiming that Sakamoto may even have staged his disappearance and planted the badge in order to frame Aum. Media coverage and consequent public interest however, forced them to open some enquiries, but after Shoko Asahara held a press conference in which he denied any responsibility and claimed that over 40,000 of those badges had been produced (in reality only 100 were made), both the media and the police strangely lost interest.

ELECTION CAMPAIGN

Despite the euphoria of getting away with this hideous crime and also of having been able to crush any attempt to upset the balance and the carefully controlled conditions of Aum, Shoko Asahara was becoming increasingly paranoid. Perhaps encouraged by his apparent invincibility, he had decided to run for parliament. The move, was generally viewed as ridiculous. Aum's policies were contradictory, their budget extortionate, their canvassing intimidating, and their campaigning – hundreds of Asahara's followers parading through the streets wearing masks depicting the face of their leader – bizarre. Unsurprisingly, they were unsuccessful. Added to this humiliating defeat, their practices were still being questioned.

FAILED REVENGE

He decided to lash out at a world which he believed to be mocking him, and instructed the scientists in the group to begin manufacturing weapons. After careful research, they reported back to him that chemical warfare would be the most effective. What's more, they could be created in their own laboratories.

The first attempt was a dismal failure. Asahara's scientists worked away for weeks in Aum's bio-labs and eventually produced clostridium botulinum, the most lethal and fast-acting poison in existence. Asahara gathered his followers together and took them to the safety of a faraway island, while the team in charge of unleashing this poison on Tokyo began equipping a truck with a spraying device. The attack was to be centred on the parliament buildings, partly for revenge, and partly so that when all the country's leaders and government officials had died, the path would be clear for Shoko Asahara to step in amongst the confusion and assume his rightful leadership of Japan. The clostridium botulinum however, failed to work, and the scientists were forced back to the labs to find a more reliable alternative.

RUSSIA

Meanwhile Asahara continued his recruitment drive overseas, this time concentrating on Russia. The response he had there was simply overwhelming. He preached to the masses, he formed alliances with government officials, he made huge donations of cash and medical supplies, and an embracing media gave him his own weekly television show to further his cause. Russian citizens flocked in their thousands to join the Aum Supreme Truth. Not only did this provide a massive injection into the finances of the cult, but it also opened the door to Russian scientists and those who had been involved in the Soviet arms and weaponry programme, through both official and clandestine channels.

So the drive began to prepare for war. Plans were made to produce or procure every weapon or method of warfare imaginable. Those who had no expertise in the manufacture of arms, nuclear weapons, chemicals or military vehicles were to be trained to fight. Every member of Aum was to be prepared for the ensuing war. The project was colossal. Factories were taken over and new premises and laboratories were built.

SECOND ATTEMPT

Throughout this time, Asahara's scientists had been working on and correcting the previously failed production of clostridium botulinum. They believed that they now had the perfected poison. Shoko Asahara saw the forthcoming wedding of Japan's Prince Naruhito as the perfect occasion to use it. This time, he personally was going to spread the poison. The truck was again loaded with its deadly cargo and on the day of the royal wedding, Asahara and his men sprayed the streets of central Tokyo. Once again, the poison failed, and the population of Tokyo, plus its despised leaders, remained unharmed.

A livid Asahara went back to his scientists who, by now, had realized that the clostridium botulinum they had produced was not going to work. Anthrax however, just might. Not fast-acting, but highly lethal, the poison takes a couple of days to work, during which time the body is subjected to fever, vomiting, boils, sores, eventual swelling of the brain, coma and death. Anthrax can be produced as either liquid or powder. Seiichi Endo, Aum's chief scientist, chose liquid.

EXPERIMENTATION

The liquid was continually sprayed over the city from the top of an eight-storey building which Aum owned on the east side of Tokyo for several days. When local residents began to complain of an unusual smell in the neighbourhood, the police came to investigate and traced the source back to the building owned by Aum. On discovering to whom the building belonged, the police discontinued any further investigation, again reluctant to contravene the religious protection laws. Asahara explained the smell as an incense he had been using to cleanse the premises, and the police were happy to leave it at that. Aside from the smell, citizens noticed that their plants were wilting, their animals were not well, and that some of them suffered stomach upsets. No one died. Asahara's scientists had used a veterinary vaccine strain, not fatal.

Frustrated, yet undeterred, Asahara ordered his team of scientists to travel the globe looking for an effective poison and more information on chemical and biological weapons.

Finally, the decision was taken to produce sarin, a deadly nerve toxin originally discovered by German scientists in 1936 but fortunately not successfully produced until the end of the war. In either liquid or gas form, one drop was fatal and it had a similarly gruesome effect as that of anthrax. Asahara could not wait to try out his new deadly weapon. The sarin was taken to Aum-owned land in Australia, where 29 sheep were subjected to the deadly gas. Each and every one died, their death-throes celebrated by a jubilant Asahara.

Choosing a human target on whom to trial the sarin proved no problem for Asahara. He had many enemies. His first attempt to spray the leader of a rival religious group, a threat to the Aum Supreme Truth, failed when the spraying machinery sprung a leak and almost killed one of Aum's own men.

Asahara then chose to take revenge on three judges who had annulled Aum's agreed purchase of a food-processing plant a few months previously. Again, the job was botched, but this time the end-result was nevertheless satisfactory to Asahara. The machinery on the vehicle which was positioned outside the residences of the three judges broke down and released a thick vapour cloud. The drivers of the vehicle had to stop their attack, as they could no longer see where they were going, and the gas was taken by the wind to a neighbouring residential area. Although not the intended target, seven people died and hundreds of casualties were treated in hospital.

Amazingly, yet again, Aum was cleared in the ensuing police investigations. Even more incredible due to the fact that police had received a warning that this had merely been a test by the Aum Supreme Truth, and that a gas attack in a confined area could prove even more tragic. The anonymous informant even quoted a crowded subway as an example.

AUM DESERTERS

Asahara had been so crazed and single-minded in his pursuit of the perfect poison, that he was failing to see the cracks appearing within the sect, and the opposition to it which was mounting outside. Disillusion within

Aum soon came to his attention however, when he was told about the disappearance of a 62-year-old female member of the group. In spite of investing all of her savings and a large part of her life to Aum, she had become increasingly disturbed by the activities of Shoko Asahara. She had fled, and one attempt to bring her back had failed. When a second Aum official was sent out to retrieve her and failed, her brother was kidnapped and tortured in order to make him divulge information. Despite horrendous suffering, he never betrayed her, remaining loyal right up to the point he died. Furthermore, having already received threatening phone calls before he was kidnapped, he had had the foresight, perhaps out of fear, to leave a note behind which simply said that should he disappear, he had been taken by the Aum Supreme Truth. The police could turn a blind eye no longer and began making the arrangements for a massive raid of the Aum Supreme Truth compound, buildings and offices. Unfortunately, this decision had come just too late for the people of Tokyo.

MARCH 20, 1995

His megalomania now uncontrollable, Shoko Asahara was still clinging on to his earlier vision of the destruction of government buildings, an attack from both the ground and the air on a massive scale. The target that Aum eventually agreed on was not attacking the individuals that Asahara had originally wanted to punish, but was equally cataclysmic in scale.

The new target was Kasumigaseki station, on the Tokyo subway, the weapon was sarin, and the attack was scheduled for the morning rush hour, 8 a.m. on Monday March 20, 1995. Sealed bags of the poison were to be taken into the subway by five chosen Aum members, punctured, and then left to diffuse.

On the chosen morning at the appointed time, the perpetrators, who had their own antidote pills to the poison, all boarded separate trains bound for Kasumigaseki station. As the trains drew nearer they released the sarin and disembarked at the next stop.

The gas took effect instantly. Commuters on the deadly trains became nauseous. Some began to collapse, and others ran from the trains to the station exits, passing more sick and collapsed passengers as they went. Railway staff immediately contacted the emergency services and soon ambulances had arrived at the scene.

Five thousand five hundred people were injured by the Aum attack that fateful morning. Some will never recover fully from the damage that the sarin gas did, and some had a relatively lucky escape with only minor injuries. Twelve people in total died. Speculation abounded regarding the cause of the attack, but when experts examined the site after everyone had been evacuated, they confirmed that it was no gas leak, but rather an attack with the manufactured gas sarin.

AFTERMATH

An elated Shoko Asahara greeted the five executors of

this evil when they returned to the compound. He paid them, praised them, and then told them to go into hiding. With the Tokyo public in shock and beseeching the authorities for answers to this tragedy, a massive impending police raid was planned. Although this was a secret operation, the plans were leaked to Asahara by Aum informers within the police, and the sect therefore began a huge clean-up operation of the compound and laboratories, hiding every trace of chemicals and any incriminating evidence or reports which could have linked them to the attack. Asahara and his followers took flight.

Aum's attempts to conceal their activities were useless. The investigators found vast amounts of dangerous substances, chemicals which could be used to produce enough sarin to kill millions of people, and the equipment to make and distribute the deadly poison. They also unearthed torture chambers, millions of dollars, gold and drugs. Although some of the followers had remained at the compound, no arrests were made.

From a secret hiding place, Asahara reacted to the police raids by launching his legal team into action. They denied all accusations of the attack, claiming that the chemicals were used for fertilisers, and even accused the American military of the sarin attack in order to frame their peaceful and innocent organization.

Neither the public nor the police believed this and the investigations increased. Aum then launched their own attack on the Tokyo police department. The chief of the national police agency was shot in the head four times as he entered his office, but miraculously survived. Warnings were issued that should the persecution of Aum continue then more police would be killed.

Slowly and painstakingly, the police did manage to track down and arrest some of the more senior Aum members for holding followers against their will, but they could not charge these individuals with the gas attack, and nothing and no one was leading them to the one man they wanted. Numerous searches revealed only a warning that should they find Asahara's hideout and attempt to enter, sarin gas would pour down on them and everyone would die together.

Refusing to give up, Asahara continued to issue threats to the police and even produced and circulated a booklet which foretold further catastrophe, this time on a phenomenal scale. He gave April 15, 1995 as the date for this impending disaster. Needless to say, mass panic spread across Tokyo. People left the city, businesses closed, nobody wanted to be around if Aum were to strike again. But the date passed without incident.

Although over 100 Aum members had been arrested, mostly only for minor offences, Tokyo was still not safe with Asahara and some of the chief architects of Aum's evil still at large. This was to be proved on May 5, a Japanese public holiday, when an already very alert police department was called to a crowded subway station after a bag had been discovered burning in one of the toilets. The flames were put out, and the deadly contents of the bag revealed. Two condoms were found inside, one filled with sodium cyanide and the other filled with sulfuric acid. Had the two condoms melted and mixed their contents, the result would have been hydrogen cyanide and it could have killed tens of thousands of subway-users.

ASAHARA CAPTURED

Finally, on May 16, 1995, police stormed the compound one more time and found Shoko Ashara hiding in one of the buildings. He was brought out to full media coverage, with the eyes of all Japan upon him.

Bringing Shoko Asahara and the inner circle of the Aum Supreme Truth to justice has been a colossal, massively time-consuming task. Beginning in April 1996, the trial made slow progress due to the large number of crimes the cult had been accused of, and the density of evidence to be presented. It was also hindered considerably by Asahara's refusal to co-operate, falling asleep during proceedings and mostly remaining silent except for occasionally mumbling inaudible comments and statements.

Originally refusing even to enter a plea and declaring only that he had 'nothing to say', Asahara eventually pleaded not-guilty in 1997 to all charges against him, diverting the blame on all counts to the followers of Aum who, he claimed, had become uncontrollable and acted against his wishes. His lawyers claimed that he was a 'genuine man of religion' and as such could never have instructed such crimes to be committed.

The scene outside the court on February 27, 2004, the day Asahara was due to receive his verdict, was chaos. Thousands of members of the public had arrived to hear the charges read against him. They were awarded their justice. Shoko Asahara, found guilty of 13 charges of murder and attempted murder, and 11 other members of Aum were sentenced to death.

Yet even with Asahara now sentenced to death and never to return to the outside world, many believe that Aum still poses a threat to Japan and the rest of the world. Aum continues to grow, led now by Fumihiro Joyu, and renamed 'Aleph' in January 2002. It has supposedly renounced violence and the former practices of Shoko Asahara, at least those which they consider dangerous. They have paid compensation to the victims of Aum's attacks – money from the group's assets and from profits gained by Aum-run computer companies.

Aleph does however, still revere Shoko Asahara as a genius in yoga and Buddhist meditation, and will continue to practise these methods taught by him. Members are still recruited, and revenue is still generated. The Japanese government claims that Aleph's followers still maintain an absolute faith in Asahara and his doctrine and it is therefore viewed with great suspicion and monitored closely. In an effort to keep a tight control on the group, legislation has been passed by parliament allowing the police freely to inspect the premises of the group.

To date, none of the convicted members of Aum have been executed. They have all launched appeals, which it is estimated will take years to settle.

At the height of its success, the net assets of the Aum Supreme Truth totalled in excess of one billion dollars. Chizuo Matsumoto could be said to have achieved his childhood dream.

Luke Woodham

High-school shootings in Mississippi

UP UNTIL OCTOBER, 1997 the Pearl High School was an average Mississippi government run school. An all singing and all dancing American dream with a mission motto to: 'instill a strong educational foundation that enables all students to become confident, self directed, lifelong learners in a changing technological world.'

There was no way that the school could have prepared for what happened on October 1, 1997 when an armed student entered the grounds and unleashed a frenzied attack which resulted in the deaths of two students and the injury of several others.

Luke Woodham was a 16-year-old second year student who throughout his school life had found it extremely difficult to fit in. He had constantly been bullied by his peers due to his inability to look the part of a trendy, popular student. He came from a broken home and was a studious type who was very awkward within himself. Even though Woodham had extreme intelligence, he lacked other skills that are held in higher regard than brain power such as physical prowess, charisma and humour, things that get you liked at school.

But it wasn't just his high-school peers who had made Woodham's life a living hell, his mother, Mary Woodham, was also guilty of emotional abuse. She regularly told him that he was the reason that his father, John Woodham had left her. She would also tell her son that he was fat, stupid and would never amount to much, unlike his extremely popular older brother.

Woodham finally found some acceptance in 1996 when he got together with his class mate Christina Menefee. Not only was Christina his first girlfriend but she was also his first 'real' friend and he fell in love instantly. He would walk her to her classes, take her to the cinema and generally dote on her. But after only two months together, the novelty had worn off for Christina, she was at the age where boyfriends changed at a vast rate. She split up with Luke and was soon making fun and taunting him just like the rest of the students at Pearl High. Little did she know the effect that breaking-up with him was going to have on both of their lives.

Luke Woodham was devastated. He could not eat or sleep, all he could think about was the girl who had made him live a little who had then gone on to knock him right back down. He believed that she was a Christian that had made him hate God, and for that he was angry.

It was shortly after their split that 19-year-old Grant Boyette befriended Woodham. Boyette told Woodham that he worshiped Satan and admired Hitler, and asked if he would like to join his group. Boyette said to Woodham: 'I think you've got the potential to do something great.'

This was the first time in a long while that Woodham had been made to feel special, for once it was him and not the high school jock who had something to offer. Woodham really took Boyette's words on board and before long he was a practicing Satanist in a group going by the name of 'The Kroth'.

What finally confirmed this new belief for Woodham was when Boyette cast a spell and the next day one of their school peers was run over and killed by a car. Woodham suddenly believed that as a member of The Kroth he had a deadly power over people and could use it however he wished.

The seven boys that made up The Kroth would participate in role-play games, such as Star Wars, and Boyette would get Woodham and the other five boys to swear allegiance to him and to Satan. They allegedly discussed and planned to overthrow the school, kill a selection of people and then flee to Cuba. They were boys who had never before in their lives fitted in with any social clique, and at long last they belonged.

It is alleged that Boyette really started to get inside Woodham's mind, by constantly bringing up his treatment by ex-girlfriend Christina. Boyette would tell Woodham that he was spineless and worthless if he didn't seek revenge on people like her.

By the summer of 1997, Luke Woodham had started

to experience hallucinations in which red cloaked demons with blood red eyes would visit him at night. He would also hear Boyette's voice telling him to command the demons to attack people on behalf of Satan.

Throughout September, Woodham's emotional state got worse, he did not care for his life any more and was reading more and more Satanic text given to him by Boyette.

On September 28, 1997, Woodham confided in his friend, Lucas Thomson, telling him that he planned to kill his mother so that he could steal her car, take his brother's gun and then drive to school and kill people he didn't like. Lucas did not tell anybody about this conversation until after the events that were about to happen.

At around 5 a.m. on October 1, 1997, Woodham got up and made his way to the kitchen where he picked up a butcher's knife and a baseball bat. He then entered the room of his still sleeping mother. He repeatedly stabbed and beat her with the bat until she was dead.

Woodham then calmly embarked on cleaning the walls and floor, and putting his blood soaked clothes in the washing machine. A couple of hours later he spoke to both Thomson and Boyette and told them what he had just done.

At around 8 a.m., Woodham climbed into his dead mother's car with his brother's rifle in tow and headed to Pearl High School. Upon arrival Woodham handed some papers to Justin Sledge, another Kroth member, and then picked up his rifle and headed towards the area where hundreds of students were waiting for lessons to begin.

Christina Menefee and best friend Lydia Dew were leaning by a post chatting when Woodham approached them. He waited until he was at point blank range and then pulled the trigger of his brother's hunting rifle. He did this twice into each of the girls bodies and then headed towards the group of students who were running for their lives. He fired the gun repeatedly until he was finally out of ammunition and then made his way back to the car to re-load.

It was here that Woodham was restrained by the deputy head and arrested.

On June 5, 1998, a circuit court jury found Luke Woodham guilty of his mother's murder and was sentenced to life behind bars. The following week on June 12, 1998, Woodham was found guilty on two counts of murder and seven counts of aggravated assault. He was sentenced to another two life imprisonments plus 20 years for each of the seven assaults.

His defence had tried to plea insanity in the hope of a lesser charge but his emotional testimony failed to convince the jury of this.

During police interviews prior to the court case Woodham said that he felt that nobody cared for him and that he could not find any reason not to go ahead with what he did.

Even though he was seen by the jury as not being insane, surely it takes quite a bit of mental instability to commit such hateful attacks? He was not forced into doing the things that he did but if one of the only people willing to be your friend is the same person brain washing you with ideas about the devil it is sure to have an effect on you if you are not 100 per cent sane. What Woodham did can never be forgiven or forgotten but he should have had the opportunity to channel this hatred through more conventional means and not through murderous worship.

PEER PRESSURE PROSECUTION QUASHED

Grant Boyette and Justin Sledge were expecting to be tried as accessories but delays occurred so that more evidence could be sought.

On December 22, 1998, 18-year-old Justin Sledge was freed when Mississippi prosecutors withdrew their request for an indictment on him due to lack of evidence.

The teenager, who had also been a member of Boyette's cult of Satanic worship – The Kroth, could have faced life imprisonment if he had been found guilty of the alleged role that prosecutors said he had had in the murders. On top of the lack of evidence, in a taped interview, Luke Woodham said that Sledge had not been involved.

Grant Boyette was a different matter. He had been the leader of the satanic group, the empowering force who had made his weak-minded and unloved followers feel special. Had he enough control that peer pressure had made Woodham commit the terrible atrocities that he did? Or would Woodham still have taken out his anger and hatred of the world on innocent people if he had never encountered Boyette? The law courts couldn't even answer this, and his trial was delayed time and time again right up until the year 2000.

In January, 2000 Boyette was still scheduled to face a murder trial on February 28 in Biloxi, but a week before the trial 20-year-old Boyette pleaded guilty to a lesser charge of conspiring to prevent a principle from doing his job. He was found guilty of this and was sentenced to a six month army-style programme called 'Regimented Inmate Discipline' and then a further five years supervised probation.

Some people believe that Boyette got off too lightly as it was alleged that he was the mastermind behind the fateful acts on that October morning. But others believe that Boyette was just a normal teenager who may have spoken of murderous acts hypothetically but never believed anyone would carry them out.

Luke Woodham and others like him, including Grant Boyette were children who expressed desperate cries for help that were never answered in time, with Woodham's final plea arriving in the form of murder. Boyette now has a chance to put his life back on track and channel his hatred of bullies in the world in a positive way, but Luke Woodham never will.

Charles Manson

The Family

An illegitimate and unwanted accident, Charles Manson began his miserable early life in Cincinnati, Ohio, on November 12, 1934. His 16-year-old mother was Kathleen Maddox, an alcoholic prostitute who passed her son off on to family and friends whenever the opportunity arose, and then disappeared for days at a time. His father, on paper, was Colonel Scott of Ashland in Kentucky, although little Charlie never knew him. In fact, he knew no father figure at all, only inheriting his surname from William Manson, to whom his mother was married for a very short time.

When Kathleen and her brother were imprisoned for armed robbery, Charles was sent to live with his devoutly religious aunt and uncle in West Virginia. The contrast between this new environment and his former home life in Ohio was marked. Charles always thought that his mother would come back for him, yet when Kathleen was subsequently released from prison, she was neither willing nor fit to look after her little boy. Consequently passed from relative to relative, Charlie, completely friendless and with no stability or continuity in his life, began to turn to crime and to his own imagination for company.

A LIFE OF CRIME

Charlie's first spell in reform school came at the age of nine, when he was caught stealing. Convicted of the same offence again at the age of 12, he was once again institutionalised and thus began the cycle of his life, in and out of reform schools and, later, prisons. In total, Charles spent more than half of his first 30 years incarcerated. The litany of offences committed by Manson was wide-ranging: burglary, armed robbery, car theft, assault, sodomy, pimping, rape, fraud.

During his extensive periods in prison, Charles Manson began to study religion and religious philosophies.

THE FAMILY IS BORN

In 1967, and in spite of his pleas to stay in prison, Charlie was awarded parole and sent to San Francisco. Re-entering the world in the 'Summer of Love' though, Charlie found it easier to adapt to the outside than he had anticipated. A keen musician, he used his guitar and the influential powers of readily-available drugs to attract friends, mainly girls, and soon followers. When he managed to sell the rights to one of his own songs, Charlie used the money to buy a bus, in which he and his entourage travelled, gathering more followers and spreading 'love'.

The bus eventually broke down, and Charles Manson and his girls moved in with Gary Hinman, a music teacher. When they had outstayed their welcome there, they moved on, and Charlie conned George Spahn into letting him and his group stay at his Ranch. With a following of such eager and attractive girls, Manson made it worth Spahn's while to agree. The group lived a decadent and carefree life at the Ranch. They scavenged for food, stealing what the supermarkets threw away each day.

Still determined to launch his music career, Charlie used his contacts to get in touch with Doris Day's son, Terry Melcher. Manson hoped that Melcher could be interested in using his music as the soundtrack for a film, and invited him to the Ranch to listen to a few of his compositions. Melcher came to listen to Charlie and his girls a couple of times, but ultimately was not interested in the music. The disappointment hit Charlie harder than Melcher could have realised, for he truly believed that this was his opening into the music business.

CHARLIE'S PROPHECY

Along with a passion for music, at the centre of 'The Family', the name which Charlie was now using to refer to his group of followers, was the development of a prophecy of impending Armageddon. Charles Manson preached to his followers that the black people of the world were going to rise up, steal from and slaughter all white men. Charlie and his followers (which he estimated would total 144,000 by this time) would survive this war, as he was going to lead them to a secret civilization in Death Valley where they would sit out the slaughter until the black men were all that remained. Then The Family would return to the cities, take back power from the black men, enslave them and rule the world. A great follower of The Beatles, Charlie gave the name 'Helter Skelter' to this race war, as he believed that the song lyrics described perfectly the Final Reckoning that was to come, and he prophesied that Helter Skelter would begin in the summer of 1969.

But when the summer days of 1969 did come and the black people had not unleashed this prophesied violence against the whites, Charlie spoke to his followers and told them that the blacks did not know what to do and therefore that they, The Family, would have to lead the way and show them. So it was that Manson's followers set out to begin the predestined and necessary slaughter.

CIELO DRIVE

The home of Sharon Tate, the heavily pregnant wife of film director Roman Polanski, was one of The Family's first targets. With her sorely missed husband away shooting a film in Europe, Sharon was spending the evening of August 9, 1969 with friends in Los Angeles. These included Abigail Folger, Folger's boyfriend Voytek Frykowski, and the internationally renowned hair stylist, Jay Sebring. Sharon was entertaining her friends, not uncommonly, in the house she rented on Cielo Drive – a house owned by Terry Melcher, who had recently shattered Charles Manson's dreams of a music career...

Shortly after 4 a.m. the following morning, the LAPD received a call from a private security guard who was on patrol in the area. He claimed to have heard gunshots. He wasn't the only one to have heard disturbing noises. Reports later came in that gunshots had also been heard earlier in the morning, and the chilling screams of a woman begging, 'Oh, God, no, please don't! Oh, God, no, don't, don't . . .' None of these earlier disturbances however, had been reported.

The morning dawned as usual over the Tate house, although on arrival at the property to begin work at around 8 a.m., Sharon Tate's housekeeper Winifred Chapman noticed the telephone wire hanging over the main gate. Swinging the gate open, she walked up the drive and saw another unfamiliar sight – a white Rambler parked on the drive. On entering the house, she made her way towards the living room, noticing as she went some unusual splashes of red across the walls. On discovery of pools of blood and what appeared to be a body on the lawn, Winifred Chapman ran screaming from the house. As she ran back up the driveway and past the white Rambler, she noticed a second body inside the car.

When the police arrived, they found the blood-soaked body in the Rambler, along with another two heavily wounded bodies on the lawn. As they entered the house, first to catch their eye was the word 'PIG', written in blood on the lower half of the front door. As they progressed cautiously through the house, they could not imagine the horror they were about to encounter. Lying on the couch in the living room was a very heavily pregnant woman, her face covered in blood, her body covered in multiple stab wounds, and a ligature around her neck. The rope had been thrown over a rafter in the ceiling, and the other end was tied around the neck of a man lying close by, equally drenched in blood.

As the police looked on in horror, they heard the voice of a man. It was the caretaker, William Garretson, and he was arrested immediately and taken away.

The victims at the Tate house were later identified as Abigail Folger and Voytek Frykowski. Theirs were the bodies on the lawn. Steve Parent, a friend of the caretaker whose body was found in the car, and Sharon Tate, her unborn baby boy, and Jay Sebring, who had died in the living room. All the victims, with the exception of Steve Parent, had been stabbed repeatedly and furiously. Parent, Frykowski and Senring had also been shot. A total of 102 stab wounds had been administered to the victims.

LABIANCA KILLINGS

No less than 48 hours later, police were called to the scene of a second bloodbath, this time in the Los Feliz area of LA. Frank Struthers, son of Rosemary LaBianca and step-son of her husband Leno LaBianca, had returned home after a camping trip to find a couple of things out of the ordinary as he walked up the drive to his parents' house. He could see Leno's speedboat still on the drive, very out of character for his step-father who would always put it away for storage in the garage. Secondly, all the window shades in the house were down, again very unusual. Frank could get no answer either at the front door or on the phone, so he called his sister Susan, and her boyfriend, and waited for them to arrive.

The three entered the house through the open back door, and the two men left Susan in the kitchen while they went to have a look around. As they entered the living room, they saw the body of Leno, covered in blood, with a pillowcase over his head and some kind of object sticking out from his stomach. The men retreated back through the house, grabbed Susan, and called the police immediately.

On further inspection by the police and ambulance-men who subsequently arrived, the protrusion from Leno's stomach was a carving knife. His hands had been tied together behind his back, a lamp-cord wound around his neck, and the word 'WAR' carved on to his body. In the bedroom, the police discovered that Rosemary had suffered a similar fate. Graffitied in the blood of the victims, in different places around the house were the statements 'DEATH TO PIGS', 'RISE', and the misspelled 'HEALTHER SKELTER'. The couple had been stabbed a combined 67 times.

UNCONNECTED CASES?

These apparently motiveless crimes left the LAPD in the dark. Even when the Los Angeles County Sheriff's Office contacted the LAPD to tell them of the similar circumstances in which they had found the body of Gary Hinman, one-time friend of Charles Manson, the LAPD made no connection between the three cases and clues were left uninvestigated. Hinman had been stabbed to death in his own home on July 31, and written in his shed blood on the wall of his living room were the words 'POLITICAL PIGGY'. Furthermore, the Sheriff's Office had arrested a man named Bobby Beausoleil in connection with the Hinman murder. Beausoleil, it transpired, had been living in a hippy commune led by the charismatic and influential Charles Manson. The LAPD just weren't interested, even though their case against William Garretson, the caretaker who claimed to have slept through the events at the Tate house had collapsed following the results of a polygraph test.

Theories and speculation as to who was behind these murders flew around, and it seemed like everyone had an opinion. The police however, were getting no further in their investigations. Until, that is, a little boy in Sherman Oaks found a gun in his back garden. He showed it to his father who immediately turned it in to the police. It was a Hi Standard .22 caliber Longhorn revolver, an exact match for the weapon which the police had traced to the Tate murders. This in itself did not offer any further information to the LAPD, but being three months since the murders, it renewed interest in the cases – so much so that the LAPD began to talk to the Sheriff's Office about the possible connection between the crimes.

The Sheriff's Office had first become interested in Beausoleil when his 13-year-old girlfriend had informed them that Beausoleil had been sent by Manson, with a woman called Susan Atkins, to Hinman's house to retrieve some money that Hinman owed Manson. When Hinman refused to pay up, the duo kept him prisoner in his own home for a couple of days before they killed him, and the girl recounted how she had heard Susan tell others that she had stabbed the victim several times in the legs during the attack. What was interesting about the young girl's story was that Hinman had not been stabbed in the leg. This therefore led the Sheriff's Office to believe that Atkins may well have been connected to one, or even both, of the other bloody attacks too.

SUSAN ATKINS'S CONFESSION

Susan Atkins confessed as much to fellow inmates at the Sybil Brand Institute, where she was awaiting trial for the Hinman murder. She gleefully announced that not only had she slashed Hinman while Beausoleil held him (believed to be the other way round by the police at the time), but that she was also the proud murderer of Sharon Tate. She claimed that Charles Manson, her lover, was Jesus Christ and that he was going to lead his Family to a civilization in a hole in Death Valley. First they had to commit a crime that would shock the world. Susan spared no details in describing the bloodthirsty and crazed way in which they had killed those at the Tate house, adding that she had wanted to go much further than they did. She wanted to cut Sharon's baby out of her womb, to gouge out the eyes of their victims, crush them against the wall, and to cut off their fingers. Throughout this history, Susan Atkins laughed manically, danced and sang. She was considered insane by those listening to her story, although she must have been convincing enough as her cellmates did report her confession to the authorities.

TRIAL

Had the police not already made a connection between the Manson Family and the murders, they may have considered Atkins mad too. With what they had already discovered though, along with Atkins's seemingly detailed knowledge of the crimes, the case came to trial.

Charles Manson and Susan Atkins stood trial, along with two other female members of The Family. There was no hard evidence against the Manson Family. Only a blood-stained fingerprint connected one of them to the Tate house, but when questioned, all but Manson did confess to the crimes, although none in quite as jubilant a fashion as Susan Atkins. Throughout the whole, agonising 22-week trial, Manson's followers never once denounced him. In fact, if ever any evidence was revealed which looked to incriminate Manson in the murders, his Family would deny his involvement, admit to all the accusations themselves and divert the attention from him. Manson's participation in the murders could not be proved, and although at least one criminologist believed that Manson was present at the murders, perhaps involved in tying up the victims or instructing his followers to kill, this could not be proved either. At one point, the lawyer for one of the other female defendants stood up and tried to implicate Charles Manson in one of the crimes his client had been accused of in order to lessen her own involvement. His client vehemently denied Manson's participation, and the lawyer's murdered body was found a couple of days later.

PECULIAR BEHAVIOUR

All of Manson's followers were present at the trial, and they behaved throughout in a very peculiar way. They imitated Charles Manson's speech and movement, and at one point, when Manson carved the sign of an 'X' into his forehead – a sign that he had exited from one world into another – the girls did the same. Manson himself created distractions whenever he could, even lunging at the judge at one point, shouting that someone should cut his head off! The court was in uproar and as the authorities tried to restrain Manson, the other three defendants began chanting loudly in

Latin. Evidence was incomplete, testimonies clearly falsified, and witnesses threatened with death – their own or of their families – if they continued.

Eventually, the trial was complete, and the jury had reached their verdict. Manson and the three women arrived at the court with shaven heads to hear the outcome of their case.

GUILTY

Charles Manson was found guilty of murder in the first degree and sentenced to death. Upon hearing the verdict, the female defendants declared that the judge had just passed sentence on himself, and that he should take to locking his own doors and carefully watching his children from that point on. All four defendants were given the death penalty, although when this was abolished in 1972, their sentences changed to life imprisonment.

The public reaction to The Manson Family after the trial was unexpected. The revulsion that had first greeted Charles Manson when he entered the courtroom had, over the course of the trial, transformed into a strange fascination and it appeared that the charisma which had seduced and hypnotised the young girls of Los Angeles into joining him and following him in his beliefs, was possibly having an effect on the general public too. Newspapers reported the story of the trial, placing Manson in a strangely favourable light. Concerns grew that his notoriety may spread to cult-hero. Fortunately, this never transpired, although Manson's story did capture the public to the extent that it has been produced and re-told on both stage and in film. The music he wrote, and so believed in, has also been performed by Guns 'n' Roses.

BEHIND BARS

Manson remains a prisoner today and is unlikely ever to be released. He receives more mail than any other prisoner in the United States and therefore, over 30 years on, perhaps he is still as dangerous as he always was – still appealing to those who need someone to follow and something to believe in. Also still dangerous physically, Manson has been isolated in prison at different times for various offences: threatening prison staff, damage to prison property, assault on an officer, drug-dealing, smuggling in a bullet and even, from within his prison walls, twice plotting to assassinate the president of the United States.

Charles Manson has been up for parole ten times. Every time, parole has been refused.

The LeBarons

*A story of a Mormon
fundamentalist family*

ALMA DAYER LEBARON was an American Mormon who relocated to a Mormon settlement in Colonia Juarez, northern Mexico in the early 1900s.

He was a member of The Church of Jesus Christ of Latter-Day Saints, that was set up by Joseph Smith in 1830, and just like many other LDS fellows of that time, Dayer LeBaron was a practising polygamist, which was usually referred to by Latter Day Saints as the act of 'Plural Marriages'.

When the United States Congress made the practice of polygamy illegal in 1862 many LDS members fled to other countries such as Canada in an attempt to set up free polygamy practicing communities without the fear of persecution or prosecution.

This was the reason that Dayer LeBaron had ended up at a settlement in Mexico and it was here that he fathered five of his seven children; Benjamin, Ross Wesley, Joel, Ervil and Alma.

It was also at this Mormon colony that Dayer LeBaron met Rulon Allred. Allred was convicted of polygamy in the US in 1947, skipped bail and escaped to Mexico where Dayer LeBaron gave him refuge whilst he sorted himself out. Rulon Allred would go on to wish that he had never encountered the LeBaron clan.

In 1944, Dayer LeBaron received a revelation from God which told him to acquire a piece of Mexican land, this became the base for Colonia LeBaron, Dayer's Mormon fundamentalist sect.

THE LEBARON CLAN

Dayer LeBaron's children were just as religiously Mormon as their father, and each one ended up setting up their own off-shoot church at some point in their lives. Three in particular became historical members of the LeBaron clan.

In 1944, Benjamin LeBaron the eldest of Dayer LeBaron's sons had a vision and proclaimed that he was in fact a prophet of God. He believed that he was the 'Lion of Israel', and to prove his point would roar at the top of his voice in the middle of the street. On top of this, Benjamin also wished to prove to the rest of humanity that he was 'Mighty and Strong'. One particular time he stopped the traffic on a motorway in the middle of Salt Lake City – the geographical heart of Mormonism and the LDS – lay face down and did 200 press-ups to show people just how mighty and strong he really was. Benjamin was soon shunned by the majority of his family and friends and spent a lot of his life in and out of mental institutes. But one person did believe him and that was his brother Ervil.

The next child of Dayer LeBaron's to have a spiritual experience was Ross Wesley. He too claimed that he was a mighty and strong prophet and related his visions to claims made by the founder of the LDS Church – Joseph Smith.

With Benjamin LeBaron in Utah State Mental Hospital and Ross Wesley's prophecies not amounting to much, Joel and Ervil were the brothers to emerge as the chosen ones.

Joel LeBaron was the third sibling to become a self-proclaimed prophet after being visited by two angel messengers from heaven in the 1960s. Joel was an extremely charismatic man who people warmed to immediately. He was softly spoken and could explain the Scriptures like no other.

Joel set up a Mormon splinter church by the name of the 'Church of the First Born of the Fullness of Time'. By the spring of 1965, Joel had organized his new church and appointed his brother Ervil as secretary.

BLOOD BROTHERS

There was a problem. Ervil LeBaron was also receiving messages from heaven, and announced that he too was 'one mighty and strong' – a prophet from God. He was the more handsome of the two brothers and although he was not as amiable as his brother, he definitely had a way with people, especially women. He had the body of a boxer, and with this came the tendency to hold a grudge, but his flip side was that he was an excellent writer of scripture. His writing became obsessive and at times Ervil would stay up for days at a time living on a diet of coffee to keep him awake but writing extremely profound holy works.

Ervil would constantly have dreams about having many wives with which he would 'multiply and replenish the earth . . .' He wanted to be a great and respected man in as many ways as possible and nobody was going to stand in his way.

The two LeBaron brothers soon started disagreeing, and with both of them needing to be the top prophet they ended up having a major fall-out. Joel wished to start an order which abided completely by the Ten Commandments. Joel believe that only when the Ten Commandments were being followed would Jesus return to Earth.

Although Ervil did agree with the idea he believed the only way to form it within the sect was by using brute force, something that pacifist Joel was not happy with doing. The finale to the brothers' relationship came in the winter of 1969. Joel, the head of the Fullness of Time Church decided to dismiss Ervil from his position within the sect due to his lack of respect for others and his rebellious tendencies towards the movement.

Ervil became extremely angry at Joel's confrontation and luckily enough it was not long before he had received some orders from God.

God had spoken to Ervil and told him that he needed to get rid of his brother Joel. The prophecy spoke of Joel as someone who even though was seen by many as 'saintly' was getting in the way of both Ervil and the Holy One's work on Earth.

On August 20, 1972, Joel LeBaron whilst at his polygamist community, Los Molinos, was shot twice, once in the throat and once the head; he was killed instantly. The murder had been organized by his own flesh and blood, Ervil LeBaron, and had been committed by one of Ervil's staunch followers.

THE CHURCH OF THE LAMB OF GOD

After the untimely death of his brother Joel, Ervil had reformed his followers under the name of the 'Church of the Blood of the Lamb of God' and preached his views to them on a daily basis.

These were the lengths that certain Mormon poly-gamists would go to to prove their cause was the most spiritually just – prophecies would come at just the right time to give people such as Ervil an excuse to murder people who held different Mormonist ideologies.

By 1975, Ervil LeBaron had murdered about five more people and seriously injured around 15 others, without getting his own hands dirty of course. Each murder was executed by one of Ervil's flock on his orders, which in turn were orders received from God.

Even when Ervil LeBaron was arrested in Mexico in

the spring of 1976, his free disciples carried on with the blood bath. His clan ran their operation from a post office box in southern most California, and they sent out circulars opposing governmental taxes, state benefits, gun control and other polygamist groups. Even the late Jimmy Carter received a death threat from Ervil's group when he stood for the presidency in 1976, the Church of the Blood of the Lamb of God believed that Carter's views were too liberal and un-godly.

In 1979, 11 months after being arrested, Ervil LeBaron was freed by the Mexican judicial system as they did not have enough proof that linked him to the murders over the previous three years, but other reports say that his freedom was more likely to have been through bribes, which were so rife in Mexico in the 1970s.

Whatever, Ervil LeBaron was once again a free man back on his rampage, cleansing the world of anyone who was not in agreement with him and did not do as he said.

Ervil arranged the murder of one of his own daughters due to her insubordination and a few months later had Rulon Allred killed.

Rulon Allred was a prominent Salt Lake City polygamist leader by this point and faced his death in an execution style manner, set up by Ervil. Ervil wanted the followers who Allred had, and thought that if he disposed of Allred he would be able to make make Allred's flock move their allegiance to the Lamb of God.

Finally the law caught up with Ervil LeBaron and this time he would go to prison for good. The Mexican authorities agreed to deport LeBaron back to the US, and in 1979 he was sentenced to life imprisonment at the maximum security prison at Point of the Mountain, Utah.

Just two years later, in the summer of 1981, Ervil LeBaron was found dead in his cell, aged just 56. He had become a rather agitated and confused man soon after his incarceration as he realised that he was never going to be free again. He had more revelations in his cell, ones which this time said that a miracle would happen which would free him. But just two years after his imprisonment, he had died of a heart attack.

Maybe Ervil's body had known more than his mind, and gave up religion even though his mind would have continued prophesying forever if he had been given half the chance.

ERVIL'S LITTLE BLACK BOOK?

Even though Ervil LeBaron was part of his own church he had still practised and accepted many of the Mormon teachings throughout his life. One teaching he adhered to always was 'blood atonement', which means 'sinners should shed their blood to save their souls'. It was his interpretation of this practice that had got him imprisoned in the first place.

Before his sudden death, Ervil LeBaron had managed to write a 400 page script called The Book of the New Covenants, which contained a list of people he believed needed to be sacrificed for his cause, people whom in his eyes were sinners, had betrayed him in the past or who had the power to betray him in the future. Again this list was based on the 'blood attonement' ideology but with his own twist.

Around 20 copies of his script were published and managed to get into the possession of his most righteous brothers. People who he could reply on, even after his death, to carry out the necessary murders. Most of these people were in fact his children. He had fathered over 50 progeny through his plural marriages and the majority of them stuck loyally by him long after he had died.

Ervil's 13-year-old son, Aaron, took over his father's leadership after his death and the clan of children, teenagers and young adults started to put their father's words into action. Many of these children had been abused by older members of the former Lamb of God clan therefore already felt a lot of hatred to the world, in their eyes they were acting upon orders from a higher force, higher than any state or congressional authority as they were orders warranted by God himself. Throughout the '80s names were crossed off the death list and by 1988 the Lambs of God were boasting about the 17 murders that they had committed.

THE DOWNFALL OF THE LEBARON CLAN

In 1993, three of Ervil LeBaron's offspring were arrested and sentenced to life in prison for their involvements in the death spree of the '80s, and in 1995 the leader of the Lambs of God, Aaron LeBaron, was found in Mexico and deported, as his father had been, back to the United States to face murder charges. He was sentenced to 45 years in prison. Where the other 50 or so LeBaron children are, is unclear. A few siblings have re-surfaced to talk about their lives within the clan, Cynthia LeBaron even testified against her brother Aaron on the second day of his trial and is now part of a witness protection scheme, and other members have written articles giving their points of view about polygamy and Mormon Fundamentalism.

The problem was that the LeBaron clan knew no different, they had been born into this lifestyle and therefore tried to abide by the rules that they were taught, how were they to know that the rules they abided by were illegal in no uncertain terms? They did not know an outside world only one of a polygamist, murdering father who's word was as divine as that of God himself.

The generations of LeBarons did not have a choice, whilst growing up, of who they were lynching and when they were legally adults they were so far within the clan that it would have been virtually impossible to change.

A quote from Aaron LeBaron's younger sister Jessica LeBaron puts their upbringing and life into perspective somewhat, even if what the family did can never be forgiven:

The thing was a nightmare, that both Aaron LeBaron and I were born into. Just like any other children we believed and tried to do what we were taught. It was not fun. Perhaps we are not good folks, but when all the bad things happened we had never been to school, were isolated on a ranch and have a family history of mental illness (treatable with medication) and other factors that contributed to extreme fanaticism. As a little child I believed all the 'stuff' the church did was right. We are not evil, even though what we did is really bad.

The Jombola Cult

Powers of the Dark

OVER 300 PEOPLE are estimated to be part of the Jombola cult, a supernatural group based in southern Sierra Leone. The group first appeared in the war-torn region at the end of the 1990s, shortly after a peace agreement was signed between the government and the barbaric rebel army, the Revolutionary United Front. Based in the southern Sierra Leone districts of Bo, Pujehan and Bonthe, the Jombola Cult strikes fear into the hearts of all who inhabit these areas. The locals are convinced of the paranormal powers of the cult members.

Terrified residents of these southern regions claim that the members of the Jombola Cult transform themselves into creatures such as rats, reptiles, cats and dogs and, in their animal guises, set off to destroy local villages and terrorize the inhabitants. Witnesses of the transformations claim that the sight is petrifying.

The mission of the Jombola Cult, disclosed by a captured cult member, is to bring down both the government and the southern Civilian Defense Force, the Kamajors. To this end, the cult uses death, destruction and the 'powers of the dark'.

This mission, and the very emergence of the Jombola Cult, is explained further by analysts who see it as a direct result of the socio-political crisis caused by the disintegration of the national army. Where the army of Sierra Leone had been weakened, the Kamajors were instrumental in keeping the Revolutionary United Front down, and now the Jombola Cult has risen up to engage them in a battle for dominance. The Kamajors are believed to have used mystical powers to combat the RUF, and these are now being challenged by the Jombola Cult

The leader of the Jombola Cult, Pa Kujah, is reported to live in the southern town of Yambama. He recruits both men and women to assist him in his mission, although the women are seen as little more than sex objects, and used mainly to attract and then sexually overpower male victims. The Jombola Cult has been held responsible for at least 30 murders committed in the regions it terrorises.

The Lafferty Brothers' Message from God

Two brothers whose lives take a turn for the worse

DANIEL AND RONALD Lafferty were brothers born into a strict Latter Day Saint family. They had four brothers and two sisters with whom they lived together with their mother and father on a farm west of Utah. Their father, Watson Lafferty, after serving a few years in the US navy as a barber, opened a barber's shop come chiropractic clinic and settled down to raise his eight children as model LDS members. With his love for religion came some strict rules, that Watson expected his wife Claudine and children to live by, and he did not think twice about beating any of them who refused to obey him.

The brothers had been born into a violent but religious family life. When they weren't facing their father's abuse personally, they often saw him inflict it on their other siblings, and also on their mother, whom Dan Lafferty described as a 'good woman and excellent mother' On the flip side of the coin, Watson Lafferty was also a loving father who would often tell his wife that he loved her, and placed his family at the centre of his life together with the LDS church. Watson complied with the Mormon doctrine but was definitely not what can be classified as a fundamentalist as he never dabbled in polygamy or even discussed the practice of plural marriages as a possibility.

DAN AND RON'S PATHS TO ADULTHOOD

Both Dan and Ronald were model Mormon children, they excelled at school, took up extra curricular activities and studied their faith at any possible opportunity. The LDS church was just as much a part of their lives as it was their father's. Ron was an outstanding sportsman and Dan had a voice of an angel, they seemed like model American men, all round 'good-guys' who would probably grow into a men akin to The Simpsons' character Ned Flanders.

After finishing high school Dan went on a religious expedition to Scotland where he met a beautiful divorcee called Matilda Loomis. Matilda had two children from her dissolved marriage, and instantly Dan felt a strong and common bond between the two of them. He returned to the United States two years later without having acted upon his feelings towards her.

Six years later at an expedition reunion, Dan re-encountered Matilda and knew that his connection with her had not weakened. After receiving a revelation from God, Dan decided that he was to marry Matilda, she agreed to his question immediately, stating that she too had been told by God that this was her calling.

Shortly after their marriage, Dan, Matilda and Matilda's two children moved south to California so that Dan could study the family business of chiropractics. Whilst in California, one of Dan and Matilda's local LDS church associates was holding a talk on the subject of plural marriages.

The couple decided to go to the lecture, just out of interest, but Dan left with an extreme thirst to know more. He had not realized just how rife the discontinued Mormon principle of polygamy was within his congregation.

After six years in California, Dan moved his wife and four children back to Utah where he started an in-depth study into the history and practice of polygamy within the LDS church and the Mormon faith.

After completing high school, Dan's brother, Ron Lafferty, signed up for the army. After a short while he realized that it was not his calling and instead went on a two-year journey as a missionary, spreading the word of the LDS church and the greatness of what it had to offer around the United States. He wanted other people to experience the pleasure and contentment that he got from being a Mormon.

It was a tough two years for Ron, as being a Mormon missionary means abiding strictly by the rules of the doctrine. Rules include: not drinking alcohol, not smoking, not ingesting caffeine, no sex before marriage, no masturbation, only reading text produced by the LDS church and only listening to religious music and watching religious programmes. He abided by these rules without complaint but now and again a rebellious streak emerged. Did this come from being brought up by such an authoritative father?

Whilst on one of his Mormon missions in Florida, Ron met a student nurse called Dianna and a few months later, at the end of his mission, they were married. The newly weds moved back to Utah so that they could be close to the rest of the Lafferty family and also so that they could be within the epicentre of the Mormon religion.

A LOOK INTO FUNDAMENTALISM

A short time into his research into polygamy, Dan Lafferty came across a text called The Peace Maker. The two-page pamphlet advocated polygamy and dealt mainly with biblical marriage laws. It is a text shrouded in mystery, as who actually wrote it remains ambiguous. Some say that a non LDS member by the name of Udney Hay Jacob was responsible for its production and that LDS founder and prophet Joseph Smith was quick to distance himself from the work, but others believe that Joseph Smith himself composed it.

Dan Lafferty received a message from God telling him that it was Smith who had written it and this was all Dan needed to begin a polygamist lifestyle. A big part of The Peace Maker deals with the need for the woman to be submissive as God had requested, and it wasn't long before Dan had Matilda abiding by these rules. She wasn't allowed to drive, handle money or speak to anyone outside of the family without Dan being there. The children were removed from school and there was to be no medical treatment, only natural homeopathic remedies.

By the late '70s Dan was treating his wife and children in the same way that his father had treated his mother, his siblings and him. According to his new sacred text, his children and his wife were his property to use as he wished.

Dan then chose his first plural wife, Rumanian immigrant called Ann Randak who he lovingly referred to as his 'gypsy bride'. Suddenly Matilda had been shoved from a happy marriage into what she described as a 'hellish situation'.

Dan and Ron Lafferty had taken dramatically different paths in their first years as men, but one thing had remained constant in both their lives, and that was the love and need they felt for their faith. Once they were both back in Utah it was Ron who acted as the glue of the family ties. He was the brother that all other siblings would turn to for advice, and he held a similar role for his children and wife. Everyone could rely on Ron to do the right thing and help in times of trouble.

Growing up, Ron had always felt a great love for his mother and it had hurt him to the core when he had witnessed the abuse that his father had inflicted on her. It was her influence and the respect he had upheld for her that had made Ron the person he was in his 20s and 30s.

It wasn't surprising when Ron was the only brother who did not attend 'chance meetings' the Lafferty brothers seemed to be having more and more frequently. Whenever there was a break at the Chiropractic clinic that Dan and Mark ran for their father, Watson Junior, Tim and Allen would arrive and discussions and seminars would take place based on the new knowledge that Dan was in ownership of regarding polygamy and 'blood atonement'. The four brothers listened to everything that Dan had to say and even though he had not yet assigned himself to a particular Fundamentalist church, his knowledge of polygamy and other abolished Mormon doctrines was vast, he had become a proficient preacher and soon he had his younger brothers mesmerized and within a few weeks they were converted Fundamentalists.

A CHANGE IN IDEAS

By the summer of 1982, Dan and Ron's four brothers had started to impose their new found ideas onto their families, but their wives were not happy about the situation that was growing and began talking about their fears to Ron's wife Dianna. Dianna was the lucky one, as she was married to the only Lafferty brother who had not been converted into the throws of polygamy and she felt that it was up to her and Ron to help the other couples out of this horrid situation.

Dianna discussed her sister-in-law's fears about the personality changes in their husbands with Ron and convinced him that he should go to one of the meetings at the Chiropractic clinic and rationally talk his five younger siblings back to the mainstream Mormon religion.

Ron Lafferty arrived at his first ever gathering held by his brothers, and they welcomed him warmly. All five of Ron's brothers held a great deal of respect and admiration for their elder brother and were happy that he had taken the time to take part in something that had become so important to them.

Ron immediately started reading an extract from an essay that had been written by the LDS church discussing the evils of fundamentalism and how it should be avoided at all costs. The brothers listened politely until Ron came to a halt and then Dan answered. And so the evening went on, Ron would quote from the Mormon scripture denouncing fundamentalism and Dan would respond with well researched knowledge on why such acts were needed in order to be as virtuous and as close to God as possible.

For the first couple of hours Ron stood his ground and refused to believe what Dan and his other four brothers were doing was in any way right. He tried to plead with Mark, Watson, Tim and Allen, telling them that Dan was brain washing them with ideas that would ruin them forever, but every word that came out of Ron's mouth was countered with an even better example backing such acts from Dan.

In the book Under the Banner of Heaven by John Krakauer, Dan Lafferty is quoted as saying:

Ron wasn't at that meeting too awfully long, before he stopped trying to convince us that we were wrong. 'What you guys are doing is right,' Ron admitted. 'It's everyone else that is wrong.' Suddenly, Ron Lafferty's views had changed dramatically. Dan had managed to brain wash his brother just as he had done to the other four.

From the moment that Ron returned home he decided it was time to bring his new found ideology into action, and this meant that his loving wife Dianna would also have to make the necessary changes to her life as well.

Ron Lafferty had been under financial pressure and he was relieved now that he had learnt from his brother's teachings that material goals no longer mattered as a Fundamentalist missionary.

Dianna was shocked with the swift and dramatic change in her husband's personality. She had sent him out to convert his brothers back to the LDS church and he had returned, in a matter of hours, as a Mormon fundamentalist. Over the weeks that followed Diana tried her hardest to talk sense into her ever changing husband, but it was impossible. He was a convert of the highest measure. Whereas before Dianna and Ron had had an extremely equal and caring relationship, one that many people around them were in envy of, he was now a strict alpha male who believed that a woman's job was to abide by the demanding rules set out for her in *The Peace Maker.* In *Under the Banner of Heaven,* Penelope Weiss, a friend of Dianna's, remarks:

He expected her to be his slave. And it was such a complete reversal from the way he'd been. Before Dan brainwashed him, Ron had treated Dianna like a queen. He was just one of the nicest men I've ever known. But when this happened, he became one of the meanest men I've ever known.

Dianna soon gave up trying to talk her husband round and surrendered to doing as he said to keep her life as pain free as possible.

A SPANNER IN THE WORKS

Dianna Lafferty had been conditioned into being a Mormon fundamentalist wife and she was not gong to complain when her husband decided it was time to take other wives. Dan, Mark, Watson and Tim had also managed to subdue their wives from their initial anger and were now living by the rules set out in *The Peace Maker.*

Allen's wife, Brenda, was a different matter, she had been angry from the moment Allen had discussed his new found views with her.

Brenda Wright Lafferty was a young, ambitious and extremely intelligent woman. She had started dating Allen after meeting him at an LDS student congregation and by April 1982 at just 21 she had married him. It was only a few months into their marriage that things had started to change. Allen did not like the thought of Brenda being a career woman, she had a degree in Broadcasting which she wished to pursue, but Allen wanted her to be a house wife, to cater for his every need. She knew she had made a mistake in marrying Allen but she was pregnant with her first child so believed she had to stay.

After giving birth to a baby girl, named Erica, Brenda was convinced that she would be able to bring Allen round and back to the person he once was, she truly believed that she could do this and she was determined to see the bad days through.

Even though Brenda believed that she could talk sense into Allen, she believed that her brother-in-law, Ron Lafferty, was so deeply involved in fundamentalism that he was never going to be converted back to his old faith. Brenda believed that because Ron had tried to hold back from Dan's teachings, the moment that he succumbed to them he did so 100 per cent.

Dianna Lafferty was good friends with Brenda and went to her to talk about her new found anguishes as Ron's wife. Brenda told Dianna that she felt that unlike Allen, Ron was never going to change and urged her to escape whilst she still could and file for divorce. It was the hardest thing Dianna was ever to do but after much deliberation she took her sister-in-law's advice, packed her bags and moved herself and her six children to Florida.

REVELATIONS FROM GOD

From the moment that Dianna left Ron his world fell apart, he was excommunicated from his LDS church and was shunned by many people who had once loved and respected him. Ron became an angry man, he felt cheated and lonely, he lost his job and was left with nothing apart from his family and his religion. He poured himself into this and soon started to have visions from God.

Dan Lafferty was so proud of his brother and they would have long discussions regarding the prophecies that Ron had received.

One of Ron's prophecies in particular was important to Dan as God had described Dan being akin to Nephi. According to the Mormon faith, Nephi was a great prophet and son of Lehi in *The First Book of Mormon.*

Dan was extremely proud that he had been spoken about by God in this way and was suddenly in awe of Ron.

The Lafferty brothers started to make their discussions open to others with similar views and it was during one of the seminars that they met Robert Crossfield. Robert was a Canadian who claimed to be a prophet. He told the Laffertys that he had received a message from God ordering him to teach the six brothers how to receive revelations and how to 'organize themselves into the School of Prophets'.

All the brothers, except Allen, started to have revelations but it was Ron's revelations that were the most intense and bloodthirsty. God spoke to him about removing certain people from the Earth that were getting in the way of the cause and it was one prophecy in particular that would change the family's life forever. Ron had a revelation of removal that stated:

Thus saith the Lord unto my servants the prophets. It is my will and commandment that ye remove the following individuals in order that my work might go forward. For they have truly become obstacles in my path and I will not allow my work to be stopped. First thy brother's wife Brenda and her baby, then Chloe Low, and then Richard Stowe. And it is my will that they be removed in rapid succession and that an example be made of them in order that others might see the fate of those who fight against the true saints of God. And it is my will that this matter be taken care of as soon as possible and I will prepare a way for my instrument to be delivered and instruction be given unto my servant Todd. And it is my will that he show great care in his duties for I have raised him up and prepared him for this important work and is he not like unto my servant Porter Rockwell. And great blessings await him if he will do my will, for I am the Lord thy God and have control over all things. Be still and know that I am with thee. Even so Amen.

When Ron discussed this revelation at The School of Prophets it was only Dan and Watson who were in agreement to carry out the order. The School disbanded due to the disagreement but Dan and Ron continued believing in what they had to do.

ROAD TO MURDER

In the spring of 1984, Ron and Dan embarked on a

road trip up through America's mid west and into Canada, they broke up their journey by dropping in on various fundamentalist communities that they knew about. They took it in turns to drive and spent the days having intense discussions about the removal revelations that Ron had had. Although Dan was proud of how far his brother had come, he also noticed he had turned into a violent and savage man.

At times Dan wondered if he should break ties with his brother, and if things had gone too far, but each time he had these thoughts something inside him told him to stick with Ron.

Ron would deliberate over the meaning of the removal revelation and commented that the four people mentioned in it had all been part of the reason that his wife and left him. Brenda being the main protagonist. His eyes would blank over when he spoke to his brother about slaughters that were soon to take place.

On July 24, 1984, Ron and Dan met up with two polygamist friends called Chip Carnes and Richard Knapp. They had planned to go to Salt Lake City – the home of the Mormons – for the day. Before leaving, Ron told the other three that he thought that they should first go to Mark Lafferty's house to pick up a hunting rifle.

Upon arriving at Mark's house Ron immediately asked for the gun. Mark gave it to him but wished to know what he was going to hunt as Ron had given up the sport years previously. Ron replied, 'Any fucking thing that gets in my way'.

The four men then headed to Allen's apartment, which was in American Fork, a sleepy suburb on the freeway between Provo and Salt Lake City. Ron had said they were going there in search for another rifle. Carnes and Knapp, who were both in the back could hear the brothers discussing whether the removal revelation was to be acted upon that day. Ron really seemed like he was on a mission.

When no one answered the door at Allen's house they got back in the car and headed for Salt Lake City.

They had not got very far when Dan felt a great urge to turn back and try Allen Lafferty's house once more. Dan knocked on the door and Brenda answered. He asked her if Allen was in and she said that he was at work. He then asked if he could step inside to use her telephone. Brenda started to sense that something was up and said that he could not enter the house.

A rage had taken over Dan by this point and he was not taking no for an answer. He pushed Brenda out of the way and let himself in. The sound of Brenda and Dan fighting could be heard from the car and it was this point that Ron made his way into the house.

The two friends were left in the car and could now hear Ron yelling expletives at Brenda at which she was yelling: 'Please don't hurt my baby! Don't hurt my baby!' A deathly silence then came over the duplex and the Lafferty brothers emerged in blood-soaked clothes.

Brenda Lafferty had received a severe beating. An incision had been made to her throat which had sliced through her trachea, both jugular veins, both cartoid arteries and her spinal column. She had then been strangled by the cord of a vaccum cleaner. She had been brutally murdered.

Fifteen month old Erica Lafferty had also had her throat cut from ear to ear – the only thing left holding her head onto her shoulders was the bone. Brenda and Erica Lafferty were to be found dead and lying in pools of their own blood by Allen Lafferty when he returned home from work later that day.

Once back in the car, Dan, Ron, Chip and Richard made their way to the Chloe Low's house. Chloe had been a good friend of Dianna's and had also coaxed her into leaving Ron. They rang the door but no one was in. After breaking in and stealing a handful of Chloe's belongings, the brothers returned to the car and spoke about heading to Richard Stowe's house – Stowe was the bishop who had excommunicated Ron soon after Dianna had left him.

Luckily for Stowe, the brothers took a wrong turn, which was enough for them to give up with completing the removal revelation. Instead they headed toward Wendover where they rented a holiday flat for the night. The Lafferty brothers cleaned themselves up and put their blood stained clothes into the boot of the car, the four men then put their heads down for the night.

Chip Carnes and Richard Knapp snuck out of the apartment in the middle of the night and made their getaway in the car, disposing of the knives and clothes on the way. They were arrested at Chip's brother's house on July 30, 1984.

The next day Dan and Ron realized that they were now on the run and they headed towards Reno. They had a female friend there who worked in a casino called Circus Circus, and had let them sleep on her floor a few months previously. Dan told Ron that they were sure to be met with arrest if they went to her as he had written about her in his diaries, which were now more than likely in the hands of the police.

Ron did not say anything so they kept walking into the Casino and whilst queueing in the restaurant for a coffee they were surrounded by FBI agents. On August 17, 1984 Ronald Watson Lafferty and Daniel Lafferty were arrested for the aggravated murders of Brenda and Erica Lafferty.

BROTHERS ON TRIAL

In 1985 the two brothers stood trial. Ron's lawyer tried to plead insanity in the hope of getting him convicted of manslaughter instead of first degree murder. Ron was found guilty on two charges of first degree murder and was sentenced to death. Dan Lafferty, was charged on two counts of first degree murder and was sentenced to life imprisonment. Dan, to this day, states that he was responsible for both murders, but Ron was sentenced to death for killing Brenda and for being the mastermind behind the plot.

If Ron Lafferty had not gone to his brothers' meeting to try and talk them out of fundamentalism maybe a lot of people's lives could have turned out different. Or was it Ron's fate to end up as he did?

The nightmare of that day in July 1984 has not been an easy one to try and get over as re-trials have occurred as recently as 2003. Ron's defence have made a number of attempts to remove him from death row but each time they have been quashed. He refuses to talk to anyone about the events that happened that year.

Dan Lafferty on the other hand has given many interviews describing the events leading up to and on that frightful day. He still believes that he and his brother were led by God to commit the murders and believes that he will not die in prison. Instead the prison walls will crumble around him and he will emerge as the biblical prophet Elijah, announcing the second coming of Christ. In an interview he gave to the Deseret News in 2002, Dan Lafferty said:

I don't feel comfortable saying I know I'm Elijah, but I'd be pretty surprised if I'm not. You could say I'm patiently awaiting to see if I'm him. I could be wrong, maybe it's all just a comfortable illusion.

The Ku Klux Klan

The White Rights Movement

- Are you now, or have you ever been a member of the Radical Republican Party?

- Did you belong to the Federal Army during the late war, and fight against the South during the existence of the same?

- Are you opposed to negro equality, both social and political?

- Are you in favour of a white man's government in this country?

These were the questions drawn up by the Ku Klux Klan in 1868 to recruit people to its organisation.

WHEN THE BLACK population of America emerged victorious from their struggle for liberation from slavery after the American Civil War, they met with a new enemy — a secret, terrorist, white-supremacist organization known as the Ku Klux Klan, who believed in the innate inferiority of the black man and therefore felt that they neither deserved, nor were welcome to, the same rights and privileges as the white man. The freedom of these slaves signified a humiliating economic and social defeat, adding salt to the wounds left by the military defeat they had already suffered. Resentment and loathing bubbled over and a campaign of terror and violence was unleashed on the southern states of America.

THE END OF THE CIVIL WAR

On March 3, 1865, the Freeman's Bureau was set up by Congress. This had as its objective the protection of freed slaves, and sought to weaken the traditional white power structure of the rebel states. They found new work for the former slaves, and provided them with better health and educational opportunities. In total, they spent 17 million dollars on improved welfare, schools and hospitals. President Andrew Johnson however, who claimed that these black slaves should be in 'subordination' and declared that he would live and die with these beliefs, sought to crush the capabilities of the Freeman's Bureau. He rejected Congress's pursuit of more powers for them, and also opposed the Civil Rights Bill which they proposed. This bill would have increased protection of the black people, and prevented unfair restrictions of their rights.

One year later however, in 1866, the number of Radical Republicans, who fought not only for the abolition of slavery but also supported complete equality for freed slaves, in Congress increased. This led to the passing of the Reconstruction Act which separated the south into districts, and allowed the freed black slaves to vote in the elections for leadership of them.

Against the backdrop of devastated towns and cities, ruined plantations and farms, and a destitute population now controlled by an occupation army, the perceived rise of the slaves was the breaking point for the white Southerners. The stage was set for the explosive arrival of the Ku Klux Klan.

The Ku Klux Klan tore across the war-ravaged South on a mission to intimidate and destroy the Reconstruction governments from the Carolinas to Arkansas. Their main targets were the blacks, and their main goal was to stop them from voting, holding office, or exercising their new, undeserved rights in any way. Also targeted however, were immigrants, and any white people who were standing up for, or sympathetic to, black rights.

The KKK frightened their targets by burning crosses within view of the victim's home. If this had no effect, then they would attack – torturing, beating, and murdering. They justified this as an essential course of action in the name of white supremacy and to protect and keep the white race pure. The Klansmen dressed in white robes with pointed hoods which covered their faces, supposedly symbolising the ghosts of dead soldiers who had returned to avenge their defeat.

THE ORIGINS OF THE KU KLUX KLAN

A group of former Confederate army members established the original group in 1865, in Pulaski,

Tennessee. Originally set up as more of a social club, there was nothing sinister about the first few gatherings of what the young men eventually decided to call the 'Ku Klux Klan'. They chose the name from the Greek word 'kuklos' meaning 'circle', and the English word 'clan'. They also decided to keep it a secret society, to make it more exciting. They gave the ranks of the society ridiculous names – Grand Cyclops, Grand Turk etc. – just to amuse themselves.

Any new members (or 'Ghouls' as they were called within the Klan) whom the group managed to recruit, were subjected to an initiation ceremony. This was a farcical procedure, involving the entrant being blindfolded, sworn in with silly oaths, and finally 'crowned'. The members all went out on horseback, dressed in sheets, with masks covering their faces. These were the very silly, and innocent beginnings of something which was to become deadly serious.

EXPANSION OF THE KU KLUX KLAN

The group began to grow, and attracted more members from adjacent neighbourhoods. The cloaked excursions became more frequent and more sinister. They would arrive at the homes of black people late at night, and give them dark warnings of more visits if they did not keep a low profile. The blacks, with their new-found freedom, ignored these warnings, and soon the threats turned into actual violence. Although the blacks were the main target of these attacks, the Klan also turned on anyone who supported black rights, Northerners who had come south, or southern unionists.

In 1867, all members of the ever-increasing Ku Klux Klan were asked to send representatives to a convention, presided over by 'Grand Wizard' General Nathan Bedford Forrest (a brilliant general in the Civil War), held in Nashville. The main objective of the convention was to discuss the Klan's response to, and encourage the opposition of, the Reconstruction effort to integrate the blacks and allow them voting rights. By now, the KKK had thousands of members all eager to further the cause and uphold white supremacy.

However, many new recruits felt uneasy about the group's activities, as did the long-standing members who were seeing the changes within the structure of the Klan. They were unhappy about the higher level of brutality, and felt that the balance had shifted since the Klan's beginnings. They were all fully supportive of the Klan's cause and agreed with terrorizing and intimidating the blacks into submission, but could not agree with the nightly rampages, robberies, rapes and murders being committed in their name.

The Reconstruction governors soon realized that this was a problem they had to address urgently. They did not however, appreciate the size of the organization they were trying to suppress. Government spies who tried to infiltrate the group were murdered by the Klan, who had been tipped off by insiders in advance. The Klan were more prolific than anyone had imagined, and the secret nature of the organization made it almost impossible to penetrate. Unbeknown to those trying to crack down on the KKK, their own colleagues were often riding out, terrorizing the towns, with the masked night riders.

When federal control of the ex-Confederate states was retracted, the whites were able to regain control and re-introduce segregation anyway. Therefore in 1869, with the main objective achieved, Forrest dissolved the Klan as he too felt that it had become increasingly violent and had abandoned its original goals in the pursuit of sheer anarchy.

Further, when President Ulysses Grant, under pressure from the Radical Republicans to do something about the terror and violence perpetrated by the KKK, signed the Klan Act and Enforcement Act in 1871, it was believed that the KKK would disappear forever. The report by the Federal Grand Jury stated that:

There has existed since 1868, in many counties of the state, an organization known as the Ku Klux Klan, or Invisible Empire of the South, which embraces in its membership a large proportion of the white population of every profession and class. The Klan has a constitution and bylaws, which provides, among other things, that each member shall furnish himself with a pistol, a Ku Klux gown and a signal instrument. The operations of the Klan are executed in the night and are invariably directed against members of the Republican Party. The Klan is inflicting summary vengeance on the colored citizens of these citizens by breaking into their houses at the dead of night, dragging them from their beds, torturing them in the most inhuman manner, and in many instances murdering.

It made the KKK an illegal organization and allowed the use of force to quash any strains of the group and any activities it engaged in. This was phenomenally successful. The Klan was completely dissolved in South Carolina, and membership in other states reduced to virtually none. Although the Klan Act was eventually declared unconstitutional in 1882, it was too late for the organization to recover.

RE-EMERGENCE OF THE KU KLUX KLAN

But the KKK never completely died, and with the outbreak of World War I, it was set to re-emerge. William J. Simmons re-formed the group in 1915. He was a preacher, who had been greatly influenced by the Thomas Dixon book, *The Ku Klux Klan,* and the film subsequently made of the book, *Birth of A Nation.*

Greatly affected by Nazi propaganda in Germany, many US citizens began to blame not only the blacks, but also the Jews, and other immigrant groups, for their economic troubles. They also targeted homosexuals, communists and organized labour. Arguably in an attempt simply to make money, Simmons took advantage of these feelings of hostility towards such groups, and established a 20th century version of the Ku Klux

Klan. Where the first KKK had been southern and of Democratic persuasion, this second version attracted both Democrats and Republicans from all over the country. Regardless of their different political beliefs they were united in their hostility towards the slaves and foreigners who were detrimental to the welfare of their white nation.

The list of those despised and victimised by the Klan grew ever longer. Klansmen were sent out to uncover society's fears and exploit them in an attempt to attract new members. Targets now included anyone who disrespected the Sabbath, had or condoned sex outside of marriage, dealt in drugs and ran or frequented night-clubs. Membership flooded in as law-abiding US citizens looked to the KKK to purge society of all its evils. At a cost of $10 per person, the money poured in too.

A greatly influential group, this organisation had over four million members at its highest point. In the 1920s, Klansmen were even occupying positions of political power. Should any members of the KKK have been arrested for their violent crimes, the southern courts were very unlikely to return a guilty verdict. The authorities turned a blind eye to the Klan's activities, even when reports were coming in of the letters 'KKK' being burnt, with acid, on to the faces of anyone considered anti-American.

A brave media eventually faced up to the Klan, but reports of immoral behaviour and corruption within the Klan headquarters and the brutal violence perpetrated by them, seemed simply to encourage more people to join. Simmons recognized this, and could give no explanation for it, but welcomed it whole-heartedly. Congress investigated further, but Simmons merely denied any knowledge of the violence, and explained the secretive nature of the group as being a feature no different from that of any other fraternal organization.

LEADERSHIP DISPUTE

The Klan's growth surge led to revolts within the organization, and eventually Simmons's leadership was overthrown by Hiram Wesley Evans and six co-conspirators. The KKK had now amassed a great fortune and owned property valued at millions of dollars. Simmons was not willing to let this go so easily, and a massive court battle exploded. When one of Simmons's lawyers was shot by Evans's publicity chief following a heated argument, Simmons backed down and agreed to a cash settlement.

Although this struggle was over, it had badly damaged the group. The internal organization of the Klan had been laid bare for the courts, the media and the public to examine, and the secrets of the group had been exposed. What was supposed to be a non-profit organization was clearly making huge amounts of money, and the claims of immorality made against both parties by each other directly contradicted the declaration of the KKK that it existed to protect the morals and the purity of America.

The continued reports of violence did not escape the

public's notice either. Men, women and children were being flogged by the KKK for immoral crimes such as missing church, or defending those who did. One divorced woman received a beating simply for remarrying, and young girls were frequently flogged if caught riding in cars with boys.

Yet still the popularity of the KKK appeared to grow and it advanced further politically. Klansmen appeared in the US Senate, and were elected to governors. Evans decided it was time to for the KKK presence to be felt in the presidential elections. He had supporters in both the Republican and Democratic parties and so felt confident that he could influence the government whichever party was elected.

DECLINE OF THE KU KLUX KLAN

But the KKK presence on such a high-profile political stage pulled the traditionally secretive Klan right into the public arena, and there they encountered as much hostility as they did support. More and more graphic news stories detailing the atrocities perpetrated by the Klan hit the headlines and this time they could not be ignored. One report detailed how a Texas man had been dowsed in oil and burned before hundreds of Klan members. Membership figures, formerly in their millions, dropped to hundreds of thousands.

The Great Depression of the 1930s saw a further reduction in membership figures and the remaining members were advised to keep a relatively low profile and stay out of the public eye. The diminishing Klan funds were hoarded by Evans and his circle.

In 1939, James A. Colescott took over leadership of the Klan, but he was to preside over it for only five years. The end for this second KKK followed a combination of events. The first was the shocking reports of a rape and murder committed by the 'Grand Dragon' of Indiana. The woman he attacked had been so badly bitten that the assault was viewed by some as cannibalistic. This stunned the nation and the KKK once again declined.

The final blow came with a lien filed by the Internal Revenue Service for a sum of over $685,000 of back taxes accrued from profits gained in the 1920s. The Klan was forced to sell all its assets in 1944, hand over any monies to the government, and cease its activities.

SPLINTER GROUPS

The Ku Klux Klan appeared again in the 1960s, but this time forming as several offshoots instead of one united body. Their main aim was to oppose the civil rights movement. With the increase in racial tolerance across the US though, these bodies, the biggest of which were the Imperial Klans of America, the White Knights of the Ku Klux Klan, and Knights of the White Kamelia, were driven underground. Yet, they still struck fear into the hearts of the black communities. In Mississippi for example, where 42 per cent of the population were black, only 2 per cent registered to vote.

The Congress of Racial Equality and another organization campaigning non-violently for black Americans, decided to concentrate their efforts in Mississippi and set up 30 'Freedom Schools' across the state. Over 3,000 students attended these schools, which now taught black history and the civil rights movement as part of their curriculum.

The schools became an obvious target for the KKK, as did those who had organized them and were campaigning for black rights. Their homes and churches were firebombed, and they were attacked and beaten. Three were murdered.

SIXTEENTH STREET BAPTIST CHURCH BOMBING

The KKK, in its various guises, was also still evading conviction for its crimes in the 1960s, even though some were so shocking that they made national headlines. One such case was the Sixteenth Street Baptist Church Bombing. On the morning of September 15, 1963, a bomb exploded underneath the church, killing four teenage girls and injuring 23 other people who had been attending the Sunday School held there.

A man, identified as Robert Chambliss, had been witnessed at the scene earlier that morning. He had placed a box under the steps of the church. Although arrested for murder and for illegal possession of explosives (122 sticks of dynamite), he was only found guilty on the second charge. He was given a fine and sentenced to six months in prison, but walked free on the murder charge.

Only 14 years later, in 1977, was Chambliss finally brought to justice for his crime. When Bill Baxley was appointed attorney general in Alabama, he requested the FBI files on the case and found masses of evidence against Chambliss which had been ignored at the trial. In November 1977, Chambliss was re-tried, convicted, and sentenced to life imprisonment. Another 25 years later, three more men were accused of having been involved in the bombing with Chambliss. The four men belonged to a KKK faction called the Cahaba Boys. One of the three had died, and one of the remaining two was given a life sentence.

MICHAEL DONALD

When a black man was taken to court in 1981 for the murder of a white policeman and released by an undecided jury, the KKK was outraged. They blamed the verdict on the fact that some of the jury were black, and decided to bring about their own justice by killing a black man in return. Henry Hays, the son of one of the most senior Klan officials in Alabama, and his friend James Knowles, searched the streets of Mobile until they found their target – a young black man named Michael Donald. Donald was forced into their car, driven out of the county and murdered.

A half-hearted investigation into the murder by local

police came to the conclusion that the murder was the result of a botched drug deal. The case, as far as they were concerned, was then closed. Donald's mother however, who knew that her son had absolutely no involvement in drugs, called upon Jessie Jackson for help. He came to Mobile and organized a protest march about the injustice served.

The case came to the attention of the assistant United States attorney in Mobile, and he raised his concerns with the FBI. Under FBI investigation, James Knowles confessed to Michael Donald's murder. He was given life imprisonment. He was also called as chief prosecution witness at Henry Hays's trial six months later, wherein Hays was was found guilty and given the death penalty for the crime.

Michael Donald's mother went even further in her pursuit of justice for her son, and for all African Americans. She set out to bring down the Ku Klux Klan in Alabama. She filed a civil suit against the Klan in 1987, which resulted in an all-white jury finding the Klan, as a body, responsible for her son's death. The Alabama Klan was ordered to pay seven million dollars.

THE KKK TODAY

The KKK is viewed by society as a racist, ignorant, violent and homophobic organization. The name of the KKK is immediately associated with crime. The Klan defends itself by attacking the members of the movement who commit the crimes. They, it claims, are not true members and joined the Klan for the wrong reasons.

However, the fact remains that they are still affiliated to this group. They attack blacks in the street, set fire to black churches, burn crosses in front of their houses and hang nooses above their doors. Media reports frequently describe murders linked to the KKK.

Generally, the name is now symbolic of hatred, racial fanaticism and bigotry. The group is unlikely ever to be able to rise above this status. It has neither the backing of society nor any kind of financial support to push it towards any kind of political credibility.

The Thugs of India

*19th Century cult worshipping Kali – the
Goddess of destruction*

IN 19TH CENTURY India there was a criminal gang who were called the Thugs. The Thugs were members of Thuggee (*tuggee*), a religious Indian cult that worshipped Kali.

Kali is the destructive and creative mother goddess of Hinduism. She is seen as the fierce aspect of God's energy and is fundamental to all of the other Hindu Gods. Kali, the Hindu word for black, is seen as the opposite to Shiva but at the same time Shiva needs her to exist. In certain forms Kali is Shiva's wife.

The Thugs were mainly found in the Vidarbha region of India, in the Central West, and although they worshiped a Hindu goddess, many cult members were Muslim – all were male. Access to the cult was hereditary and would be passed down from father to son and most of the time the women family members would be ignorant to what went on.

The original mission of the Thugs was to murder and then steal from their victims as sacrifices to their Goddess Kali. The unlucky victim would always be an affluent Indian man travelling for the purpose of business or a celebration such as a wedding. This class choice was because the Thugs believed that the Brahams, who were the top and wealthiest caste in India, were enemies of Kali and therefore had to be exterminated.

The Thugs were a well-oiled machine. They would work in groups of between 20 and 100 and each individual of the group would have a specific role. The 'lughaees' would prepare the graves, the 'sothaees' would lure travellers and the 'bhuttotes' performed the ritualistic murders. Even Thugs who were either too old or infirm to take part in the actual murder would still have a role. They would act as spies and cooks and would find out when a wealthy party were due to pass.

The Thugs also had their own language called 'Ramasee' which even members in the remotest parts of India were knowledgeable of.

THE RITUAL OF DEATH

To begin with the Thugs did everything in a ritualistic manner. The ritual would start out with the 'sothaees' becoming involved with the group of travellers that they wished to prey on. The Thugs were excellent cooks and it would not take long before they were entertaining the people they wished to murder and mug, with their victims soon becoming off-guard and relaxed in the Thugs' company.

Once the travellers were enjoying eating, drinking and dancing with the Thugs a code phrase of 'Bring the

Tobacco' would be uttered. This code meant that it was time to begin the slaughter. Each Thug would move towards a male member of the travelling party and then another coded order would be issued. Each Thug would then pull a long silk scarf, called an 'arm', out of their pockets which had a copper coin tied in the middle of it. In a matter of seconds the scarf would be around the victims neck with the copper coin positioned over the neck bone. With one powerful tug the victim would start to suffocate and then have a broken neck due to the pressure of the coin on the bone. Within a few minutes the strangled man would be dead.

The Thugs would then tie up all women and children, take anything of value from the dead men and then dedicate the corpses to Kali. The women and children would be left unharmed. The whole ritual was extremely silent and clean, not a drop of blood was ever spilled. As soon as they put their scarves away they would look no different from the next man who was to pass.

STEALING FROM THE RICH

The Thugs were seen by some as holy people whose destiny it was to follow such a path. They followed the command of Kali, who came to them through a series of omens, or as an inner God and told them to perform the sacrifices in her honour. To murder for monetary gain was a religious duty for them, in which the morality of the act was never thought about. In the eyes of the Thugs they were part of an honourable profession in which doing something for a higher power was of much more importance than the lives of mere mortals.

Over the years the Thugs' ceremonial acts became slack and it was soon just murder for money in the style of Robin Hood. Although they were still sacrificing the Brahams for Kali, bodies were not buried and could be seen scattered around the Indian countryside.

They went for years performing their murderous operation and due to their tight-knit community and the security of their work they managed to practise their craft well into the 20th Century. They were tax-payers and under the banner of religion it was hard for the governments over the years to do anything about it.

Many Indians, due to the caste system, knew that they were not to fear as they were too poor to be affected, but the Brahams lived in constant fear of attack by this silent group of murderers who disappeared as quickly as they had arrived – without a leaving a trace.

Maybe the Thugs were just as much a group angry about class division as they were about pleasing their Goddess?

In the 1830s the British rulers in India managed to stop a lot of the Thug action that had been going on. A British man called William Sleeman started the witch-hunt which consisted of profiling, detective intelligence and execution.

A lot of mystery still surrounds the history of the Thuggee, it is even believed that they may have just been a bunch of highway-men who were demonized by the British in order to get the Indians on side when they were taking power and it helped them secure Indian loyalty to the British Raj.

The word Thuggee came from the Sanskrit word 'sthaga' which means to conceal, and is usually used in conjunction with fraudulent concealment. Why would the Indian people have named the Thugs so if they were in fact a group of heartless murderers? Would they not have been named something that showed the extent of their crimes?

It is believed that the Thuggee cult were responsible for over one and a half million deaths but it is hard to know what is propaganda and what is fact when the history of the country is hugely written by the colonizer. Maybe the British Raj feared this group as they were anti-class and anti-imperialism, two things that the British Raj relied heavily upon when colonizing India.

But if the colonizers have written the truth then the Thuggee cult holds the record for the most murders committed by one group of people.

Roch Theriault

The Ant Hill Kids Commune

ONE OF CANADA'S most disturbing criminals, Roch Theriault abused the members of his commune physically, sexually and psychologically. He led a staggering reign of fear, which involved torturing, castrating and killing. A polygamist, he took 12 wives, one of whom he killed, and one he disabled by hacking off her arm with a meat cleaver. Roch Theriault believed that God had charged him with a mission to help construct a better world. God had told him that the apocalypse was approaching, and that it was his task to guide God's followers out of the despair to a new beginning.

Over a period of 12 years, approximately 20 people left their friends and families in order to follow Roch Theriault and to lead what they believed to be an existence outside of sin and temptation. Beginning with the desire to rid themselves of their dependances, their reasons for joining the group soon changed and became more of a need to help Roch achieve his divine mission.

During this period the group members lived their

dream – being the people elected by God. For some, the experience was sometimes difficult, yet generally satisfactory. For others, the pursuit of this ideal became a nightmare. Some suffered greatly as they strove to be recognized as faithful servants and dignified of being accepted into the kingdom of God. They suffered daily physical and psychological abuse, and gave away all their money and possessions to belong in the group.

Roch's view of the world was of a universe split into two: the good and the bad; rule-abiding members, and rule-breaking members; members and non-members. Using this vision, he isolated his followers from the outside world. They were not permitted to speak to non-members for fear they may become corrupted, influenced, and therefore impure, through contact with them.

Roch believed that he was God's representative on Earth. He was different from everyone else, and had been elected by God. His followers were spiritually inferior to him. That is why they could not accompany him right to the top. He was the last prophet on Earth, and God spoke to him as he had done to his ancestor, Moses.

ROCH THERIAULT

Born in Chicoutimi, Quebec, in 1947, Theriault showed signs of abnormal behaviour from a young age. This could perhaps be attributed to his lack of a particularly healthy role-model to set him an example. His father was a member of the 'White Berets', a radical and fanatical Catholic group. One of his favourite pastimes was to gather his young son, with his three brothers, to sit together at the table and play a game called 'bone'. This involved kicking each other's shins as hard as possible, wearing heavy boots, until one of them finally gave in.

Roch Theriault claims to have spent a lot of time in the Quebec bush as a boy. It was here, he says, that he first learned to talk to the trees and the animals. Not long after his eighth birthday, he discovered another talent – he was able to heal the sick. His first patient was a friend who had broken his teeth, and from there he moved on to performing the castration of farm animals, which after a while he was able to achieve without causing any bleeding whatsoever.

He joined a Catholic group called the 'Aramis Club', but quickly went about trying to re-direct their worship, telling members to wear the image of Satan on their backs. The group was not comfortable with Roch Theriault, and so he was asked to leave.

Roch went instead to the Seventh Day Adventist church, where he found the existing members much more willing to listen to his views and beliefs. Only two months after joining the Adventists, the charismatic Theriault had already attracted the attention of six women and two men who saw him as their religious teacher. Possessed by a desire to help the population to rid themselves of their dependencies on drugs and cigarettes, he decided to hold sessions, across Quebec, on health and how to give up smoking. The sessions were a programme of five days, and focused on a healthy diet, psychology and group therapy. He claimed these delivered excellent results. A strict vegetarian himself, he also held vegetarian banquets to promote a healthier diet.

EXPULSION

When Roch indirectly caused the death of a woman suffering from Leukemia, by persuading her husband that he should take her away from hospital and let Roch heal her with a healthy diet, he was asked to leave the church. He took his following, which now consisted of six men, 12 women and two children, with him.

Although Roch's original mission was not to establish a group or a commune, several of those who had joined him decided to live with him and to follow him in his mission. According to Roch, the creation of the commune was more of a fortuitous development than a planned occurrence. He claimed that, originally, the arrival of these volunteers posed a serious organizational problem. They had all left paid jobs to devote themselves full time to this new work. Given that the sessions were free and that those who attended gave only as much as they wanted to at the end of each one, it was impossible for Roch to put any of his helpers on a fixed salary. That is why they decided to embark on communal living.

After several months, the progressive disinterest of the Quebec citizens for the detox programmes Roch offered led the group to retreat into their own isolated part of Quebec.

GASPE REGION

On 5 June, 1978, several of the members went out to research the Gaspe region in east Quebec, looking for a new residence. Roch had decided to leave Beauce in the south. The group had been living together for almost one year when the decision to move was taken. He claimed that the group was unified in this decision, and that although he had been at the heart of the creation of the group, all big decisions were made with the consent of the whole group. Without hesitation apparently, they all agreed to leave for the mountains of Gaspe, where they settled in July, 1978.

MOSES

Shortly after their arrival in Gaspe, Roch consigned a new name to each of the members in order to mark their new departure. He wrote biblical names on pieces of paper, and one by one, each member chose. When they all had their names, they decided on a name for Roch. He was to be known as Moses. At the same time, and again on Roch's instructions, the members adopted identical tunic uniforms.

Roch, who felt that the world was becoming intransigent towards the group, ordered his members to reduce contact with their families and friends. He backed up this order with the Bible's instructions to keep evil far away. This command was just one of a set of guidelines which Roch established for them to follow in their daily lives. He expected them to:

Live the lives of the first Christians
Live without sin
Release their goods and all their possessions
Spend their time working for the community
Eat as little as possible to avoid the sin of greed
Attend community confessions
Consult Moses before every decision
Respect Moses's dress-code

He instructed them to build a commune, the construction of which he oversaw, rather than participated in as he was suffering from stomach problems and cancer which, he claimed, did not permit him to help. His followers toiled on the building for long hours every day.

In the Autumn of the first year in the Gaspe region, Roch married each of his 12 women followers. This was necessary, he claimed, in order to create large families as the biblical kings Saul, David and Solomon had done before him. But with 12 women now at his every beck and call, his attentions were diverted from his pure and healthy lifestyle, and concentrated more on sexual gratification.

On January 3, 1979, Moses's first child was born in the commune. Over the whole 12 years which the group existed, over 20 children, from five different women, were born into the group. Moses was the father of most of them.

FEBRUARY 17, 1979

Roch foretold of impending disaster based on the biblical prophecy in the Book of Revelation. He forecast this doomsday for February 17, 1979, but he told his followers not to fear, for he had been chosen by God to lead them away from the wickedness of the world and to form a new social order which would embrace God's 1,000-year reign.

The day came, and nothing happened. To explain this hiccup, Roch told his members that although God had given him this date, nothing was certain. He explained that one second in the life of God could equate to 40 years of life on Earth, and conversely, one second of time on Earth could represent 40 years of God's existence. It is likely therefore, that the calculations were inaccurate. The members were not disillusioned by this error in Roch's prediction. They were fixed on their sole objective – to help Roch in his divine mission.

HYPOCRISY

Over time, Roch either forgot, or chose to ignore, the vegetarian diet he had previously advocated and began regularly to eat large quantities of meat, washed down with 'Pepsi Cola'. His attitude to his followers however, did not slacken at all. He still made them work ceaselessly, now on minimal amounts of food. There was no breakfast, and only a small lunch. No one dared to complain because they knew this meant that the portions would decrease further. One of the women, pregnant at the time, was so hungry that she stole two pancakes – a crime for which Roch hit her so hard that he broke two of her ribs.

Moses justified any deviation from his original rules as part of the secret nature of his role in the group, and therefore he was unable to give away too many details. He did explain his new diet by saying that fresh foods had a bad effect on his body, and that by eating them, he was forcing himself to suffer, not indulging in greed. He also explained that he was allowed to have sexual relations with whomever he chose as he was God's representative and was sowing God's seed on earth. Members who wanted to have a sex life had to receive Moses's blessing first. He had to approve of any procreation, and he decided with whom the members were allowed to have sexual relations.

However, no one was allowed to question Moses anyway. Members had to follow his every word. They should not think for themselves, or query anything he said. Any private thought they had, encouraging them to speak up, was the voice of the devil.

POLICE INTERVENTION

Following an agreed radio interview given by Roch, the police became interested in the group and issued a court order which insisted that one member of the group be taken to hospital for psychiatric tests. The police also took Roch and three other members to the police station to answer further enquiries.

All members were free to go shortly afterwards, but Roch was accused of keeping the members at the commune against their will, when he refused to let one of the group be taken to the hospital for a mental health assessment. Following a psychiatric evaluation however, Roch was deemed unfit to undergo trial. He was transmitted to a psychiatric institution in the Quebec region. After a second evaluation, he was deemed fit, and went to trial. He was found guilty of the charges and given a suspended sentence. Roch returned to the commune on April 27, 1979.

INCREASED VIOLENCE

Shortly after Roch's return, the violence at the commune greatly increased. Gabrielle Lavallée was punched by him for falling asleep during one of his speeches.

After this, the punishments became more frequent. He also began drinking heavily. He would keep the already exhausted group members up throughout the night, and anybody who fell asleep would be beaten with a wooden club.

It was not only he who conducted this violence, the members themselves were forced to impose punishments on each other. Moses would get members to admit that they were worthless and that he had to punish them. He would then instruct the other followers to administer the punishment, kicking, punching and hair-pulling.

On one occasion, Roch ordered one commune member to cut off the toe of his wife, as a punishment for disobedience. He told the sobbing man that he had to learn how to discipline her in order to keep her under control. The man could not bring himself to do the deed, but knew that if he didn't, then Roch would do it himself and with much less accuracy and compassion. So, with tears in his eyes, he brought the axe down on his poor wife's delicate foot.

During one of his punishment sessions, he ordered two of his followers to go out into the winter air, totally naked. One protested, telling him that they would freeze outside and fall ill. He told them that they would not fall ill as long as he decided so. He told them that nothing happened at the commune without his express endorsement, which was the will of God. He ordered them outside.

Moses saw himself as the enforcer of purity and of making the members respect the rules. Sinners were punished by him, or by other members of the group. Moreover, it was a privilege to be punished by Moses himself. Completely naked, they were beaten by him until they bled.

Through punishment, the members would find the inspiration to record their faults in The Diary of the Children of Israel – the reference book of the community.

Roch went some way towards explaining his insistence on complete submission by saying that he had to prepare them to obey him. When the end of the world arrives, they will need a guide. The Hebrews could not have escaped Egyptian slavery without Moses, and now he was there for them. Even if he did not understand God's will, as he was not chosen to be an interpreter, he would guide them. If his members chose to follow him, then they had to follow him to his word, and not criticize him – no matter what may come. He was not acting on his will, but on that of God. They were not following him, but through him they were following God.

Roch Theriault began to see himself as more and more powerful. He even began to believe that he had shaman and healing powers and began to treat his followers when they fell ill.

GUY VEER

In November 1980, the commune was joined by Guy

Veer, a mental patient who had had enough of society and had heard about Roch Theriault's group on 'Eternal Mountain'. He joined, and was sent by Roch to sleep in the storage shed, along with one of the other member's son, Samuel.

Samuel had been severely mistreated by Roch, who was angry because the boy was not his own son. If he cried, his father was instructed to roll him in the snow. One night in March, 1981, the drunk Roch decided to circumsize Samuel, and to prepare him, poured ethanol into his mouth. Samuel was found dead the next morning. The blame was instantly passed to Guy Veer. Roch claimed that he had punched the young boy over and over again to stop him crying. A mock court, set up by Roch months later, also came to this conclusion. Guy's punishment for murdering Samuel was castration, for which Guy even signed a consent form. Roch gave Guy some alcohol, and wound an elastic band around his genitals to perform the operation.

Guy Veer eventually went to the police, and on December 9, 1981, after having received Veer's statement, the police made another visit to the commune. They arrested four members, including Moses, concerning the death of the child. They were convicted of criminal responsibility and child abandonment. Further, Gabrielle Lavallée was also convicted for having helped Moses with the castration, despite being a nurse and knowing that this operation could have resulted in death.

On December 23, the judge sent an eviction notice to

the members still in the commune, and on January 18, 1982, the members still at the commune were evacuated by forest guards.

On September 28, 1982, the four accused members were all found guilty of practising illegal medicine which caused the death of the child. They all received prison sentences, ranging from between nine months to one year. During his time in prison, Moses wrote a book about the life of the commune in the Gaspe forest.

On his release from prison, Roch moved his community to Burnt River, an area just north of Toronto. The locals and authorities were very suspicious of Roch and his followers and treated them very warily. They were caught shop-lifting, and consequently banned, from local stores and they were not granted welfare from the social services, on the basis that they were not a family.

In order to raise some money, Roch set up his own business making and selling bread and pastries door to door. He called the company 'The Ant Hill Kids' because of how hard they worked together. With a little more money coming in, Roch began drinking again. His stomach condition worsened, but every time he felt pain, he sent one of his followers to buy him a case of beer to ease it.

In June 1985, the Ontario Provincial Police were alerted to distress calls which had been made from the commune. They arrived to find a drunken Roch, totally naked, clinging to a tree calling 'Mayday' into a two-way radio. The other commune members, who had been told that the day had of judgement had finally arrived and to prepare themselves for the end of the world, were found cringing in a shelter.

PUNISHMENT

Roch became increasingly violent. In drunken rages, he would proclaim that all the members of the commune were evil and that he had to strike the devil from them. Mostly, the punishments were humiliating. Sometimes Roch would order his followers to lie down while he urinated on them, other times he ordered them to wipe their faces with each other's excrement.

When one of the members could take no more of such rituals, he hit Roch in the face, smacking him against the wall. The punishment for this outburst? Circumcision. A small comfort was that Roch ordered another member of the commune to carry out the procedure. Had Roch done it himself, it would have been much worse.

One of the children, who could bear life in the commune no longer having been severely beaten by Roch, fled from the camp. He went to the police and told them that Moses had sexually abused him.

CHILDREN'S AID SOCIETY

The commune was visited by social workers from the Children's Aid Society, and they remarked how subservient the women of the commune were. None dared to speak unless given permission from Roch.

Roch told the social workers that only one of the women was his wife. The others were just his lovers. He was asked if the eldest girl in the commune, aged nine years, would eventually become his lover, to which he replied that he hoped so.

The Children's Aid Society kept a close eye on Roch and the commune, and made frequent visits which he greatly disliked. One woman spoke to the CAS workers and told them of Roch's division of the children into the chosen ones and mere slaves. The 'slaves' were used to gratify him sexually, or served as punchbags when he had been drinking and become violent. He would throw them against trees or into the lake. One boy, whom Roch particularly disliked because his droopy eyes were the mark of the devil, was left outside in a wheelbarrow for two hours – the temperature being −10°C. An ambulance was called but the boy had already died by the time it arrived.

Seventeen children were removed from the commune, under warrants issued by the CAS, and placed in foster homes. Their carers reported very unusual behaviour. One boy was scared of men with beards, another terrified by a light being turned on. One eight-year-old child told his foster parents how it had been his job to wash the commune women's sanitary towels.

More horrific stories emerged from the commune. Roch, seemingly always drunk, used to suspend babies by their ankles above the fire, and ask of their crying mothers which one should be dropped first. Having thrown a child into the lake to cleanse it of the devil, he would not allow the mother to swim out and rescue her drowning baby until it had bobbed up at least three times.

Outside of the commune and in the safety of caring homes, the children were assessed psychologically. All, the reports showed, had been subjected to sexual acts too early in their development. They spoke naively of having had to masturbate Roch, one girl having been forced to do so at the same time as her mother.

Yet despite such intervention and the constant supervision of the police, still the strange practices did not stop. On September 29, 1988, one of the women, Solange Boilard, died after being operated on by Moses. The aim of the procedure was to relieve her of stomach aches, but Roch partially disembowelled her with a kitchen knife during the gruesome operation. The group buried the body, but it was later exhumed. This was repeated three times before they finally left her in peace. Moses took a small piece of her bone which he kept beneath his beard.

GABRIELLE LAVALLÉE

On November 5, 1988, Moses tore out eight of Gabrielle's teeth with pliers as punishment for a reduction in bread sales. After this, Gabrielle fled, but she returned to the group a few days later. She repeated this a couple of times more, leaving but always coming back. She was scared of Moses, but admitted she couldn't live without him.

Moses noticed that Gabrielle had a paralysed finger and ordered her to show it to him. As she held it out, he cut into it with a hunting knife. He told her she needed to have her hand amputated, explaining that there was a risk of gangrene. He then cut her arm off and attempted to cauterize the wound using a steel rod heated with a blow torch. After this, Gabrielle waited for the right time to leave the group again.

On August 14, Gabrielle left for good. As soon as she arrived in the village she was hospitalized. In hospital, she told a police officer about the treatment she had been subjected to in the commune and disclosed details of Solange Boilard's 'operation'. After her statement the police went looking for Moses. Five days later, Moses, two wives and two children were arrested as they prepared to flee Canada for the US.

In October 1990, he was charged with many counts of assault on Gabrielle, and for having caused the death of Solange Boilard. For the latter, he pleaded guilty to second-degree murder and was sentenced to 25 years.

He admitted that many things had happened at Burnt River, and that his alcoholism had brought on his psychological imbalance. He said he would never be able to forgive himself for Solange's death.

IMPRISONED

Roch Theriault is still in prison. Since his imprisonment in 1989, he has been moved from different prisons across Canada. Yet he still casts a spell over some of his disciples. In each prison, he has received visits from three female members of the group, and has fathered a total of four children by them during this time.

In July 2002, an appeal was launched for his release. This was refused on the grounds that he was still considered a danger to society, and still had drug and alcohol problems. Unusually, Roch welcomed the verdict. Prior to the actual hearing he had even asked *not* to be released as he had begun to fear the treatment which he anticipated would be waiting for him on the outside.

Gabrielle Lavallée campaigns constantly to keep Roch Theriault in prison. She has written a book about the ordeals she suffered, testified at his parole hearing, and believes that he is a 'monster' who should stay behind bars for the rest of his life.

Francisco Bezerra de Morais

Toto and his prophecies of death

BRAZILIAN, FRANCISCO BEZERRA de Morais was 35 when he and his followers murdered six people in order to 'wipe out the enemies of God'.

Morais was the leader of a religious sect deep in the Amazon rain forest which was an off shoot group of the United Pentecostal Church of Brazil.

Even though Brazil's largest religion is Catholicism, over the years there has been a vast increase in other religions and sects that have been influenced by Christianity and Ancient African spirituality.

On November 17, 1998, Morais, known to his followers as Toto, commanded for murders to take place after he started receiving prophecies from God ordering him to kill certain people within his church community.

The voices were said to state that Satanical people had become members of his congregation, and these evil people needed to be wiped out as soon as possible.

Six members of the 30-strong sect were arrested at a rubber plantation, which had been the site of the ritualistic murders.

Leader, Toto, had been helped by his wife and four other men after the three children and three adults had started to turn into demons. One of Toto's followers, Francisco Lopes da Silva killed his own 13-year-old child after the boy apparently 'transformed into a demon in front of a large crowd'. Lopes took his son to the rubber plantation and inflicted a ritualistic beating upon him, which ended in his death. The beatings took place using a number of different weapons such as bare knuckles, wooden clubs and metal chains whilst a continual chant of 'Out, Satan!' was cried.

Another father, Adalberto Taviera de Souza was also arrested for the murder of his two young children aged three and five. He killed them by repeatedly stamping on their heads after they had 'turned into monsters with wide faces, fat legs and long fingernails.'

Souza then calmly watched his wife be murdered by Toto. Toto believed that it was necessary for her to be killed as she had given birth to the two miscreated children, so it was more than likely that she also had monstrous, demonic tendencies.

The other adults who were killed on Toto's orders were two men who had apparently performed miracles such as changing the colours of the sun.

Toto believed that nearly all of his followers were 'infected' by demons and marked for death by God. It was his job whilst here on Earth to cleanse his congregation of the evil within.

Toto and his wife were arrested two weeks after the first murder had taken place when a former leader of the church who had been left for dead after an obligatory beating had raised the alarm. Francisco Oliviera de Franca had pretended to be dead as Toto's followers beat him with sticks and chains. As soon as the men and women had left him to rot away, he mustered up enough strength and courage to get to his feet. The former minister was then confronted with a three-day hike through the Amazon before he reached a town where he was able to notify the local police force of the events that were occuring in the jungle.

When the police arrived at the scene they were met with the foul smell of decomposing flesh. The bodies had not even been disposed of. They still lay where they had taken their final breath and were rapidly rotting, with chunks of missing flesh where wild animals had eaten from them.

If de Franca, had not survived his beating, who is to say how many more murders would have been committed?

Toto is still adamant that there is nothing wrong with him or with his actions. The only thing he did was to act upon orders given to him by God and what can be so wrong with that? Whilst being held in a secure unit in a town close to the Peruvian unit Toto stated:

These were the words of God. I have been communicating with him since the age of eight. This is in God's hands and he will tell me what to do next.

Yahweh Ben Yahweh

God, the son of God

YAHWEH BEN YAHWEH proclaims himself, and is believed by his followers, to be the Black Christ. He founded the 'Nation of Yahweh', also known as the Temple of Love, in 1979, with the intention of leading the blacks out of oppression and into the promised land. He is now serving the last stretch of his 18-year prison sentence in Lewisburg Federal Prison.

Yahweh Ben Yahweh, born Hulon Mitchell, Jr., in Oklahoma in 1935, believes that the black people are the lost tribe of Israel. They are the true Jews, and God and Jesus are black. White people are devils, and need to be eliminated in his prophesised race war.

Mitchell moved to Miami in 1979, and began to circulate his beliefs. He demanded that those who follow him should give up their 'slave' names, and assume Hebrew names. He established the Nation of Yahweh, and the laws which governed its members. He instructed them to cut their ties with their families and instead offer complete loyalty and devotion to him. Allegiance to this sect grew, and by 1980, Mitchell was able to purchase a property in Miami which he named The Temple of Love. He set up businesses inside the building, including a supermarket and beauty parlour, and used the Temple's members as full-time workers. Those who lived and worked within the temple worked without payment and donated all their possessions to Mitchell and the Temple.

EXPANSION OF THE TEMPLE

As the Temple flourished in the early 1980s, Mitchell declared himself to be the son of God, and thus renamed himself 'Yahweh Ben Yahweh', meaning 'God, son of God'. He established a new, standardized dress code for his followers, consisting of white robes and turbans, and he became much stricter on the Temple members' contact with non-believers. He placed security guards at the entrance to the Temple who were ordered to search all who entered. These guards were named 'The Circle of Ten' and, armed with clubs and machetes, they were told that anyone who attempted to enter the Temple without an invitation should be prevented, using whatever means necessary. This Circle of Ten also served as Ben Yahweh's personal bodyguards and swore allegiance to him and to his protection.

The Nation of Yahweh began to expand in the years which followed. Trusted elders were sent out to distribute pamphlets and to set up temples elsewhere. By the mid-80s several new temples had been established in some of the larger cities in the US.

The expectations Ben Yahweh placed on his followers, and his subsequent control of them, also increased. He used sleep deprivation and malnutrition to control all members. Weakened, and unable to protest, they were forced to work long hours to earn more money for the Temple. Anyone who disobeyed his orders, either intentionally or unintentionally, was subjected to ridicule and beatings. Although he happily intimidated and humiliated those who dared to rebel against him, Ben Yahweh didn't conduct the physical punishment himself. Rather, one of his other more 'loyal' followers, who were keen to show their devotion and please their leader, administered the beatings.

RACE WAR

Ben Yahweh went one step further in his test of the Temple members' allegiance. At meetings he repeatedly instructed them that they should be prepared to fight and die for God and the Nation of Yahweh, and they responded by shouting back their enthusiasm and complete acceptance of both these requirements. Ben Yahweh's insistence on his members' acceptance of these requirements began to increase at the same time as his beliefs and prophecies were becoming more and more radical, violent and racist. He prophesied a race war – the will of the one true, terrible, black God. Members were told that God had cursed 'white America' and that it was the mission of the blacks, the 'death angels', to wipe the 'white devils' from existence. Perhaps some of them agreed in principle, but thought that it was something they would never actually be asked to do.

Others however, who had been in attendance at secondary, sinister, and strictly confidential meetings of an elite group called 'The Brotherhood' held a very different, and much more informed, opinion.

THE BROTHERHOOD

The Brotherhood were Ben Yahweh's private assassins, and they performed every task he gave them. Initiation into the Brotherhood involved the slaughter of a white person, and the consequent presentation to the group of evidence of this murder – usually the head. Although the white devils were the primary target of The Brotherhood, they were also charged to kill any of the misguided, sinful blacks who stood in the way of Ben Yahweh or the collection of funds for the Temple. This deathly force was sent out into Miami on countless occasions to do Ben Yahweh's bidding.

Conflict grew between the Temple of Love and the residents of Miami, who viewed Ben Yahweh's activities with suspicion. Ben Yahweh was now in charge of a multi-million dollar enterprise and there were rumours of fire-bombing, extortion and murder. Eventually, on November 7, 1990, 300 law enforcement agents raided the Temple and arrested Ben Yahweh and a group of Temple members.

One of the most fearful members of The Brotherhood was former National Football League player, Robert Rozier. His Hebrew name was Neariah Israel, meaning 'Child of God', and Ben Yahweh placed him in charge of the Newark Temple. He was eventually captured in 1992 and convicted of the murder of a homeless white man whom he had stabbed to death in a ritual sacrifice in preparation for Ben Yahweh's visit.

IMPRISONMENT

Ben Yahweh was convicted of the murders of 14 individuals. Twelve other Temple members were charged with the same offences, and it was also alleged that they were planning to bomb federal buildings.

On imprisonment, Ben Yahweh demanded that he be allowed access to sacred texts and literature of the Nation of Yahweh. That he was not allowed to read such texts was, he claimed, a denial of his religious freedom. The authorities disagreed, arguing that these were dangerous, criminal and racist documents, and if circulated within the prison could threaten prison security.

Ben Yahweh's followers consider the government entirely corrupt, and guilty of tampering with evidence and providing untruthful reports. They see his conviction and punishment as reminiscent of that of the white Christ, and they draw parallels between Judas and Robert Rozier, who betrayed their black Christ for a reduced sentence himself. Rozier, who was released after serving time for four murders (having actually admitted to seven) and placed on a witness protection programme, committed cheque fraud and consequently his new identity was revealed. He now, justifiably, fears for his life.

The future of the Temple of Love is uncertain, but Ben Yahweh's followers await his release. Once a week, from within the prison walls, he sends a three-minute message to his followers on the outside. The message, which he sends via telephone from the prison cafeteria, is broadcast as a voice-over against the backdrop of a still portrait of him and is a feature of a weekly 30-minute programme which is aired in most of the US's main cities. The programme also includes advertisements for texts and tapes to educate his followers.

SECTION THREE

CAUSE FOR CONCERN?

Twelve Tribes

Messianic Communities

THE TWELVE TRIBES began as an essentially well-meaning, religious group, but over time evolved into a far more sinister organization, responsible for the devastation of many lives. The founder, Elbert Eugene Spriggs, believed, or at least preached to his followers, that he had a direct link to God. Those who accepted this as the truth were in a very vulnerable position.

ELBERT EUGENE SPRIGGS

Elbert Eugene Spriggs was born in East Ridge, Tennessee on 18 May, 1937. He married in 1957, but was divorced three years later, and thus entered the '60s at a turbulent time in his life. He married again in 1962, and had a son, but this marriage lasted only three years longer than the previous one. During the last couple of years of the marriage, Spriggs's father died, and the young man was thrown into turmoil.

Only a year after his second divorce, Spriggs married for a third time. During the past few years he had been employed in a number of different jobs, including a stint in the Army, and now found himself working in a carnival. It was while working there that Spriggs claims the Lord spoke to him for the first time, asking him, 'Is this what I created you for?' He witnessed sin first hand, and decided to leave in order to find a life in which he could avoid it.

Against the backdrop of the Civil Rights Movement, the Vietnam War and the assassination of their president, many other young Americans were equally unsettled at this time, and began to question the customs and principles of their society. To help them in their search for answers, many turned to religion. Elbert Eugene Spriggs was amongst them.

CALIFORNIA

Spriggs travelled to California, where he became involved with the Jesus Movement. His family had always been religious and he had been raised religiously, often going to church three times a week as a child, but his encounter with this group, also known as the Jesus People Revival, stimulated him more than he had ever been before. He realized the need for Jesus in his empty life, and committed to Christ on a beach in Carpenteria. By this time, his third marriage had failed.

With his devotion to Jesus Christ reaffirmed, Spriggs began working with the homeless at the Santa Barbara Rescue Mission but after only a short time he left to preach his Christian beliefs around the country. While doing this, he met Marsha Ann Duvall, who was to be his fourth wife. She became a Christian and they married in 1972. They moved back to Tennessee together, and settled in Chattanooga.

In the years which followed, Spriggs spent his time preaching the word of God to teenagers in the local areas, and encouraged many of them to turn to Christ themselves. He had soon drawn in enough young people to begin his own church group, which he called the 'Light Brigade', aimed specifically at teens. Spriggs acquired a house on Vine Street in which to hold prayer meetings and before long, many of the young people had actually moved in, and were living communally at the house.

Young people from all walks of life were welcome at the Vine Street house. Race, class and culture were of no consequence to Spriggs, but as a result he was becoming the target of much criticism from the local churches. He therefore began to turn away from these established religions, whose commitment to Jesus he had already begun to question. He felt that the churches did not hold the Gospel in the high regard which it deserved, and was particularly disgusted on one occasion when he learned that his church service had been cancelled due to the Superbowl.

VINE COMMUNITY CHURCH

He therefore established his own church at the house, and named it the 'Vine Community Church'. Followers began to worship there instead of at the hypocritical churches. Spriggs's congregation became quite active, and embarked on fund-raising and business enterprises to spread their word and raise money for the Vine Community Church. One such business enterprise was the establishment of a chain of restaurants called 'Yellow Deli', throughout Tennessee, Georgia, and Alabama. Their menu included a dish entitled 'Fruit of the Spirit', with the subheading – 'Why don't you ask us?'.

These activities were drawing unwelcome attention from the established churches, who felt that Spriggs had gone over the top with his restaurants and businesses, and worried about the lifestyle at Vine Street. In 1976, when Spriggs opened an even larger restaurant named 'Areopagus', where all Christians were encouraged to meet for support and fellowship, and ordained a follower there, the churches really questioned his ability. Added to this, there was growing nationwide concern about the emergence of cults. With its strange practices, and the intense focus on Spriggs as its leader, the Vine Community Church became a target. Members of other Christian groups were advised to avoid Spriggs and the Vine followers, and not to eat in any of the Yellow Deli restaurants.

Spriggs, who was increasingly disillusioned with the churches anyway, took this criticism very badly and responded by calling all churches the 'whores of Babylon'. He cut any remaining ties with these institutions, and the Vine Community Church became more and more inward-looking. Spriggs's beliefs were also becoming more extreme. He claimed that mainstream Christianity appeared to have renounced religion itself, and that the world outside of his own church was dark and evil. His followers must be protected from this outside world and therefore contact with families and friends who did not share the firm beliefs of the church was to be discontinued, or at the very least limited. These people were harmful and viewed as enemies.

THE NORTHEAST KINGDOM COMMUNITY CHURCH, ISLAND POND

With the Chattanooga society becoming increasingly suspicious and uneasy about the activities of the Vine Community Church, Spriggs decided it was time to leave. He had been offered a position as a pastor in northern Vermont, which he did not take, but which encouraged him to look to Vermont for the next stage of his mission. He settled in Island Pond, and his followers from Chattanooga began to join him in stages. The group adopted the new name, 'The Northeast Kingdom Community Church'.

As they had done in Tennessee, Spriggs and his followers began setting up businesses in this new location. These were again used as both money-raising enterprises as well as for evangelical purposes.

But just as the group had met with disapproval and mistrust in Chattanooga, so the residents of Island Pond began to feel the same. Not only had a couple of hundred new people arrived in their small town, capable of upsetting the balance of the quiet and closely-knit community, but many religious leaders had been monitoring the practices of Elbert Eugene Spriggs, and word had spread that his church was unconventional and had been very unpopular in Chattanooga.

DISCIPLINE

One of the most controversial practices employed by Spriggs and The Northeast Kingdom Community Church was their harsh discipline of children. Spriggs believed that it was God's will for disobedient children to be physically punished and he neither made excuses for it, nor tried to hide it from the distressed residents of Island Pond. He told his followers that when disciplining a child, it was necessary to 'bend his neck and bruise his ribs while he is young'.

The fundamental belief of the Twelve Tribes is in the return of 'Yahshua', the Messiah. Everything they practise is done in preparation for his coming and this is the reason they feel they must keep their children so pure and wholesome. Yahshua must have a following (The Body or The Bride) of perfect individuals, therefore children must be disciplined severely in order to keep them righteous. Children are to be punished the first time they commit sin or are disobedient to an adult. Their punishment is to be beaten with a wooden rod, intended to cleanse the conscience. Following their beating, the child is expected to thank whoever administered it, normally a parent, for correcting them, and certainly not to cry. The only rule which governs this punishment is that it be conducted out of love, and with self-control.

Children are not allowed to play with toys or invent their own games. They cannot watch television, or eat sweets. They are however, permitted to play with building blocks and practise with sewing kits. They are educated at home.

In spite of threats of violence made against them by the Island Pond locals, and even intervention by the State who raised issues regarding their treatment of children, Spriggs's church did settle successfully in the area, and went about their primary objective of serving God peacefully. They believed themselves to be the restoration of the Messianic Jewish New Testament Community of the first century, God's people on earth. They instituted a standardized dress code of loose-fitting clothes, and head-scarves for the women, and consequently became quite conspicuous and recognisable as a group. Spriggs decreed that, on entry into the community, all members had to give up their material possessions. He claimed that this was in pursuit of harmony – they had to live together equally, sharing everything they owned, as the Christian disciples had done before them.

By the early 1980s therefore, the now quite affluent Spriggs had acquired a lot of property and began to expand into New England, forming communities in Boston and Nova Scotia, amongst other places. In keeping with the belief that they were the restoration of God's people, they re-named the group 'The Twelve Tribes', representing Abraham and the Twelve Tribes of Israel.

CHILD ABUSE?

With the growing size and success of the group, knowledge of its treatment of children also became quite widespread and when stories of child abuse hit the headlines, the American public turned decidedly against the group. In 1983, Spriggs's 'deputy', Eddie Wiseman, was charged with assault on a 13-year-old girl. He had reportedly whipped the girl for seven whole hours as a punishment for disobedience. Before the case could come to trial though, the girl's father dropped all charges, retracted his first statement and refused to testify if brought to court.

In light of continued reports of suspected abuse, the State authorities raided the communities in 1984 and took more than 100 children away from the church. However, having acted illegally in doing so, the State was forced to return every child to their family within 24 hours. The warrant obtained for the raid on the group was declared 'grossly unconstitutional' by the judge in the case, and he was provided with no evidence to support the allegations of child abuse. It appeared that the group had just been targeted by their enemies, and that none of the charges were true. Spriggs saw the outcome as a triumph. But it neither satisfied nor appeased those who were still convinced that something very sinister was going on behind the closed doors of the Twelve Tribes.

Accusations of child abuse are registered frequently against the group, and include allegations of both beatings and paedophilia. Yet, the charges are always dropped before the cases come to court. Ex-members of the group vehemently denounce the practices of Spriggs and claim that the abuse within the community is widespread.

NEGLECT

Charges of abuse by neglect are also regularly reported. One baby, suffering from spinal meningitis, was diagnosed by the group's improvised health facility as having an ear infection. The infant died as a result of insufficient treatment. Several babies are known to have died at the community, one of which was aged eight months but weighed a mere 13kg, and are buried in unmarked graves. Most of the babies in these graves were stillborn – an apparently common occurrence at the Twelve Tribes.

Authorities also investigated the case of one young mother who endured labour for five days before it was eventually decided that she should be taken to hospital. By the time she reached the hospital, the baby had died inside her. No charges were pressed.

Serious childhood illnesses such as whooping cough and hepatitis have also gone undetected and therefore untreated, leading to death. One couple who did receive a prison term for causing the death of their son were Michael Ginhoux and Dagmar Zoller, whose 19-month-old son died of malnutrition and a curable heart disorder.

Zeb Wiseman, the son of Eddie Wiseman, eventually left the group and spoke out about the death of his mother within the Twelve Tribes. She had beensuffering from uterine cancer but was denied medical care, and had died a drawn-out and painful death. The young Zeb was beaten, locked up, and told that his mother had died because she was a sinner, and because she had once voiced her disapproval of the apostle Spriggs.

Also accused of practising child labour, Spriggs does confirm that children are asked to assist their parents in the factories and the farms from a young age, yet he claims that the group is not in violation of any child labour laws. The group formerly supplied furniture to Robert Redford's *Sundance* mail order catalogue, but this range has since been cancelled. Estée Lauder also pulled a huge contract from them when they discovered that children were being used to help make their products.

No amount of negative media attention has yet brought down the Twelve Tribes or Eugene Elbert Spriggs, and the group continues to grow. There are currently more than 25 communities across the world, mainly in the US, but also in England, France, Germany, Spain, Argentina, Brazil, Australia and Canada. Across these nine countries there are an approximate 2,500 members – it is estimated that half of this number are children under 15 years old.

Falun Gong

*The Practice of the Wheel
of the Dharma*

BY THE END of the 1990s, a decade which had witnessed the mass suicides of the Branch Davidians in Waco, Texas, and the attempt by the Aum Supreme Truth in Tokyo to kill thousands of commuters in a sarin gas attack on the Tokyo subway, there was a climate of fear and suspicion surrounding spiritual or religious movements with large groups of followers. As a result of this paranoia, the government in China decided to launch a crackdown on various spiritual groups, and amongst those targeted was the Falun Gong. Meaning 'The practice of the wheel of Dharma', Falun Gong (originally named Falun Dafa but renamed after this practice), was reported by the Chinese government to have two million members. This figure was perhaps an attempt by the government to play down the actual membership, for the Falun Gong movement itself claimed to have over 100 million.

The Falun Gong's response to this move by the Chinese government was to hold a silent and peaceful protest in front of the Communist Party headquarters in Beijing. Ten thousand of its members participated in this demonstration on April 25, 1999. Yet, instead of reassuring the Chinese authorities of the harmless intentions of the group, the silent protest threw the government into an even greater panic. Both the size of the assembled group, and the fact that they had been leaked no details of it by the Chinese intelligence services, terrified them. To them, it demonstrated a frightening level of secrecy and organization within the movement and so they concentrated their efforts against it with a renewed vigour.

OUTLAWED

The Falun Gong movement was outlawed in July 1999, and its members were discriminated against. Some members had their properties broken into by the police and their possessions taken, and others were denied the retirement pension to which they were entitled. Some were simply harassed on the street, or as they performed their group exercises in public. Falun Gong claims that some members simply disappeared and were never seen again, or were taken to prison and labour camps on fictitious charges and never released. Chinese lawyers were not allowed to defend the members of the Falun Gong unless agreed with the government, and no international legal representation was permitted. They were accused of fraud and deception and of posing a threat not only to the government but to the very foundation of Chinese society.

The Falun Gong was branded a 'cult' by the Chinese government, and even held responsible for the unsolved murders of many Chinese citizens. Consequently, an arrest warrant was issued for Li Hongzhi, the leader of this movement. The government accused him of carrying out these murders through his followers, by influencing them to commit the crimes. He was even accused of the deaths of 1,559 of the members themselves. Also wanted for the organization of 'illegal' demonstrations, Li Hongzhi fled to New York in 1996, and China has been pursuing America for his arrest and repatriation since.

INTERNATIONAL INVOLVEMENT

Not only has the US refused to deport Li Hongzhi, but they have condemned the Chinese government for its persecution of the Falun Gong and have passed resolutions which state that China should observe the UN Declaration of Human Rights and put a stop to the false imprisonment and abuse of the Falun Gong members. Yet the Chinese government maintains that the Falun Gong is a dangerous cult, and not the passive, inoffensive movement which America mistakenly perceives it to be. The government even claims that America's pursuit of these resolutions is a direct attack on Chinese autonomy.

Recognizing their support in the US, 700 members of the Falun Gong went to the World Trade Organization meetings in Seattle in November 1999 to begin a worldwide drive for acceptance of their movement, and to encourage the Chinese government to enter into negotiations with them. Yet the government did not relent, and fought back with an even greater campaign of discrimination against them. The plight of the Falun Gong became internationally known, and the popularity of the group began increasing. They were seen as victims of China's religious bigotry, and consequently global institutions began to cease trade links with China in support.

FOUNDATION OF THE FALUN GONG

The Falun Gong was founded by Li Hongzhi in 1992. Hongzhi claims to have been born on May 13, 1951 – the birthday of the Buddha, Siddhartha Gautama – but the government refutes this, declaring that their official records state that he was born on July 7, 1952. They maintain that he is falsifying his birthdate in order to claim some kind of link to the Buddha, a link which Hongzhi himself has never asserted. Whether this is true, or whether they are merely attempting to discredit him is unproven.

HONESTY, COMPASSION AND TOLERANCE

The basis of Falun Gong and Hongzhi's teachings are the achievement of a higher level of spirituality and enlightenment. This is attained through a combination of exercise, to advance body and mind, and belief in a mixture of Confucian, Taoist and Buddhist philosophies which promote honesty, compassion and tolerance. Followers must demonstrate these three virtues in every situation with which they are confronted. There are many levels of this enlightenment and it is an individual pursuit to achieve them. Falun Gong concentrates on the development of each human being as opposed to the advancement of the group.

According to Hongzhi the secrets of the Falun Gong were previously only disclosed by the master to an elite group of students. Such had been the tradition since ancient times in China as the teachings were very valuable and confidential. Li Hongzhi however, apparently on the directives of his own masters, made the teachings available to the public in 1992. As a result, the popularity of the movement grew.

The accusation that Falun Gong is a 'cult' is fiercely denied by its members. They protest that it is not even a religion, but rather a discipline. Members of Falun Gong are free to follow any faith they choose. The movement is purely about the progression of the individual and maintains that no one should have their beliefs imposed upon them. Li Hongzhi, although the leader of the movement, is not revered as a God, and does not accept donations to Falun Gong or encourage any activity which raises money in its name. There is no hierarchy within Falun Gong; all members are equal and practice together as such.

APRIL 25, 2000

Yet, the government persisted in its persecution of the movement. On April 25, 2000, the anniversary of the first silent protest against the government action towards the Falun Gong, the authorities in Beijing were placed on high alert. They had warned Beijing in the weeks leading up to the anniversary that there would be a showdown with the 'doomsday cult' which was still capable of raising the Devil in China.

They had anticipated the movements of the Falun Gong correctly, as members did return to Tiananmen Square to hold another protest. Yet although the government's fears had been justified, the action they took against these peaceful protesters was not.

In small groups, the Falun Gong protesters would unfurl a banner or would raise their fists in silent solidarity. Some simply sat in a circle to meditate. Plain-clothed policemen launched themselves at the groups, knocking down men, women and children indiscriminately. But throughout the day, as one group was led away by the authorities, another would arrive in its place and continue the protest. So, the day went on, with the police becoming more and more heavy-handed in their treatment of the protesters. Over the course of a very long day, many members of the Falun Gong were injured and many arrested.

Yet in spite of the arrests and the police brutality, the events of that day proved that the government were unable to crush the Falun Gong, who just kept rising up time and time again. That there was no decisive conclusion, or the anticipated 'showdown', was seen as a failure for the government.

INTERNATIONAL DISAPPROVAL

The events were seen in a negative light internationally, and the Clinton administration in the US attacked the Chinese government, claiming that they had again violated international human rights. At a time when the US was debating whether to pass a trading deal with China which would allow it the same low-tariff privileges as its other trading partners, the government's action and the arrest of innocent and peaceful protesters caused the US great concern. China retaliated by accusing America of hypocrisy. The US was fighting its own domestic terrorism, yet criticized China for its crackdown on the Falun Gong.

VICTIMISATION

Several theories have been put forward as to why China so vehemently victimizes the members of the Falun Gong and stamps down on the movement itself. Some claim that the Communist Party fears the Internet and the global access and international membership possibilities with which the Internet can provide the Falun Gong. For a country which had traditionally been so cut-off from the rest of the world, this was a frightening prospect. Also unnerving, the membership numbers of Falun Gong (according to the movement itself yet denied by the government) had exceeded that of the Communist Party, and it was also rumoured that members of the Communist Party had joined the Falun Gong themselves. Perhaps the most contentious feature of the Falun Gong movement was its focus on spirituality. This directly contravened the Chinese government's atheist principles.

THE FUTURE FOR THE FALUN GONG?

Some believe that although the Falun Gong has won a lot of favour globally, the government will eventually win over and the movement will disintegrate. Currently, it is believed that China has arrested tens of thousands of Falun Gong members, and sent over 5,000 to labour camps without trial. The precedent set by the Falun Gong cannot be destroyed though, and if the movement itself does crumble under the enormous governmental pressure, it is thought that in its place more religious and spiritual movements will rise up as Chinese citizens strive to challenge communist dictates and look for meaning and guidance through the meditation and exercise which the Falun Gong promoted.

The Church of
Scientology

Constantly under a cloud of bad press

SCIENTOLOGY MAY BE one of the most well known and widespread 'Personal Development' religions in the world but it is also one that comes under the most attack and scrutiny.

The Church of Scientology was founded in 1952 by science fiction writer Lafayette Ron Hubbard. Hubbard was on the one hand seen as an outspoken liar verging on madness but on the other as an intelligent artist and philosopher who was open to new ways of thinking.

Born in Tilden, Nabraska in the US in 1911, not much is known about Hubbard's life prior to the founding of his ideology and church, and what is known is rather ambiguous. It is alleged that he led a very eventful childhood and early man hood, and by the age of 19 had travelled more than a quarter of a million nautical miles.

In the 1930s Hubbard discovered his talent for writing and although he is most famous for his science fiction titles he also wrote westerns and mysteries and was a successful screen-play writer.

By the end of the 1930s Hubbard was becoming increasingly philosophical and in 1938 he wrote a manuscript entitled *Excalibur* which theorized that life was made up of just two parts; the 'Material Universe' and the 'X-Factor'. Hubbard believed that with training, the X-Factor would be able to run the Material Universe. This theory was soon to become the foundations for his future.

It is also reported that Hubbard was associated with Jack Parsons, a rocket propulsion researcher who was a friend of Alistair Crowley, the notorious occultist who was self-styled as 'The Beast 666'. Allegedly Parsons and Hubbard engaged in ritual magic but again this has never been proved.

Hubbard joined the United States Navy in 1941 but left in 1945 in order to work on his ever increasing theories that were soon to make him richer and more successful than his sci-fi books had made him.

THE THEORY OF DIANETICS

Before Hubbard founded his Church of Scientology he came up with a theory called 'Dianetics' that was a step up from his previous works, it was this publication that changed the path of many lives and is still changing people today.

According to Hubbard the word dianetics came from

the Greek 'dia' meaning through and 'nous' meaning soul, and can basically be described as what the soul does to the body. Hubbard believed that the unconsciousness in every human mind stores the trauma of every bad or unpleasant thing that happens to us from the day we are conceived in pictorial form which he called an 'engram'. Although the actual incident may be long forgotten the trauma can be triggered by association and can end up causing mental health problems.

The theory of dianetics deals with deleting these engrams from the subconsciousness through a process called 'auditing'. The process of auditing is a counselling based technique in which the auditor asks the subject a list of questions which then result in the subject back tracking and coming face to face with past traumas.

Hubbard published his theories of self-improvement and its techniques in a book entitled *Dianetics: The Modern Science of Mental Health* on May 9, 1950 and it soon became a best-seller. Many of his sci-fi fans were rather confused with what to make of it as it was a text layered with science fact and science fiction.

Dianetics groups began appearing all over America and Hubbard set up his own foundation called 'The Hubbard Dianetic Research Foundation'.

By 1952 the interest in Dianetics had grown in popularity and intrigue but his Foundation was failing fast. It ran into massive financial problems and by 1952 had gone bankrupt. Hubbard ended up having to sell the rights to Don Purcell who had been the financial backing at the beginning of the venture.

But Ron Hubbard was a fighter, he knew that something could be made of his ideas and was quick to expand his theory into what started out as a seemingly non-religious, non-spiritual philosophy which he called 'Scientology'. At the same time he started suing Purcell for using his ideas.

Hubbard was an extremely good story-teller and he was renowned for weaving tales out of thin air but keeping people's attention firmly on what he was saying and nothing else. Hubbard soon realized that this talent could come in handy when promoting his philosophy to the world.

By December 1953 Hubbard's non-profit making secular organisation was declared a religion and he founded the first Church of Scientology in Camden, New Jersey, in the US.

The goal of Scientology was and still is to:

Fully rehabilitate the spiritual nature of an individual, including rehabilitating all abilities and realising one's full potential, whereas, the goal of Dianetics is to rid the individual of his reactive mind and become 'Clear'.

What Hubbard meant by Clear was: to make a person free with his emotions and be a stronger and more creative individual.

Hubbard went on in this year to regain control of his

Dianetics text and also to invent a type of lie detector that he called an 'E-meter' that he believed would help with the auditing of patients.

He founded his Scientology headquarters in Phoenix Arizona and issued himself with a degree and title of Doctor of Scientology. It could be viewed that science and fiction were getting ever more blurred within Hubbard's universe.

SELF-HELP OR SELF-DEPRIVATION?

From the outside the theories of Scientology seem rather plausible and who wouldn't want to rid their inner self from past traumas that could have an adverse effect later in life? The thought of being a happier, more intelligent person who is completely in tune with the material and ethereal world that encompasses us sounds like a state of perfected euphoria, and being told that it is just a few lessons away sounds too good to be true – and maybe The Church of Scientology is just that?

In the summer of 1959, Hubbard moved with his wife and children to East Grinstead in Sussex, England to set up a central training and management centre for what was now growing into a big business. One of the first offices to be completed at Hubbard's premises, which was called 'Saint Hill', was the shipping department. Books and manuals on Dianetics and Scientology were being requested by people from all over the world that it was extremely hard to keep up with supply and demand.

Individuals started arriving at 'Saint Hill' to take part in auditing courses and lectures, and were extremely happy to part with their hard earned cash in order to reach a new level of being.

Once 'Saint Hill' was up and running, Hubbard embarked on trips around the world organizing lectures and setting up new Scientology churches and learning centres.

Hubbard was back in the US in 1963 when the US Food and Drug Administration raided Scientology offices and confiscated thousands of E-metres, stating that they were illegal medical devices. Hubbard got around this set back by issuing a disclaimer with each piece of equipment stating that they were only religious artifacts that did not treat illness.

PROBLEM AFTER PROBLEM

The E-metre scandal was the first piece of bad press of many to be given to The Church of Scientology. The more Scientology has grown in popularity the more worrying it has become to official agencies all over the world.

The Church has been investigated by governmental agencies including the FBI in the US as it is alleged time and time again that The Church of Scientology has been involved in illegal actions. The majority of times these allegations have been quashed but a few incidents have led to criminal convictions for members of The Church.

In 1979, a number of Scientologists from the Guardian Office (GO) were found guilty of a wide range of criminal activities. The GO had been set up in 1966 as an intelligence unit to help infiltrate the bad press that was ever increasing against The Church. The GO officers, which included Hubbard's third wife Mary Sue Hubbard, managed to enter many government offices and foreign embassies in Washington DC in the US and steal hundreds of Scientology related documents and investigations – which they called 'black propaganda'. When they were finally caught and convicted in 1969 the eight members were fined $10,000 and sentenced to five years in prison.

Mary Sue, appealed against her conviction but she was finally imprisoned in 1983 where she served just one year.

After this The Church of Scientology stated that the convicted GO members had been influenced by another force and had not acted under the command of The Church. It will never be known what the truth of this really is.

OLD MAN HUBBARD

By the early '80s Hubbard's health was rapidly deteriorating and by the winter of 1980 he was a complete recluse who began to work on his ten volume Mission Earth science fiction series. Not many Scientologists were to ever see him again.

It seemed, on the outside, that Scientology was on its

way out. With the founding leader in the last years of his life, and the years of bad press that had led to a dramatic decrease of Scientology members, it seemed like only a matter of time before Scientology and its theories would be an endangered movement, if not altogether extinct.

Yet this was not to be, as The Church seemed to have a second, or is that third, wind . . .

In 1981 one of Hubbard's most trusted advisors began to take over a lot of the work that Hubbard had once done. Although he was only 23 years old, David Miscavige had been working closely with Hubbard since he was a teenager and if anyone was going to do justice to the cause it would be him.

By 1982, Miscavige had taken over control of The Church and started to set up organizations that he stated, would help with the overall running of The Church. The Church now stands in a triangular shaped maze of bureaucracy with Miscavige at the top as Chairman of the Board.

Miscavige is described by other Church officials as being: 'An initiator with the tremendous ability to cut through the bull and get to the point' but former high-ranking Scientologists have been quick to describe another side to his personality. Former members believe that he 'has a volatile temper and is a ruthless in-fighter who punctuates his speech with expletives'.

By the time of Hubbard's death in 1986, and to the disappointment of some Scientologists, Miscavige was leader – and at the time of writing still is.

THE DEATH OF LISA MCPHERSON

The Church of Scientology is believed to have around eight million members worldwide, and individuals can gain membership on many different levels. With this number of members, there must be a lot of positive work and beliefs that The Church is involved in, but it is the negative points that get recorded.

A recent controversy that The Church has been involved in is the death of Lisa McPherson in December 1995. Lisa died in the care of Scientologists and her family believed that her death was due to her not being cared for in the proper or necessary way.

Lisa McPherson had joined The Church of Scientology in 1977 at the age of 36. In 1994, after living and working for a Scientology owned publisher in Dallas she moved with her colleagues to Clearwater in order to be close to the head quarters of The Church,

At the beginning of 1995 it was announced that she was 'clear' – free from inhibitions and painful memories and traumas – and she reportedly spoke to non-Scientologist friends about it being time for her to leave The Church.

In November 1995 Lisa was involved in a minor car crash in which she was not physically injured but had behaved in a strange way.

Immediately after the crash she had got out of the car and removed all of her clothes and started walking along the street. When a paramedic reached her she said: 'I need help, I need to talk to someone.' The paramedics took her to a psychiatric hospital but she was signed out by Scientologists against the doctor's advice a few hours later. Scientologists are opposed to non-Scientology psychiatric treatment.

Lisa was moved to a Scientology-owned hotel called Fort Harrison where she got progressively weaker over the 17 days that she was there.

On December 5, 1995, Scientologists started to worry about the state of her health and drove her to a hospital in the next state that had a Scientologist member as a doctor. She was pronounced dead on arrival.

A year later, in 1996, a State Attorney charged The Church with two felonies – practising medicine without a licence and abuse of a disabled adult. The McPherson estate believed that if she had been left at the psychiatric hospital she had been in straight after the accident, she would still be alive today.

After years of legal wrangling in June 2000, criminal charges were finally dropped due to lack of concrete evidence. But the civil case continued.

Finally, in May 2004, the estate of Lisa McPherson and The Church of Scientology reached a settlement, the terms of which were made confidential.

So legally, The Church was proved to be innocent, but only because the evidence was full of ambiguities. But the fact that a settlement was reached in the civil case means that The Church wanted closure to what had happened in 1995 – if they had been totally innocent would they not have fought the battle right until the end?

FREEDOM OF THOUGHT

There are hundreds of websites and publications that can be found slating The Church and alleging that they are responsible for even more deaths and suicides than that of Lisa McPherson.

There have also been claims made that The Church cleverly steals money from its members by using brain washing techniques and subliminal pressuring. Due to the confidentiality and secrecy within the movement it is impossible to find out if members are free and happy as Scientologists or in fact scared and imprisoned sheep.

Whilst in The Church members do not have a bad word to say about the religion but members who have left for whatever reason are usually quick to bring up the negative sides to life within. Is this because there is genuinely something to be worried about, or is it because it just wasn't right for that individual.

For many years Germany refused to see Scientology as a religion and the late Helmut Kohl believed that The Church was a threat to Germany's democracy. Since 2000 Germany have relaxed many laws for Scientologists and it has now become slightly easier to practice the religion there.

This paranoia might be seen as discriminating to members of The Church but with the secrecy that they seem to work under, governments cannot be blamed for keeping their eyes open, especially in a world where fanatical religious groups are closely connected to terrorism.

Of course violent acts of terrorism cannot be linked to movements such as The Church of Scientology, but within every organization there are people who can make the world hell for the rest of us if they are left to their own devices. If we were all really free, the world would probably be in even more carnage than it is already.

In a free world humans should be allowed to believe what they like and be part of whatever organization they wish, but do all adults have strong enough minds to realize when they are involved in something that could spiral out of control?

If The Church of Scientology wants to rid itself of the bad press surrounding it, it needs to work alongside its critics and prove itself to the world as more than the stereotype 'cult' that it is fast becoming.

DISCLAIMER

There have been so many words written and uttered on the subject of Scientology that it is very hard to sieve the truth from the propaganda, and this is true of both pro- and anti-Scientology groups.

As with every single issue in the whole of the world, there are always two sides, and life would be very boring if only one opinion was ever expressed. Maybe movements such as The Church of Scientology should be seen as innocent until proven guilty and so long as nobody is being physically or mentally harmed through being a member, individuals should be left to follow their beliefs whatever they may be – that is, as long as illegal acts are not passing unnoticed.